The Wisdom Of
Orison Swett Marden Vol. I

by Orison Swett Marden

How to Succeed
An Iron Will
Cheerfulness as a Life Power

How to Succeed:
Or, Stepping-Stones to Fame and Fortune

Contents:

First, Be a Man

The great need at this hour is manly men. We want no goody-goody piety; we have too much of it. We want men who will do right, though the heavens fall, who believe in God, and who will confess Him. —Rev. W. J. Dawson

All the world cries, Where is the man who will save us? We want a man! Don't look so far for this man. You have him at hand. This man—it is you, it is I; it is each one of us!... How to constitute one's self a man? Nothing harder, if one knows not how to will it; nothing easier, if one wills it. —Alexander Dumas

"I thank God I am a Baptist," said a little, short Doctor of Divinity, as he mounted a step at a convention. "Louder! louder!" shouted a man in the audience; "we can't hear." "Get up higher," said another. "I can't," replied the doctor, "to be a Baptist is as high as one can get."

But there is something higher than being a Baptist, and that is being a *man*.

Rousseau says: "According to the order of nature, men being equal, their common vocation is the profession of humanity; and whoever is well educated to discharge the duty of a man cannot be badly prepared to fill any of those offices that have a relation to him. It matters little to me whether my pupil be designed for the army, the pulpit, or the bar. To live is the profession I would teach him. When I have done with him, it is true he will be neither a soldier, a lawyer, nor a divine. *Let him first be a man*; Fortune may remove him from one rank to another, as she pleases, he will be always found in his place."

"First of all," replied the boy James A. Garfield, when asked what he meant to be, "I must make myself a man; if I do not succeed in that, I can succeed in nothing."

"Hear me, O men," cried Diogenes, in the market place at Athens; and, when a crowd collected around him, he said scornfully, "I called for men, not pigmies."

One great need of the world to-day is for men and women who are good animals. To endure the strain of our concentrated civilization, the coming man and woman must have an excess of animal spirits. They must have a robustness of health. Mere absence of disease is not health. It is the overflowing fountain, not the one half full, that gives life and beauty to the valley below. Only he is healthy who exults in mere animal existence; whose very life is a luxury; who feels a bounding pulse throughout his body; who feels life in every limb, as dogs do when scouring over the field, or as boys do when gliding over fields of ice.

Dispense with the doctor by being temperate; the lawyer by keeping out of debt; the demagogue, by voting for honest men; and poverty, by being industrious.

"Nephew," said Sir Godfrey Kneller, the artist, to a Guinea slave trader, who entered the room where his uncle was talking with Alexander Pope, "you have the honor of seeing the two greatest men in the world." "I don't know how great men you may be," said the Guinea man, as he looked contemptuously upon their diminutive physical proportions, "but I don't like your looks; I have often bought a much better man than either of you, all muscles and bones, for ten guineas."

A man is never so happy as when he suffices to himself, and can walk without crutches or a guide. Said Jean Paul Richter: "I have made as much out of myself as could be made of the stuff, and no man should require more."

"The body of an athlete and the soul of a sage," wrote Voltaire to Helvetius; "these are what we require to be happy."

Although millions are out of employment in the United States, how difficult it is to find a thorough, reliable, self-dependent, industrious man or woman, young or old, for any position, whether as a domestic servant, an office boy, a teacher, a brakeman, a conductor, an engineer, a clerk, a bookkeeper, or whatever we may want. It is almost impossible to find a really *competent* person in any department, and oftentimes we have to make many trials before we can get a position fairly well filled.

It is a superficial age; very few prepare for their work. Of thousands of young women trying to get a living at typewriting, many are so ignorant, so deficient in the common rudiments even, that they spell badly, use bad grammar, and know scarcely anything of punctuation. In fact, they murder the English language. They can copy, "parrot like," and that is about all.

The same superficiality is found in nearly all kinds of business. It is next to impossible to get a first-class mechanic; he has not learned his trade; he has picked it up, and botches everything he touches, spoiling good material and wasting valuable time.

In the professions, it is true, we find greater skill and faithfulness, but usually they have been developed at the expense of mental and moral breadth.

The merely professional man is narrow; worse than that, he is in a sense an artificial man, a creature of technicalities and specialties, removed alike from the broad truth of nature and from the healthy influence of human converse. In society, the most accomplished man of mere professional skill is often a nullity; he has sunk his personality in his dexterity.

"The aim of every man," said Humboldt, "should be to secure the highest and most harmonious development of his powers to a complete and consistent whole."

Some men impress us as immense possibilities. They seem to have a sweep of intellect that is grand; a penetrative power that is phenomenal; they seem to know everything, to have read everything, to have seen everything. Nothing seems to escape the keenness of their vision. But somehow they are forever disappointing our expectations. They raise great hopes only to dash them. They are men of great promise, but they never pay. There is some indefinable want in their make-up.

What the world needs is a clergyman who is broader than his pulpit, who does not look upon humanity with a white neckcloth ideal, and who would give the lie to the saying that the human race is divided into three classes: men, women and ministers. Wanted, a clergyman who does not look upon his congregation from the standpoint of old theological books, and dusty, cobweb creeds, but who sees the merchant as in his store, the clerk as making sales, the lawyer pleading before the jury, the physician standing over the sick bed; in other words, who looks upon the great throbbing, stirring, pulsing, competing, scheming, ambitious, impulsive, tempted, mass of humanity as one of their number, who can live with them, see with their eyes, hear with their ears, and experience their sensations.

The world has a standing advertisement over the door of every profession, every occupation, every calling: "Wanted—A Man."

Wanted, a lawyer, who has not become the victim of his specialty, a mere walking bundle of precedents.

Wanted, a shopkeeper who does not discuss markets wherever he goes. A man should be so much larger than his calling, so broad and symmetrical in his culture, that he would not talk shop in society, that no one would suspect how he gets his living.

Nothing is more apparent in this age of specialties than the dwarfing, crippling, mutilating influence of occupations or professions. Specialties facilitate commerce, and promote efficiency in the professions, but are often narrowing to individuals. The spirit of the age tends to doom the lawyer to a narrow life of practice, the business man to a mere money-making career.

Think of a man, the grandest of God's creations, spending his life-time standing beside a machine for making screws. There is nothing to call out his individuality, his ingenuity, his powers of balancing, judging, deciding.

He stands there year after year, until he seems but a piece of mechanism. His powers, from lack of use, dwindle to mediocrity, to inferiority, until finally he becomes a mere part of the machine he tends.

Wanted, a man who will not lose his individuality in a crowd, a man who has the courage of his convictions, who is not afraid to say "No," though all the world say "Yes."

Wanted, a man who, though he is dominated by a mighty purpose, will not permit one great faculty to dwarf, cripple, warp, or mutilate his manhood; who will not allow the over-development of one faculty to stunt or paralyze his other faculties.

Wanted, a man who is larger than his calling, who considers it a low estimate of his occupation to value it merely as a means of getting a living. Wanted, a man who sees self-development, education and culture, discipline and drill, character and manhood, in his occupation.

As Nature tries every way to induce us to obey her laws by rewarding their observance with health, pleasure and happiness, and punishes their violation by pain and disease, so she resorts to every means to induce us to expand and develop the great possibilities she has implanted within us. She nerves us to the struggle, beneath which all great blessings are buried, and beguiles the tedious marches by holding up before us glittering prizes, which we may almost touch, but never quite possess. She covers up her ends of discipline by trial, of character building through suffering by throwing a splendor and glamour over the future; lest the hard, dry facts of the present dishearten us, and she fail in her great purpose. How else could Nature call the youth away from all the charms that hang around young life, but by presenting to his imagination pictures of future bliss and greatness which will haunt his dreams until he resolves to make them real. As a mother teaches her babe to walk, by holding up a toy at a distance, not that the child may reach the toy, but that it may develop its muscles and strength, compared with which the toys are mere baubles; so Nature goes before us through life, tempting us with higher and higher toys, but ever with one object in view—the development of the man.

In every great painting of the masters there is one idea or figure which stands out boldly beyond everything else. Every other idea or figure on the canvas is subordinate to this idea or figure, and finds its real significance not in itself, but, pointing to the central idea, finds its true expression there. So in the vast universe of God, every object of creation is but a guide-board with an index finger pointing to the central figure of the created universe—Man. Nature writes this thought upon every leaf; she thunders it in every creation; it exhales from every flower; it twinkles in every star.

Open thy bosom, set thy wishes wide,
And let in manhood—let in happiness;
Admit the boundless theatre of thought
From nothing up to God ... which makes a man! —Young

Seize Your Opportunity

"The blowing winds are but our servants
When we hoist a sail."

You must come to know that each admirable genius is but a
successful diver in that sea whose floor of pearls is all your own.—Emerson

Who waits until the wind shall silent keep,
Who never finds the ready hour to sow,
Who watcheth clouds, will have no time to reap.—Helen Hunt Jackson

The secret of success in life is for a man *to be ready for his opportunity* when
it comes.—Disraeli

Do the best you can where you are; and, when that is accomplished, God
will open a door for you, and a voice will call, "Come up hither into a higher
sphere."—Beecher

Our grand business is, not to see what lies dimly at a distance, but to do
what lies clearly at hand.—Carlyle

"When I was a boy," said General Grant, "my mother one morning found
herself without butter for breakfast, and sent me to borrow some from a
neighbor. Going into the house without knocking, I overheard a letter read
from the son of a neighbor, who was then at West Point, stating that he had
failed in examination and was coming home. I got the butter, took it home,
and, without waiting for breakfast ran to the office of the congressman for our
district. 'Mr. Hamer,' I said, 'will you appoint me to West Point?' 'No, —— is
there, and has three years to serve.' 'But suppose he should fail, will you send
me?' Mr. Hamer laughed. 'If he don't go through, no use for you to try, Uly.'
'Promise me you will give me the chance, Mr. Hamer, anyhow.' Mr. Hamer
promised. The next day the defeated lad came home, and the congressman,
laughing at my sharpness, gave me the appointment. Now," said Grant, "it
was my mother's being without butter that made me general and president."
But he was mistaken. It was his own shrewdness to see the chance, and the
promptness to seize it, that urged him upward.

"There is nobody," says a Roman Cardinal, "whom Fortune does not visit
once in his life; but when she finds he is not ready to receive her, she goes in
at the door, and out through the window." Opportunity is coy. The careless,
the slow, the unobservant, the lazy fail to see it, or clutch at it when it has
gone. The sharp fellows detect it instantly, and catch it when on the wing.

The utmost which can be said about the matter is, that circumstances will,
and do combine to help men at some periods of their lives, and combine to
thwart them at others. Thus much we freely admit; but there is no fatality in
these combinations, neither any such thing as "luck" or "chance," as commonly

understood. They come and go like all other opportunities and occasions in life, and if they are seized upon and made the most of, the man whom they benefit is fortunate; but if they are neglected and allowed to pass by unimproved, he is unfortunate.

"Charley," says Moses H. Grinnell to a clerk born in New York City, "take my overcoat tip to my house on Fifth Avenue." Mr. Charley takes the coat, mutters something about "I'm not an errand boy. I came here to learn business," and moves reluctantly. Mr. Grinnell sees it, and at the same time one of his New England clerks says, "I'll take it up." "That is right, do so," says Mr. G., and to himself he says, "that boy is smart, he will work," and he gives him plenty to do. He gets promoted, gets the confidence of business men as well as of his employers, and is soon known as a successful man.

The youth who starts out in life determined to make the most of his eyes and let nothing escape him which he can possibly use for his own advancement, who keeps his ears open for every sound that can help him on his way, who keeps his hands open that he may clutch every opportunity, who is ever on the alert for everything which can help him to get on in the world, who seizes every experience in life and grinds it up into paint for his great life's picture, who keeps his heart open that he may catch every noble impulse and everything which may inspire him, will be sure to live a successful life; there are no ifs or ands about it. If he has his health, nothing can keep him from success.

Zion's Herald says that Isaac Rich, who gave one million and three quarters to found Boston University of the Methodist Episcopal Church, began business thus: at eighteen he went from Cape Cod to Boston with three or four dollars in his possession, and looked about for something to do, rising early, walking far, observing closely, reflecting much. Soon he had an idea: he bought three bushels of oysters, hired a wheelbarrow, found a piece of board, bought six small plates, six iron forks, a three-cent pepper-box, and one or two other things. He was at the oyster-boat buying his oysters at three o'clock in the morning, wheeled them three miles, set up his board near a market, and began business. He sold out his oysters as fast as he could get them, at a good profit. In that same market he continued to deal in oysters and fish for forty years, became king of the business, and ended by founding a college. His success was won by industry and honesty.

"Give me a chance," says Haliburton's Stupid, "and I will show you." But most likely he has had his chance already and neglected it.

"Well, boys," said Mr. A., a New York merchant, to his four clerks one winter morning in 1815, "this is good news. Peace has been declared. Now *we* must be up and doing. We shall have our hands full, but we can do as much as anybody."

He was owner and part owner of several ships lying dismantled during the war, three miles up the river, which was covered with ice an inch thick. He knew that it would be a month before the ice yielded for the season, and that thus the merchants in other towns where the harbors were open, would have time to be in the foreign markets before him. His decision therefore was instantly taken.

"Reuben," he continued, addressing one of his clerks, "go and collect as many laborers as possible to go up the river. Charles, do you find Mr.——, the rigger, and Mr.——, the sailmaker, and tell them I want them immediately. John, engage half-a-dozen truckmen for to-day and to-morrow. Stephen, do you hunt up as many gravers and caulkers as you can, and hire them to work for me." And Mr. A. himself sallied forth to provide the necessary implements for icebreaking. Before twelve o'clock that day, upward of an hundred men were three miles up the river, clearing the ships and cutting away ice, which they sawed out in large squares, and then thrust under the main mass to open up the channel. The roofing over the ships was torn off, and the clatter of the caulkers' mallets was like to the rattling of a hail-storm, loads of rigging were passed up on the ice, riggers went to and fro with belt and knife, sailmakers busily plied their needles, and the whole presented an unusual scene of stir and activity and well-directed labor. Before night the ships were afloat, and moved some distance down the channel; and by the time they had reached the wharf, namely, in some eight or ten days, their rigging and spars were aloft, their upper timbers caulked, and everything ready for them to go to sea.

Thus Mr. A. competed on equal terms with the merchants of open seaports. Large and quick gains rewarded his enterprise, and then his neighbors spoke depreciatingly of his "good luck." But, as the writer from whom we get the story says, Mr. A. was equal to his opportunity, and this was the secret of his good fortune.

A Baltimore lady lost a valuable diamond bracelet at a ball, and supposed it was stolen from the pocket of her cloak. Years afterward, she walked the streets near the Peabody Institute to get money to purchase food. She cut up an old, worn out, ragged cloak to make a hood of, when lo! in the lining of the cloak, she discovered the diamond bracelet. During all her poverty she was worth thirty-five hundred dollars, but did not know it.

Many of us who think we are poor are rich in opportunities if we could only see them, in possibilities all about us, in faculties worth more than diamond bracelets, in power to do good.

In our large eastern cities it has been found that at least ninety-four out of every hundred found their first fortune at home, or near at hand, and in meeting common everyday wants. It is a sorry day for a young man who cannot see any opportunities where he is, but thinks he can do better somewhere else. Several Brazilian shepherds organized a party to go to California to dig gold, and took along a handful of clear pebbles to play checkers with on the voyage. They discovered after arriving at Sacramento, after they had thrown most of the pebbles away, that they were all diamonds. They returned to Brazil only to find that the mines had been taken up by others and sold to the government.

The richest gold and silver mine in Nevada was sold for forty-two dollars by the owner, to get money to pay his passage to other mines where he thought he could get rich.

Professor Agassiz told the Harvard students of a farmer who owned a farm of hundreds of acres of unprofitable woods and rocks, and concluded to sell out and try some more remunerative business.

He studied coal measures and coal oil deposits, and experimented for a long time. He sold his farm for two hundred dollars and went into the oil business two hundred miles away. Only a short time afterward the man who bought the farm discovered a great flood of coal oil, which the farmer had ignorantly tried to drain off.

A man was once sitting in an uncomfortable chair in Boston talking with a friend as to what he could do to help mankind. "I should think it would be a good thing," said the friend, "to begin by getting up an easier and cheaper chair."

"I will do it," he exclaimed, leaping up and examining the chair. He found a great deal of rattan thrown away by the East India merchant ships, whose cargoes were wrapped in it. He began the manufacture of rattan chairs and other furniture, and has astonished the world by what he has done with what was before thrown away. While this man was dreaming about some far off success, he at that very time had fortune awaiting only his ingenuity and industry.

If you want to get rich, study yourself and your own wants. You will find millions of others have the same wants, the same demands. The safest business is always connected with men's prime necessities. They must have clothing, dwellings; they must eat. They want comforts, facilities of all kinds, for use and pleasure, luxury, education, culture. Any man who can supply a great want of humanity, improve any methods which men use, supply any demand or contribute in any way to their well-being, can make a fortune.

But it is detrimental to the highest success to undertake anything merely because it is profitable. If the vocation does not supply a human want, if it is not healthful, if it is degrading, if it is narrowing, don't touch it.

A selfish vocation never pays. If it belittles the manhood, blights the affections, dwarfs the mental life, chills the charities and shrivels the soul, don't touch it. Choose that occupation, if possible, which will be the most helpful to the largest number.

It is estimated that five out of every seven of the millionaire manufacturers began by making with their own hands the articles on which they made their fortune.

One of the greatest hindrances to advancement and promotion in life is the lack of observation and the disinclination to take pains. A keen, cultivated observation will see a fortune where others see only poverty. An observing man, the eyelets of whose shoes pulled out, but who could ill afford to get another pair, said to himself, "I will make a metallic lacing hook, which can be riveted into the leather." He succeeded in doing so and now he is a very rich man.

An observing barber in Newark, N. J., thought he could make an improvement on shears for cutting hair, and invented "clippers" and became very rich. A Maine man was called from the hayfield to wash out the clothes for his invalid wife. He had never realized what it was to wash before. He invented the washing-machine and made a fortune. A man who was suffering terribly with toothache, said to himself, "There must be some way of filling teeth to prevent them aching;" he invented gold filling for teeth.

The great things of the world have not been done by men of large means. Want has been the great schoolmaster of the race: necessity has been the mother of all great inventions. Ericsson began the construction of a screw-propeller in a bath-room. John Harrison, the great inventor of the marine chronometer, began his career in the loft of an old barn. Parts of the first steamboat ever run in America were set up in the vestry of an old church in Philadelphia by Fitch. McCormick began to make his famous reaper in an old grist-mill. The first model dry-dock was made in an attic. Clark, the founder of Clark University of Worcester, Mass., began his great fortune by making toy wagons in a horse-shed.

Opportunities? They crowd around us. Forces of nature plead to be used in the service of man, as lightning for ages tried to attract his attention to electricity, which would do his drudgery and leave him to develop the God-given powers within him.

There is power lying latent everywhere, waiting for the observant eye to discover it.

First find out what the people need and then supply that want. An invention to make the smoke go the wrong way in a chimney might be a very ingenious thing, but it would be of no use to humanity. The patent office at Washington is full of wonderful devices, ingenious mechanism; not one in hundreds is of earthly use to the inventor or to the world, and yet how many families have been impoverished and have struggled for years mid want and woe, while the father has been working on useless inventions. These men did not study the wants of humanity. A. T. Stewart, as a boy, lost eighty-seven cents when his capital was one dollar and a half, in buying buttons and thread which people would not purchase. After that he made it a rule never to buy anything which people did not want.

The first thing a youth, entering the city to make his home there, needs to do is to make himself a necessity to the person who employs him, according to the Boston *Herald*. Whatever he may have been at home, it counts for nothing until he has done something that makes known the quality of the stuff that is in him. If he shirks work, however humble it may be, the work will soon be inclined to shirk him. But the youth who comes into a city to make his way in the world, and is not afraid of doing his best whether he is paid for it or not, is not long in finding remunerative employment. The people who seem so indifferent to employing young people from the country are eagerly watching for the newcomers, but they look for qualities of character and service in actual work before they manifest confidence or give recognition. It is the youth who is deserving that wins his way to the front, and when once he has been tested his promotion is only a question of time. It is the same with young women. There are seemingly no places for them where they can earn a decent living, but the moment they fill their places worthily there is room enough for them, and progress is rapid. What the city people desire most is to find those who have ability to take important places, and the question of gaining a position in the city resolves itself at once into the question of what the young persons have brought with them from home. It is the staying qualities that have been in-wrought from childhood which are now in requisition, and the success of the boy or girl is determined by the amount of energetic character that has been developed in the early years at home. Take up the experience of every man or woman who has made a mark in the city for the last hundred years, and it has been the sterling qualities of the home training that have constituted the success of later years.

Don't think you have no chance in life because you have no capital to begin with. Most of the rich men of to-day began poor. The chances are you would be ruined if you had capital. You can only use to advantage what has become a part of yourself by your earning it. It is estimated that not one rich man's son in ten thousand dies rich. God has given every man a capital to start with; we are born rich. He is rich who has good health, a sound body, good muscles; he is rich who has a good head, a good disposition, a good heart; he is rich who has two good hands, with five chances on each. Equipped? Every man is equipped as only God could equip him. What a fortune he possesses in the marvelous mechanism of his body and mind. It is individual effort that has accomplished everything worth accomplishing in this world. Money to start with is only a crutch, which, if any misfortune knocks it from under you, would only make your fall all the more certain.

How Did He Begin?

There can be no doubt that the captains of industry to-day, using that term in its broadest sense, are men who began life as poor boys. —Seth Low

Poverty is very terrible, and sometimes kills the very soul Within us, but it is the north wind that lashes men into Vikings; it is the soft, luscious south wind which lulls them to lotus dreams. —Ouida

'Tis a common proof, that lowliness is young ambition's ladder—Shakespeare

"Fifty years ago," said Hezekiah Conant, the millionaire manufacturer and philanthropist of Pawtucket, R. I., "I persuaded my father to let me leave my home in Dudley, Mass., and strike out for myself. So one morning in May, 1845, the old farm horse and wagon was hitched up, and, dressed in our Sunday clothes, father and I started for Worcester. Our object was to get me the situation offered by an advertisement in the Worcester County *Gazette* as follows:

Boy Wanted
Wanted Immediately.—At the *Gazette* Office, a well disposed boy, able to do heavy rolling. Worcester, May 7.

"The financial inducements were thirty dollars the first year, thirty-five the next, and forty dollars the third year and board in the employer's family. These conditions were accepted, and I began work the next day. The *Gazette* was an ordinary four-page sheet. I soon learned what 'heavy rolling' meant for the paper was printed on a 'Washington' hand-press, the edition of about 2000 copies requiring two laborious intervals of about ten hours each, every week. The printing of the outside was generally done Friday and kept me very busy all day. The inside went to press about three or four o'clock Tuesday afternoon, and it was after three o'clock on Wednesday morning before I could go to bed, tired and lame from the heavy rolling. In addition, I also had the laborious task of carrying a quantity of water from the pump behind the block around to the entrance in front, and then up two flights of stairs, usually a daily job. I was at first everybody's servant. I was abused, called all sorts of nicknames, had to sweep out the office, build fires in winter, run errands, post bills, carry papers, wait on the editor, in fact I led the life of a genuine printer's devil; but when I showed them at length that I had learned to set type and run the press, I got promoted, and another boy was hired to succeed to my task, with all its decorations. That was my first success, and from that day to this I have never asked anybody to get me a job or situation, and never used a letter of recommendation; but when an important job was in prospect the proposed employers were given all facilities to learn of my abilities and character. If some young men are easily discouraged, I hope they may gain encouragement and strength from my story. It is a long, rough road at first, but, like the ship on the ocean, you must lay your course for the place where you hope to land, and take advantage of all favoring circumstances."

"Don't go about the town any longer in that outlandish rig. Let me give you an order on the store. Dress up a little, Horace." Horace Greeley looked down on his clothes as if he had never before noticed how seedy they were, and replied: "You see, Mr. Sterrett, my father is on a new place, and I want to help him all I can." He had spent but six dollars for personal expenses in seven months, and was to receive one hundred and thirty-five from Judge J. M. Sterrett of the Erie *Gazette* for substitute work. He retained but fifteen dollars and gave the rest to his father, with whom he had moved from Vermont to Western Pennsylvania, and for whom he had camped out many a night to guard the sheep from wolves. He was nearly twenty-one; and, although tall and gawky, with tow-colored hair, a pale face and whining voice, he resolved to seek his fortune in New York City. Slinging his bundle of clothes on a stick over his shoulder, he walked sixty miles through the woods to Buffalo, rode on a canal boat to Albany, descended the Hudson in a barge, and reached New York, just as the sun was rising, August 18, 1831.

For days Horace wandered up and down the streets, going into scores of buildings and asking if they wanted "a hand;" but "no" was the invariable reply. His quaint appearance led many to think he was an escaped apprentice. One Sunday at his boarding-place he heard that printers were wanted at "West's Printing-office." He was at the door at five o'clock Monday morning, and asked the foreman for a job at seven. The latter had no idea that the country greenhorn could set type for the Polyglot Testament on which help was needed, but said: "Fix up a case for him and we'll see if he *can* do anything." When the proprietor came in, he objected to the newcomer and told the foreman to let him go when his first day's work was done. That night Horace showed a proof of the largest and most correct day's work that had then been done. In ten years Horace was a partner in a small printing-office. He founded the *New Yorker*, the best weekly paper in the United States, but it was not profitable. When Harrison was nominated for President in 1840, Greeley started *The Log Cabin*, which reached the then fabulous circulation of ninety thousand. But on this paper at a penny a copy, he made no money. His next venture was the New York *Tribune*, price one cent. To start it he borrowed a thousand dollars and printed five thousand copies of the first number. It was difficult to give them all away. He began with six hundred subscribers, and increased the list to eleven thousand in six weeks. The demand for the *Tribune* grew faster than new machinery could be obtained to print it. It was a paper whose editor always tried to be *right*.

At the World's Fair in New York in 1853 President Pierce might have been seen watching a young man exhibiting a patent rat trap. He was attracted by the enthusiasm and diligence of the young man, but never dreamed that he would become one of the richest men in the world. It seemed like small business for Jay Gould to be exhibiting a rat trap, but he did it well and with enthusiasm. In fact he was bound to do it as well as it could be done. Young Gould supported himself by odd jobs at surveying, paying his way by erecting sundials for farmers at a dollar apiece, frequently taking his pay in board. Thus he laid the foundation for the business career in which he became so rich.

Fred. Douglass started in life with less than nothing, for he did not own his own body, and he was pledged before his birth to pay his master's debts. To reach the starting-point of the poorest white boy, he had to climb as far as the distance which the latter must ascend if he would become President of the United States. He saw his mother but two or three times, and then in the night, when she would walk twelve miles to be with him an hour, returning in time to go into the field at dawn. He had no chance to study, for he had no teacher, and the rules of the plantation forbade slaves to learn to read and write. But somehow, unnoticed by his master, he managed to learn the alphabet from scraps of paper and patent medicine almanacs, and no limits could then be placed to his career. He put to shame thousands of white boys. He fled from slavery at twenty-one, went North and worked as a stevedore in New York and New Bedford. At Nantucket he was given an opportunity to speak in an anti-slavery meeting, and made so favorable an impression that he was made agent of the Anti-Slavery Society of Massachusetts. While traveling from place to place to lecture, he would study with all his might. He was sent to Europe to lecture, and won the friendship of several Englishmen, who gave him $750, with which he purchased his freedom. He edited a paper in Rochester, N. Y., and afterward conducted the *New Era* in Washington. For several years he was Marshal of the District of Columbia. He became the first colored man in the United States, the peer of any man in the country, and died honored by all in 1895.

"What has been done can be done again," said the boy with no chance who became Lord Beaconsfield, England's great prime minister. "I am not a slave, I am not a captive, and by energy I can overcome greater obstacles." Jewish blood flowed in his veins, and everything seemed against him, but he remembered the example of Joseph, who became prime minister of Egypt four thousand years before, and that of Daniel, who was prime minister to the greatest despot of the world five centuries before the birth of Christ. He pushed his way up through the lower classes, up through the middle classes, up through the upper classes, until he stood a master, self-poised upon the topmost round of political and social power. Rebuffed, scorned, ridiculed, hissed down in the House of Commons, he simply said, "The time will come when you shall hear me." The time did come, and the boy with no chance but a determined will, swayed the sceptre of England for a quarter of a century.

"I learned grammar when I was a private soldier on the pay of sixpence a day," said William Cobbett. "The edge of my berth, or that of the guard-bed, was my seat to study in; my knapsack was my bookcase; a bit of board lying on my lap was my writing table, and the task did not demand anything like a year of my life. I had no money to purchase candles or oil; in winter it was rarely that I could get any evening light but that of the fire, and only my turn, even of that. To buy a pen or a sheet of paper I was compelled to forego some portion of my food, though in a state of half starvation. I had no moment of time that I could call my own, and I had to read and write amidst the talking, laughing, singing, whistling, and bawling of at least half a score of the most thoughtless of men, and that, too, in the hours of their freedom from all control. Think not lightly of the *farthing* I had to give, now and then, for pen, ink, or paper. That farthing was, alas! a great sum to me. I was as tall as I am now, and I had great health and great exercise. The whole of the money not expended for us at market was *twopence a week* for each man. I remember, and well I may! that upon one occasion I had, after all absolutely necessary expenses, on a Friday, made shift to have a half-penny in reserve, which I had destined for the purchase of a red herring in the morning, but when I pulled off my clothes at night, so hungry then as to be hardly able to endure life, I found that I had lost my half-penny. I buried my head under the miserable sheet and rug, and cried like a child.

"If I, under such circumstances, could encounter and overcome this task," he added, "is there, can there be in the world, a youth to find any excuse for its non-performance?"

"I have talked with great men," Lincoln told his fellow-clerk and friend, Greene, according to *McClure's Magazine*, "and I do not see how they differ from others."

He made up his mind to put himself before the public, and talked of his plans to his friends. In order to keep in practice in speaking he walked seven or eight miles to debating clubs. "Practicing polemics," was what he called the exercise.

He seems now for the first time to have begun to study subjects. Grammar was what he chose. He sought Mentor Graham, the schoolmaster, and asked his advice.

"If you are going before the public," Mr. Graham told him, "you ought to do it."

But where could he get a grammar? There was but one in the neighborhood, Mr. Graham said, and that was six miles away.

Without waiting for more information the young man rose from the breakfast-table, walked immediately to the place, borrowed this rare copy of Kirkham's Grammar, and before night was deep in its mysteries. From that time on for weeks he gave every moment of his leisure to mastering the contents of the book. Frequently he asked his friend Greene to "hold the book" while he recited, and when puzzled by a point he would consult Mr. Graham.

Lincoln's eagerness to learn was such that the whole neighborhood became interested. The Greenes lent him books, the schoolmaster kept him in mind and helped him as he could, and even the village cooper let him come into his shop and keep up a fire of shavings sufficiently bright to read by at night. It was not long before the grammar was mastered.

"Well," Lincoln said to his fellow-clerk, Greene, "if that's what they call science, I think I'll go at another."

He had made another discovery—that he could conquer subjects.

The poor and friendless lad, George Peabody, weary, footsore and hungry, called at a tavern in Concord, N. H., and asked to be allowed to saw wood for lodging and breakfast. Half a century later he called there again, but then

George Peabody was one of the greatest millionaire bankers of the world. Bishop Fowler says: "It is one of the greatest encouragements of our age, that ordinary men with extraordinary industry reach the highest stations."

Greeley's father, because the boy tried to yoke the off ox on the near side, said: "Ah! that boy will never get along in the world. He'll never know enough to come in when it rains."

He was too poor to wear stockings. But Horace persevered, and became one of the greatest editors of his century.

Handel's father hated music, and would not allow a musical instrument in the house; but the boy with an aim secured a little spinet, hid it in the attic, where he practiced every minute he could steal without detection, until he surprised the great players and composers of Europe by his wonderful knowledge of music. He was very practical in his work, and studied the taste and sensitiveness of audiences until he knew exactly what they wanted; then he would compose something to supply the demand. He analyzed the effect of sounds and combinations of sounds upon the senses, and wrote directly to human needs. His greatest work, "The Messiah," was composed in Dublin for the benefit of poor debtors who were imprisoned there. The influence of this masterpiece was tremendous. It was said it out-preached the preacher, out-prayed prayers, reformed the wayward, softened stony hearts, as it told the wonderful story of redemption, in sound.

A. T. Stewart began life as a teacher in New York at $300 a year. He soon resigned and began that career as a merchant in which he achieved a success almost without precedent. Honesty, one price, cash on delivery, and business on business principles were his invariable rules. Absolute regularity and system reigned in every department. In fifty years he made a fortune of from thirty to forty million dollars. He was nominated as Secretary of the Treasury in 1869, but it was found that the law forbids a merchant to occupy that position. He offered to resign, or to give the entire profits of his business to the poor of New York as long as he should remain in office. President Grant declined to accept such an offer.

Poor Kepler struggled with constant anxieties, and told fortunes by astrology for a livelihood, saying that astrology as the daughter of astronomy ought to keep her mother; but fancy a man of science wasting precious time over horoscopes. "I supplicate you," he writes to Moestlin, "if there is a situation vacant at Tübingen, do what you can to obtain it for me, and let me know the prices of bread and wine and other necessaries of life, for my wife is not accustomed to live on beans." He had to accept all sorts of jobs; he made almanacs, and served anyone who would pay him.

Who could have predicted that the modest, gentle boy, Raphael, without either riches or noted family, would have worked his way to such renown, or that one of his pictures, but sixty-six and three-quarter inches square (the Mother of Jesus), would be sold to the Empress of Russia, for $66,000? His Ansedei Madonna, was bought by the National Gallery for $350,000. Think of Michael Angelo working for six florins a month, and eighteen years on St. Peter's for nothing!

Dr. Johnson was so afflicted with king's-evil that he lost the use of one eye. The youth could not even engage in the pastimes of his mates, as he could not see the gutter without bending his head down near the street. He read and studied terribly. Finally a friend offered to send him to Oxford, but he failed to keep his promise, and the boy had to leave. He returned home, and soon afterward his father died insolvent. He conquered adverse fortune and bodily infirmities with the fortitude of a true hero.

Ichabod Washburn, a poor boy born near Plymouth Rock, was apprenticed to a blacksmith in Worcester, Mass., and was so bashful that he scarcely dared to eat in the presence of others; but he determined that he would make the best wire in the world, and would contrive ways and means to manufacture it in enormous quantities. At that time there was no good wire made in the United States. One house in England had the monopoly of making steel wire for pianos for more than a century. Young Washburn, however, had grit, and was bound to succeed. His wire became the standard everywhere. At one time he made 250,000 yards of iron wire daily, consuming twelve tons of metal, and requiring the services of seven hundred men. He amassed an immense fortune, of which he gave away a large part during his life, and bequeathed the balance to charitable institutions.

John Jacob Astor left home at seventeen to acquire a fortune. His capital consisted of two dollars, and three resolutions,—to be honest, to be industrious and not to gamble. Two years later he reached New York, and began work in a fur store at two dollars a week and his board. Soon learning the details of the business, he began operations on his own account. By giving personal attention to every purchase and sale, roaming the woods to trade with the Indians, or crossing the Atlantic to sell his furs at a great profit in England, he soon became the leading fur dealer in the United States. His idea of what constitutes a fortune expanded faster than his acquisitions. At fifty he owned millions; at sixty his millions owned him. He invested in land, becoming in time the richest owner of real estate in America. Generous to his family, he seldom gave much for charity. He once subscribed fifty dollars for some benevolent purpose, when one of the committee of solicitation said, "We did hope for more, Mr. Astor. Your son gave us a hundred dollars." "Ah!" chuckled the rich furrier, "William has a rich father. Mine was poor."

Elihu Burritt wrote in a diary kept at Worcester, whither he went to enjoy its library privileges, such entries as these: "Monday, June 18, headache, 40 pages Cuvier's 'Theory of the Earth,' 64 pages of French, 11 hours' forging. Tuesday, June 19, 60 lines Hebrew, 30 Danish, 10 lines Bohemian, 9 lines Polish, 15 names of stars, 10 hours' forging. Wednesday, June 20, 25 lines Hebrew, 8 lines Syriac, 11 hours' forging." He mastered eighteen languages and thirty-two dialects. He became eminent as the "Learned Blacksmith," and for his noble work in the service of humanity. Edward Everett said of the manner in which this boy with no chance acquired great learning: "It is enough to make one who has good opportunities for education hang his head in shame."

"I was born in poverty," said Vice-President Henry Wilson. "Want sat by my cradle. I know what it is to ask a mother for bread when she has none to give. I left my home at ten years of age, and served an apprenticeship of eleven years, receiving a month's schooling each year, and, at the end of eleven years of hard work, a yoke of oxen and six sheep, which brought me eighty-four dollars. I never spent the sum of one dollar for pleasure, counting every penny from the time I was born till I was twenty-one years of age. I know what it is to travel weary miles and ask my fellow-men to give me leave to toil. In the first month after I was twenty-one years of age, I went into the woods, drove a team, and cut mill-logs. I rose in the morning before daylight and worked hard till after dark, and received the magnificent sum of six dollars for the month's work! Each of these dollars looked as large to me as the moon looks to-night."

"Many a farmer's son," says Thurlow Weed, "has found the best opportunities for mental improvement in his intervals of leisure while tending 'sap-bush.' Such, at any rate, was my own experience. At night you had only to feed the kettles and keep up the fires, the sap having been gathered and the wood cut before dark. During the day we would always lay in a good stock of 'fat-pine' by the light of which, blazing bright before the sugar-house, in the posture the serpent was condemned to assume, as a penalty for tempting our first grandmother, I passed many a delightful night in reading. I remember in this way to have read a history of the French Revolution, and to have obtained from it a better and more enduring knowledge of its events and horrors and of the actors in that great national tragedy, than I have received from all subsequent reading. I remember also how happy I was in being able to borrow the books of a Mr. Keyes after a two-mile tramp through the snow, shoeless, my feet swaddled in remnants of rag carpet."

"That fellow will beat us all some day," said a merchant, speaking of John Wanamaker and his close attention to his work. What a prediction to make of a young man who started business with a little clothing in a hand cart in the streets of Philadelphia. But this youth had *the indomitable spirit of a conqueror in him*, and you could not keep him down. General Grant said to George W. Childs, "Mr. Wanamaker could command an army." His great energy, method, industry, economy, and high moral principle, attracted President Harrison, who appointed him Postmaster-General.

Jacques Aristide Boucicault began his business life as an employé in a dry goods house in a small provincial town in France. After a few years he went to Paris, where he prospered so rapidly that in 1853 he became a partner and later the sole proprietor of the Bon Marché, then only a small shop, which became under his direction the most unique establishment in the world. His idea was to establish a combined philanthropic and commercial house on a large scale. Every one who worked for him was advanced progressively, according to his length of employment and the value of the services he rendered. He furnished free tuition, free medical attendance, and a free library for employés; a provident fund affording a small capital for males and a marriage portion for females at the expiration of ten or fifteen years of service; a free reading room for the public; and a free art gallery for artists to exhibit their paintings or sculptures. After his sudden death in 1877, his only son carried forward his father's projects until he, too, died in 1879, when his widow, Marguerite Guerin, continued and extended his business and beneficent plans until her death in 1887. So well did this family lay the foundations of a building covering 108,000 square feet, with many accessory buildings of smaller size, and of a business employing 3600 persons with sales amounting to nearly $20,000,000 annually, that every department is still conducted with all its former success in accordance with the instructions of the founders. They are here no longer in their bodily presence, but their spirit, their ideas, still pervade the vast establishment. Everything is still sold at a small profit and at a price plainly marked, and any article which may have ceased to please the purchaser can, without the slightest difficulty, be exchanged or its value refunded.

When James Gordon Bennett was forty years old, he collected all his property, three hundred dollars, and in a cellar with a board upon two barrels for a desk, himself his own type setter, office boy, publisher, newsboy, clerk, editor, proof-reader and printer's devil, he started the New York *Herald*. In all his literary work up to this time he had tried to imitate Franklin's style; and, as is the fate of all imitators, he utterly failed.

He lost twenty years of his life trying to be somebody else. He first showed the material he was made of in the "Salutatory," of the *Herald*, viz., "Our only guide shall be good, sound and practical common-sense applicable to the business and bosoms of men engaged in everyday life. We shall support no party, be the organ of no faction or coterie, and care nothing for any election or any candidate from President down to constable. We shall endeavor to record facts upon every public and proper subject stripped of verbiage and coloring, with comments when suitable, just, independent, fearless and good-tempered."

Joseph Hunter was a carpenter, Robert Burns a ploughman, Keats a druggist, Thomas Carlyle a mason, Hugh Miller a stone mason. Rubens, the artist, was a page, Swedenborg, a mining engineer. Dante and Descartes were soldiers. Ben Johnson was a brick layer and worked at building Lincoln Inn in London with trowel in hand and a book in his pocket. Jeremy Taylor was a barber. Andrew Johnson was a tailor. Cardinal Wolsey was a butcher's son. So were Defoe and Kirke White. Michael Faraday was the son of a blacksmith. He even excelled his teacher, Sir Humphry Davy, who was an apprentice to an apothecary.

Virgil was the son of a porter, Homer of a farmer, Pope of a merchant, Horace of a shopkeeper, Demosthenes of a cutler, Milton of a money scrivener, Shakespeare of a wool stapler, and Oliver Cromwell of a brewer.

John Wanamaker's first salary was $1.25 per week. A. T. Stewart began his business life as a school teacher. James Keene drove a milk wagon in a California town. Joseph Pulitzer, proprietor of the New York *World*, once acted as stoker on a Mississippi steamboat. When a young man, Cyrus Field was a clerk in a New England store. George W. Childs was an errand boy for a bookseller at $4 a month. Andrew Carnegie began work in a Pittsburg telegraph office at $3 a week. C. P. Huntington sold butter and eggs for what he could get a pound or dozen. Whitelaw Reid was once a correspondent of a newspaper in Cincinnati at $5 per week. Adam Forepaugh was once a butcher in Philadelphia.

Sarah Bernhardt was a dressmaker's apprentice. Adelaide Neilson began life as a child's nurse. Miss Braddon, the novelist, was a utility actress in the provinces. Charlotte Cushman was the daughter of poor people.

Mr. W. O. Stoddard, in his "Men of Business," tells a characteristic story of the late Leland Stanford. When eighteen years of age his father purchased a tract of woodland, but had not the means to clear it as he wished. He told Leland that he could have all he could make from the timber if he would leave the land clear of trees. A new market had just then been created for cord wood, and Leland took some money that he had saved, hired other choppers to help him, and sold over two thousand cords of wood to the Mohawk and Hudson River Railroad at a net profit of $2600. He used this sum to start him in his law studies, and thus, as Mr. Stoddard says, chopped his way to the bar.

It is said that the career of Benjamin Franklin is full of inspiration for any young man. When he left school for good he was only twelve years of age. At first he did little but read. He soon found, however, that reading, alone, would not make him an educated man, and he proceeded to act upon this discovery at once. At school he had been unable to understand arithmetic. Twice he had given it up as a hopeless puzzle, and finally left school almost hopelessly ignorant upon the subject. But the printer's boy soon found his ignorance of figures extremely inconvenient. When he was about fourteen he took up for the *third time* the *"Cocker's Arithmetic," which had baffled him at school,* and *ciphered all through it with ease and pleasure.* He then mastered a work upon navigation, which included the rudiments of geometry, and thus tasted "the inexhaustible charm of mathematics." He pursued a similar course, we are told, in acquiring the art of composition, in which, at length, he excelled most of the men of his time. When he was but a boy of sixteen, he wrote so well that the pieces which he slyly sent to his brother's paper were thought to have been written by some of the most learned men in the colony.

Henry Clay, the "mill-boy of the slashes," was one of seven children of a widow too poor to send him to any but a common country school, where he was drilled only in the "three R's." But he used every spare moment to study without a teacher, and in after years he was a king among self-made men.

The most successful man is he who has triumphed over obstacles, disadvantages and discouragements.

It is Goodyear in his rude laboratory enduring poverty and failure until the pasty rubber is at length hardened; it is Edison biding his time in baggage car and in printing office until that mysterious light and power glows and throbs at his command; it is Carey on his cobbler's bench nourishing the great purpose that at length carried the message of love to benighted India;—these are the cases and examples of true success.

Out of Place

The high prize of life, the crowning fortune of a man, is to be born with a bias to some pursuit, which finds him in employment and happiness. —Emerson

The art of putting the right man in the right place is perhaps the first in the science of government, but the art of finding a satisfactory position for the discontented is the most difficult. —Talleyrand

It is a celebrated thought of Socrates, that if all the misfortunes of mankind were cast into a public stock, in order to be equally distributed among the whole species, those who now think themselves the most unhappy would prefer the share they are already possessed of, before that which would fall to them by such a division. —Addison

I was born to other things. —Tennyson

How many a rustic Milton has passed by,
Stifling the speechless longings of his heart,
In unremitting drudgery and care!
How many a vulgar Cato has compelled
His energies, no longer tameless then,
To mould a pin, or fabricate a nail.—Shelley

"But I'm good for something," pleaded a young man whom a merchant was about to discharge for his bluntness. "You are good for nothing as a salesman," said his employer. "I am sure I can be useful," said the youth. "How? Tell me how." "I don't know, sir, I don't know." "Nor do I," said the merchant, laughing at the earnestness of his clerk. "Only don't put me away, sir, don't put me away. Try me at something besides selling. I cannot sell; I know I cannot sell." "I know that, too," said the principal; "that is what is wrong." "But I can make myself useful somehow," persisted the young man; "I know I can." He was placed in the counting-house, where his aptitude for figures soon showed itself, and in a few years he became not only chief cashier in the large store, but an eminent accountant.

"Out of an art," says Bulwer, "a man may be so trivial you would mistake him for an imbecile—at best, a grown infant. Put him into his art, and how high he soars above you! How quietly he enters into a heaven of which he has become a denizen, and unlocking the gates with his golden key, admits you to follow, an humble reverent visitor."

A man out of place is like a fish out of water. Its fins mean nothing, they are only a hindrance. The fish can do nothing but flounder out of its element. But as soon as the fins feel the water, they mean something. Fifty-two per cent of our college graduates studied law, not because, in many cases, they have the slightest natural aptitude for it, but because it is put down as the proper road to promotion.

A man never grows in personal power and moral stamina when out of his place. If he grows at all, it is a narrow, one-sided, stunted growth, not a manly growth. Nature abhors the slightest perversion of natural aptitude or deviation from the sealed orders which accompany every soul into this world.

A man out of place is not half a man. He feels unmanned, unsexed. He cannot respect himself, hence he cannot be respected.

You can enter all kinds of horses for a race, but only those which have natural adaptation for speed will make records; the others will only make themselves ridiculous by their lumbering, unnatural exertions to win. How many truck and family-horse lawyers make themselves ridiculous by trying to speed on the law track, where courts and juries only laugh at them. The effort to redeem themselves from scorn may enable them by unnatural exertions to become fairly passable, but the same efforts along the line of their strength or adaptation would make them kings in their line.

"Jonathan," said Mr. Chace, when his son told of having nearly fitted himself for college, "thou shalt go down to the machine-shop on Monday morning." It was many years before Jonathan escaped from the shop to work his way up to the position of a man of great influence as a United States Senator from Rhode Island.

Galileo was sent to the university at Pisa at seventeen, with the strict injunction not to neglect medical subjects for the alluring study of philosophy or literature. But when he was eighteen he discovered the great principle of the pendulum by a lamp left swinging in the cathedral.

John Adams' father was a shoemaker; and, trying to teach his son the art, gave him some "uppers" to cut out by a pattern which had a three-cornered hole in it to hang it up by. The future statesman followed the pattern, hole and all.

There is a tradition that Tennyson's first poems were published at the instigation of his father's coachman. His grandfather gave the lad ten shillings for writing an elegy on his grandmother. As he handed it to him, he said; "There, that's the first money you ever earned by your poetry, and take my word for it, it will be the last."

Murillo's mother had marked her boy for a priest, but nature had already laid her hand upon him and marked him for her own. His mother was shocked on returning from church one day to find that the child had taken down the sacred family picture, "Jesus and the Lamb," and had painted his own hat on the Saviour's head, and had changed the lamb into a dog.

The poor boy's home was broken up, and he started out on foot and alone to seek his fortune. All he had was courage and determination to make something of himself. He not only became a famous artist, but a man of great character.

"Let us people who are so uncommonly clever and learned," says Thackeray, "have a great tenderness and pity for the folks who are not endowed with the prodigious talents which we have. I have always had a regard for dunces,—those of my own school days were among the pleasantest of the fellows, and have turned out by no means the dullest in life; whereas, many a youth who could turn off Latin hexameters by the yard, and construe Greek quite glibly, is no better than a feeble prig now, with not a pennyworth more brains than were in his head before his beard grew."

"In the winter of 1824, there set in a great flood upon the town of Sidmouth, the tide rose to a terrible height. In the midst of this sublime and terrible storm, Dame Partington, who lived upon the beach, was seen at the door of her house, with mop and pattens, trundling her mop, squeezing out the sea-water, and vigorously pushing away the Atlantic Ocean. The Atlantic was roused. Mrs. Partington's spirit was up: but I need not tell you the contest was unequal; the Atlantic Ocean beat Mrs. Partington. She was excellent at a slop or a puddle, but she should not have meddled with a tempest."

How many Dame Partingtons there are of both sexes, and in every walk of life!

The young swan is restless and uneasy until she finds the element she has never before seen. Then,

"With archéd neck
Between her white wings mantling proudly, rows
Her state with oary feet."

What a wretched failure was that of Haydon the painter. He thought he failed through the world's ingratitude or injustice, but his failure was due wholly to his being out of place. His bitter disappointments at his half successes were really pitiable because to him they were more than failures. He had not the slightest sense of color, yet went through life under the delusion that he was an artist.

"If it is God's will to take any of my children by death, I hope it may be Isaac," said the father of Dr. Isaac Barrow. "Why do you tell that blockhead the same thing twenty times over?" asked John Wesley's father. "Because," replied his mother, "if I had told him but nineteen times, all my labor would have been lost, while now he will understand and remember."

A man out of place may manage to get a living, but he has lost the buoyancy, energy and enthusiasm which are as natural to a man in his place as his breath. He is industrious, but he works mechanically and without heart. It is to support himself and family, *not because he cannot help it.* Dinner time does not come two hours before he realizes it; a man out of place is constantly looking at his watch and thinking of his salary.

If a man is in his place he is happy, joyous, cheerful, energetic, fertile in resources. The days are all too short for him. All his faculties give their consent to his work; say "yes" to his occupation. He is a man; he respects himself and is happy because all his powers are at play in their natural sphere. There is no compromising of his faculties, no cramping of legal acumen upon the farm; no suppressing of forensic oratorical powers at the shoemaker's bench; no stifling of exuberance of physical strength, of visions of golden crops and blooded cattle amid the loved country life in the dry clergyman's study, composing sermons to put the congregation to sleep.

To be out of place is demoralizing to all the powers of manhood. We can't cheat nature out of her aim; if she has set all the currents of your life toward medicine or law, you will only be a botch at anything else. Will-power and application cannot make a farmer of a born painter any more than a lumbering draught horse can be changed into a race horse. When the powers are not used along the line of their strength they become demoralized, weakened, deteriorated. Self-respect, enthusiasm and courage ooze out; we become half-hearted and success is impossible.

Scott was called the great blockhead while in Edinburgh College. Grant's mother called the future General and President, "Useless Grant," because he was so unhandy and dull.

Erskine had at length found his place as a lawyer; he carried everything before him at the bar. Had he remained in the navy he would probably never have been heard from. When elected to Parliament, his lofty spirit was chilled by the cold sarcasm and contemptuous indifference of Pitt, whom he was expected by his friends to annihilate. But he was again out of his place; he was shorn of his magic power and his eloquent tongue faltered from a consciousness of being out of his place.

Gould failed as a storekeeper, tanner and surveyor and civil engineer, before he got into a railroad office where he "struck his gait."

When extracts from James Russell Lowell's poem at Harvard were shown his father at Rome, instead of being pleased the latter said, "James promised me when I left home, that he would give up poetry and stick to books. I had hoped that he had become less flighty." The world is full of people at war with their positions.

Man only grows when he is developing along the lines of his own individuality, and not when he is trying to be somebody else. All attempts to imitate another man, when there is no one like you in all creation, as the pattern was broken when you were born, is not only to ruin your own pattern, but to make only an echo of the one imitated. There is no strength off the lines of our own individuality.

Anywhere else we are dwarfs, weaklings, echoes, and the echo even of a great man is a sorry contrast to even the smallest human being who is himself.

What Shall I Do?

No man ever made an ill-figure who understood his own talents, nor a good one who mistook them. —Swift

Blessed is he who has found his work,—let him ask no other blessing. —Carlyle

Whatever you are by nature, keep to it; never desert your line of talent. Be what nature intended you for, and you will succeed; be anything else, and you will be ten thousand times worse than nothing. —Sydney Smith

He who is false to present duty breaks a thread in the loom, and will find the flaw when he may have forgotten its cause. —Beecher

I am glad to think
I am not bound to make the world go round;
But only to discover and to do,
With cheerful heart, the work that God appoints.—Jean Ingelow

"Do that which is assigned you," says Emerson, "and you cannot hope too much or dare too much. There is at this moment for you an utterance brave and grand as that of the colossal chisel of Phidias, or trowel of the Egyptians, or the pen of Moses or Dante, but different from all these."

"I felt that I was in the world to do something, and thought I must," said Whittier, thus giving the secret of his great power. It is the man who must enter law, literature, medicine, the ministry, or any other of the overstocked professions, who will succeed. His certain call—that is, his love for it, and his fidelity to it—are the imperious factors of his career. If a man enters a profession simply because his grandfather made a great name in it, or his mother wants him to, with no love or adaptability for it, it were far better for him to be a day laborer. In the humbler work, his intelligence may make him a leader; in the other career he might do as much harm as a boulder rolled from its place upon a railroad track, a menace to the next express.

Lowell said: "It is the vain endeavor to make ourselves what we are not, that has strewn history with so many broken purposes, and lives left in the rough."

"The age has no aversion to preaching as such," said Phillips Brooks, "it may not listen to your preaching." But though it may not listen to your preaching, it will wear your boots, or buy your flour, or see stars through your telescope. It has a use for every person, and it is his business to find out what that use is.

The following advertisement appeared several times in a paper without bringing a letter:

"**Wanted**.—Situation by a Practical Printer, who is competent to take charge of any department in a printing and publishing house. Would accept a professorship in any of the academies. Has no objection to teach ornamental painting and penmanship, geometry, trigonometry, and many other sciences. Has had some experience as a lay preacher. Would have no objection to form a small class of young ladies and gentlemen to instruct them in the higher branches. To a dentist or chiropodist he would be invaluable; or he would cheerfully accept a position as bass or tenor singer in a choir."

At length there appeared this addition to the notice:

"P.S. Will accept an offer to saw and split wood at less than the usual rates."

This secured a situation at once, and the advertisement was seen no more.

Don't wait for a higher position or a larger salary. Enlarge the position you already occupy; put originality of method into it. Fill it as it never was filled before. Be more prompt, more energetic, more thorough, more polite than your predecessor or fellow-workmen. Study your business, devise new modes of operation, be able to give your employer points. The art lies not in giving satisfaction merely, not in simply filling your place, but in doing better than was expected, in surprising your employer; and the reward will be a better place and a larger salary.

"He that hath a trade," says Franklin, "hath an estate; and he that hath a calling hath a place of profit and honor. A ploughman on his legs is higher than a gentleman on his knees."

Follow your bent. You cannot long fight successfully against your aspirations. Parents, friends, or misfortune may stifle and suppress the longings of the heart, by compelling you to perform unwelcome tasks; but, like a volcano, the inner fire will burst the crusts which confine it and pour forth its pent-up genius in eloquence, in song, in art, or in some favorite industry. Beware of "a talent which you cannot hope to practice in perfection." Nature hates all botched and half-finished work, and will pronounce her curse upon it.

Your talent is your *call*. Your legitimate destiny speaks in your character.

If you have found your place, your occupation has the consent of every faculty of your being.

If possible, choose that occupation which focuses the largest amount of your experience and tastes. You will then not only have a congenial vocation, but will utilize largely your skill and business knowledge, which is your true capital.

There is no doubt that every person has a special adaptation for his own peculiar part in life. A very few—the geniuses, we call them—have this marked in an unusual degree, and very early in life.

A man's business does more to make him than anything else. It hardens his muscles, strengthens his body, quickens his blood, sharpens his mind, corrects his judgment, wakes up his inventive genius, puts his wits to work, starts him on the race of life, arouses his ambition, makes him feel that he is a man and must fill a man's shoes, do a man's work, bear a man's part in life, and show himself a man in that part. No man feels himself a man who is not doing a man's business. A man without employment is not a man. He does not prove by his works that he is a man. A hundred and fifty pounds of bone and muscle do not make a man. A good cranium full of brains is not a man. The bone and muscle and brain must know how to do a man's work, think a man's thoughts, mark out a man's path, and bear a man's weight of character and duty before they constitute a man.

Whatever you do in life, be greater than your calling. Most people look upon an occupation or calling as a mere expedient for earning a living. What a mean, narrow view to take of what was intended for the great school of life, the great man-developer, the character-builder; that which should broaden, deepen, heighten, and round out into symmetry, harmony and beauty, all the God-given faculties within us! How we shrink from the task and evade the lessons which were intended for the unfolding of life's great possibilities into usefulness and power, as the sun unfolds into beauty and fragrance the petals of the flower.

"Girls, you cheapen yourselves by lack of purpose in life," says Rena L. Miner. "You show commendable zeal in pursuing your studies; your alertness in comprehending and ability in surmounting difficult problems have become proverbial; nine times out of ten you outrank your brothers thus far; but when the end is attained, the goal reached, whether it be the graduating certificate from a graded school, or a college diploma, for nine out of every ten it might as well be added thereto, 'dead to further activity,' or, 'sleeping until marriage shall resurrect her.'

"Crocheting, placquing, dressing, visiting, music, and flirtations, make up the sum total for the expense and labor expended for your existence. If forced to earn your support, you are content to stand behind a counter, or teach school term after term in the same grade, while the young men who graduated with you walk up the grades, as up a ladder, to professorship and good salary, from which they swing off into law, physics, or perhaps the legislative firmament, leaving difficulties and obstacles like nebulæ in their wake.—You girls, satisfied with mediocrity, have an eye mainly for the 'main chance'—marriage. If you marry wealthy,—which is marrying well according to the modern popular idea,—you dress more elegantly, cultivate more fashionable society, leave your thinking for your husband and your minister to do for you, and become in the economy of life but a sentient nonentity. If you are true to the grand passion, and accept with it poverty, you bake, brew, scrub, spank the children, and talk with your neighbor over the back fence for recreation, spending the years literally like the horse in a treadmill, all for the lack of a purpose,—a purpose sufficiently potent to convert the latent talent into a gem of living beauty, a creative force which makes all adjuncts secondary, like planets to their central sun. Choose some one course or calling, and master it in all its details, sleep by it, swear by it, work for it, and, if marriage crowns you, it can but add new glory to your labor."

Dr. Hall says that the world has urgent need of "girls who are mother's right hand; girls who can cuddle the little ones next best to mamma, and smooth out the tangles in the domestic skein when things get twisted; girls whom father takes comfort in for something better than beauty, and the big brothers are proud of for something that outranks the ability to dance or shine in society. Next, we want girls of sense,—girls who have a standard of their own regardless of conventionalities, and are independent enough to live up to it; girls who simply won't wear a trailing dress on the street to gather up microbes and all sorts of defilement; girls who don't wear a high hat to the theatre, or lacerate their feet with high heels and endanger their health with corsets; girls who will wear what is pretty and becoming and snap their fingers at the dictates of fashion when fashion is horrid and silly. And we want good girls,—girls who are sweet, right straight out from the heart to the lips; innocent and pure and simple girls, with less knowledge of sin and duplicity and evil-doing at twenty than the pert little schoolgirl of ten has all too often. And we want careful girls and prudent girls, who think enough of the generous father who toils to maintain them in comfort, and of the gentle mother who denies herself much that they may have so many pretty things, to count the cost and draw the line between the essentials and non-essentials; girls who strive to save and not to spend; girls who are unselfish and eager to be a joy and a comfort in the home rather than an expense and a useless burden. We want girls with hearts,—girls who are full of tenderness and sympathy, with tears that flow for other people's ills, and smiles that light outward their own beautiful thoughts. We have lots of clever girls, and brilliant girls, and witty girls. Give us a consignment of jolly girls, warm-hearted and impulsive girls; kind and entertaining to their own folks, and with little desire to shine in the garish world. With a few such girls scattered around, life would freshen up for all of us, as the weather does under the spell of summer showers."

Will You Pay the Price?

The gods sell anything and to everybody at a fair price. —Emerson
All desire knowledge, but no one is willing to pay the price. —Juvenal

There is no royal path which leads to geometry. —Euclid

There is no road to success but through a clear, strong purpose. A purpose underlies character, culture, position, attainment of whatever sort. —T. T. Munger

Remember you have not a sinew whose law of strength is not action; you have not a faculty of body, mind, or soul, whose law of improvement is not energy. —E. B. Hall

"We have but what we make, and every good with the part of Saul, I read and reread the Bible, so as to become impregnated with the appropriate sentiments, manners and local color. When I took up Othello, I pored over the history of the Venetian Republic and that of the Moorish invasion of Spain. I studied the passions of the Moors, their art of war, their religious beliefs, nor did I overlook the romance of Giraldi Cinthio, in order the better to master that sublime character. I did not concern myself about a superficial study of the words, or of some point of scenic effect, or of greater or less accentuation of certain phrases with a view to win passing applause; a vaster horizon opened out before me—an infinite sea on which my bark could navigate in security, without fear of falling in with reefs."

His method was not new, but he considered it so, and gives his opinion in quotation-marks. He speaks of characters with which, his name is not always associated by writers on the stage, but is correct, I think, in the main.

Many years ago a little boy entered Harrow school and was put in a class beyond his years, wherein all the other boys had the advantage of previous instruction. His master used to reprove his dullness, but all his efforts could not raise him from the lowest place in the class. The boy finally procured the elementary books which the other boys had studied. He devoted the hours of play and many of the hours of sleep to mastering the elementary principles of these books. This boy was soon at the head of his class and the pride of Harrow. The statue of that boy, Sir William Jones, stands to-day in St. Paul's Cathedral; for he lived to be the greatest Oriental scholar of Europe.

"What is the secret of success in business?" asked a friend of Cornelius Vanderbilt. "Secret! there is no secret about it," replied the commodore; "all you have to do is to attend to your business and go ahead." If you would adopt Vanderbilt's method, know your business, attend to it, and keep down expenses until your fortune is safe from business perils.

"Work or starve," is nature's motto,—and it is written on the stars and the sod alike,—starve mentally, starve morally, starve physically. It is an inexorable law of nature that whatever is not used, dies. "Nothing for nothing," is her maxim. If we are idle and shiftless by choice, we shall be nerveless and powerless by necessity.

The mottoes of great men often give us glimpses of the secret of their characters and success. "Work! work! work!" was the motto of Sir Joshua Reynolds, David Wilkie, and scores of other men who have left their mark upon the world. Voltaire's motto was "Toujours au travail" (always at work). Scott's maxim was "Never be doing nothing." Michael Angelo was a wonderful worker. He even slept in his clothes ready to spring to his work as soon as he awoke. He kept a block of marble in his bedroom that he might get up in the night and work when he could not sleep. His favorite device was an old man in a go-cart, with an hour-glass upon it, bearing this inscription: "Ancora imparo" (still I'm learning). Even after he was blind he would ask to be wheeled into the Belvidere, to examine the statues with his hands. Cobden used to say, "I'm working like a horse without a moment to spare." It was said that Handel, the musician, did the work of a dozen men. Nothing ever daunted him. He feared neither ridicule nor defeat. Lord Palmerston worked like a slave, even in his old age. Being asked when he considered a man in his prime, he replied, "Seventy-nine," that being his own age. Humboldt was one of the world's great workers. In summer he arose at four in the morning for thirty years. He used to say work was as much of a necessity as eating or sleeping. Sir Walter Scott was a phenomenal worker. He wrote the "Waverley Novels" at the rate of twelve volumes a year. He averaged a volume every two months during his whole working life. What an example is this to the young men of to-day, of the possibilities of an earnest life! Edmund Burke was one of the most prodigious workers that ever lived.

George Stephenson used to work at meal time, getting out loads of coal while the miners were at dinner in order that he might earn a few extra shillings to buy a spelling-book and an arithmetic. His associates thought he was very foolish, and asked him what good it would do to learn to read and cipher. He told them he was determined to improve his mind; so he studied whenever he could snatch a minute before the engine's fire, and in every possible situation until he had a good, practical, common-sense education.

Garibaldi's father decided that Guiseppe should be a minister, because the boy was so sorry for a cricket which lost its leg. Samuel Morse's father concluded that his son would preach well because he could not keep his head above water in a dangerous attempt to catch bait in the Mystic River. President Dwight told young Morse he would never make a painter, and hinted that he never would amount to much any way if he did not study more. Although under the teaching of West and Allston in London, he became a tolerable portrait painter, he did not find his sphere until returning from England on a sailing vessel, he heard Professor Jackson explain an electrical experiment in Paris, when the thought of the telegraph flashed into his mind and he found no rest, until he flashed over the wire the first message, "What hath God wrought!" on the experimental line between Baltimore and Washington: this was May 24, 1844.

William H. Vanderbilt was by far the wealthiest man in the world. Chauncey M. Depew estimated his fortune at two hundred millions. He left his eight children ten millions each, except Cornelius and William K., who had sixty-five millions each. Commodore Vanderbilt, his father, amassed a fortune of eighty millions of dollars in his own lifetime, and that too at a time when it was more difficult to make money than it is now.

Mr. C. P. Huntington is a good example of a self-made man. His father was a Connecticut farmer. The farm was left to him, but he traded it off for a lot of clocks which he peddled in mining districts for gold dust and nuggets. He and Mark Hopkins formed a partnership and opened a hardware store in California. They united with Leland Stanford in the construction of a railroad, and they all got rich rapidly. Mr. Huntington is one of the greatest railroad operators of the country. He always acted upon the principle that he would control the stock of any road in which he was interested. He is one of the most methodical men of all the millionaires of this country. He is very plain in his manner, strictly temperate, and very abstemious in his living. He said he never knew what it was to be tired.

Russell Sage used to keep a grocery store in Troy, N. Y. He finally associated himself with Jay Gould, who used to be a constant borrower of money of him. Mr. Sage probably keeps more ready money on hand than any other millionaire. He can nearly always control ten millions or more at call. He has never speculated in stocks to any extent. Mr. Sage's word is as good as any bond. He has no taste for ordinary diversions, except driving.

Philip D. Armour, who has the appearance of a prosperous farmer, was born on a farm near Watertown, N. J. He became fired with a desire to see the "Boundless West." His mind seemed to run to hogs, and with a financial instinct he made up his mind that there was a fortune in transporting the hogs from where they were so plenty to where there were so few of them and so many to eat them. He could now purchase every hog in the world and then have money left to buy a railroad or two.

Mrs. Hetty Green is probably the richest woman in the world. Her fortune has grown from the little industry of her father in New Bedford, Mass. She has raised the nine millions left her by her father and nine millions left her by her aunt to thirty millions. She is a woman of great ability and courage. She once took with her five millions of dollars of securities in a satchel on a street car to deposit with her banker on Wall street.

The probabilities are that billionaires will be as plentiful in the twentieth century as millionaires are to-day, through hard work, self-denial, rigid economy, method, accuracy, and strict temperance, for not one of the self-made millionaires are intemperate. John D. Rockefeller never tastes intoxicating liquor. He seems as unvarying in his method and system as the laws of the universe. Jay Gould did not use wine or intoxicating liquor of any kind. Mr. Huntington does not even drink coffee, while William Waldorf Astor merely takes a sip of wine for courtesy's sake. Not one of the leading millionaires uses tobacco, and not one of them is profane. Very rich men are almost always honest in their dealings, so far as their word is concerned. William Waldorf Astor, until recently, has been considered the richest man in the world, but John D. Rockefeller surpasses him now, it is said. The whole wealth of Croesus was little more than the income of this modern Croesus for one year. Mr. Rockefeller controls about eighty or ninety millions of capital stock in the Standard Oil Trust. The Standard Oil Company is one of the best managed corporations in the world.

Two centuries and a quarter ago, a little, tempest-tossed, weather-beaten bark, barely escaped from the jaws of the wild Atlantic, landed upon the bleakest shore of New England. From her deck disembarked a hundred and one careworn exiles.

To the casual observer no event could seem more insignificant. The contemptuous eye of the world scarcely deigned to notice it. Yet the famous vessel that bore Cæsar and his fortunes, carried but an ignoble freight compared with that of the Mayflower. Though landed by a treacherous pilot upon a barren and inhospitable coast, they sought neither richer fields nor a more congenial climate, but liberty and opportunity.

A lady once asked Turner the secret of his great success.

"I have no secret, madam, but hard work."

"This is a secret that many never learn, and they don't succeed because they fail to learn it. Labor is the genius that changes the world from ugliness to beauty, and the great curse to a great blessing."

See Balzac, in his lonely garret, toiling, toiling, waiting, waiting, amid poverty and hunger, but neither hunger, debt, poverty nor discouragement could induce him to swerve a hair's breadth from his purpose. He could wait, even while a world scoffed.

"Mankind is more indebted to industry than to ingenuity," says Addison; "the gods set up their favors at a price and industry is the purchaser."

Rome was a mighty nation while industry led her people, but when her great conquests of wealth and slaves placed her citizens above work, that moment her glory began to fade, and vice and corruption, induced by idleness, doomed the proud city to an ignominious history. Even Cicero, Rome's great orator, said, "All artisans are engaged in a disgraceful occupation;" and Aristotle said, "The best regulated states will not permit a mechanic to be a citizen, for it is impossible for one who lives the life of a mechanic, or hired servant, to practice a life of virtue. Some were born to be slaves." But, fortunately there came a mightier than Rome, Cicero or Aristotle, whose magnificent life and example forever lifted the false ban from labor and redeemed it from disgrace. He gave dignity to the most menial service, and significance to labor.

Christ did not say, "Come unto me all ye pleasure hunters, ye indolent and ye lazy;" but "Come all ye that *labor* and are *heavy laden.*"

Columbus was a persistent and practical, as well as an intellectual hero. He went from one state to another, urging kings and emperors to undertake the first visiting of a world which his instructed spirit already discerned in the far-off seas. He first tried his own countrymen at Genoa, but found none ready to help him. He then went to Portugal, and submitted his project to John II., who laid it before his council. It was scouted as extravagant and chimerical. Nevertheless, the king endeavored to steal Columbus's idea. A fleet was sent forth in the direction indicated by the navigator, but, being frustrated by storms and winds, it returned to Lisbon after four days' voyaging.

Columbus returned to Genoa, and again renewed his propositions to the Republic, but without success. Nothing discouraged him. The finding of the

New World was the irrevocable object of his life. He went to Spain, and landed at the town of Palos, in Andalusia. He went by chance to a convent of Franciscans, knocked at the door and asked for a little bread and water. The prior gratefully received the stranger, entertained him, and learned from him the story of his life. He encouraged him in his hopes, and furnished him with an admission to the Court of Spain, then at Cordova. King Ferdinand received him graciously, but before coming to a decision he desired to lay the project before a council of his wisest men at Salamanca. Columbus had to reply, not only to the scientific arguments laid before him, but to citations from the Bible. The Spanish clergy declared that the theory of the antipodes was hostile to the faith. The earth, they said, was an immense flat disk; and if there was a new earth beyond the ocean, then all men could not be descended from Adam. *Columbus was considered a fool.*

Still bent on his idea, he wrote to the King of England, then to the King of France, without effect. At last, in 1492, Columbus was introduced by Louis de Saint Angel to Queen Isabella of Spain. The friends who accompanied him pleaded his cause with so much force and conviction that he at length persuaded the queen to aid him.

Lord Ellenborough was a great worker. He had a very hard time in getting a start at the bar, but was determined never to relax his industry until success came to him. When he was worked down to absolute exhaustion, he had this card which he kept constantly before his eyes, lest he might be tempted to relax his efforts: "Read or Starve."

Show me a man who has made fifty thousand dollars, and I will show you in that man an equivalent of energy, attention to detail, trustworthiness, punctuality, professional knowledge, good address, common sense, and other marketable qualities. The farmer respects his savings bank book not unnaturally, for it declares with all the solemnity of a sealed and stamped document that for a certain length of time he rose at six o'clock each morning to oversee his labors, that he patiently waited upon seasonable weather, that he understood buying and selling. To the medical man, his fee serves as a medal to indicate that he was brave enough to face small pox and other infectious diseases, and his self-respect is fostered thereby.

The barrister's brief is marked with the price of his legal knowledge, of his eloquence, or of his brave endurance during a period of hope-deferred brieflessness.

A rich man asked Howard Burnett to do a little thing for his album. Burnett complied and charged a thousand francs. "But it took you only five minutes," objected the rich man. "Yes, but it took me thirty years to learn how to do it in five minutes."

"I prepared that sermon," said a young sprig of divinity, "in half an hour, and preached it at once, and thought nothing of it." "In that," said an older minister, "your hearers are at one with you, for they also thought nothing of it."

Virgil seems to have accomplished about four lines a week; but then they have lasted eighteen hundred years and will last eighteen hundred more.

Seven years Virgil is said to have expended in the composition of the Georgics, and they could all be printed in about seven columns of an ordinary newspaper. Tradition reports that he was in the habit of composing a few lines in the morning and spending the rest of the day in polishing them. Campbell used to say that if a poet made one good line a week, he did very well indeed; but Moore thought that if a poet did his duty, he could get a line done every day.

What an army of young men enters the success-contest every year as raw recruits! Many of them are country youths flocking to the cities to buy success. Their young ambitions have been excited by some book, or fired by the story of some signal success, and they dream of becoming Astors or Girards, Stewarts or Wanamakers, Vanderbilts or Goulds, Lincolns or Garfields, until their innate energy impels them to try their own fortune in the magic metropolis. But what are you willing to pay for "success," as you call it, young man? Do you realize what that word means in a great city in the nineteenth century, where men grow gray at thirty and die of old age at forty,—where the race of life has become so intense that the runners are treading on the heels of those before them; and "woe to him who stops to tie his shoestring?" Do you know that only two or three out of every hundred will ever win permanent success, and only because they have kept everlastingly at it; and that the rest will sooner or later fail and many die in poverty because they have given up the struggle.

There are multitudes of men who never rely wholly upon themselves and achieve independence. They are like summer vines, which never grow even ligneous, but stretch out a thousand little hands to grasp the stronger shrubs; and if they cannot reach them, they lie dishevelled in the grass, hoof-trodden, and beaten of every storm. It will be found that the first real movement upward will not take place until, in a spirit of resolute self-denial, indolence, so natural to almost every one, is mastered. Necessity is, usually, the spur that sets the sluggish energies in motion. Poverty, therefore, is often of inestimable value as an incentive to the best endeavors of which we are capable.

Foundation Stones

In all matters, before beginning, a diligent preparation should be Made.—Cicero

How great soever a genius may be, ... certain it is that he will never shine in his full lustre, nor shed the full influence he is capable of, unless to his own experience he adds that of other men and other ages. —Bolingbroke

It is for want of the little that human means must add to the wonderful capacity for improvement, born in man, that by far the greatest part of the intellect, innate in our race, perishes undeveloped and unknown. —Edward Everett

If any man fancies that there is some easier way of gaining a dollar than by squarely earning it, he has lost his clue to his way through this mortal labyrinth and must henceforth wander as chance may dictate. —Horace Greeley

What we do upon some great occasion will probably depend on what we already are; and what we are will be the result of previous years of self-discipline. —H. P. Liddon

Learn to labor and to wait. —Longfellow

"What avails all this sturdiness?" asked an oak tree which had grown solitary for two hundred years, bitterly handled by frosts and wrestled by winds. "Why am I to stand here useless? My roots are anchored in rifts of rocks; no herds can lie down under my shadow; I am far above singing birds, that seldom come to rest among my leaves; I am set as a mark for storms, that bend and tear me; my fruit is serviceable for no appetite; it had been better for me to have been a mushroom, gathered in the morning for some poor man's table, than to be a hundred-year oak, good for nothing."

While it yet spoke, the axe was hewing at its base. It died in sadness, saying as it fell, "Weary ages for nothing have I lived."

The axe completed its work. By and by the trunk and root form the knees of a stately ship, bearing the country's flag around the world. Other parts form keel and ribs of merchantmen, and having defied the mountain storms, they now equally resist the thunder of the waves and the murky threat of scowling hurricanes. Other parts are laid into floors, or wrought into wainscoting, or carved for frames of noble pictures, or fashioned into chairs that embosom the weakness of old age. Thus the tree, in dying, came not to its end, but to its beginning of life. It voyaged the world. It grew to parts of temples and dwellings. It held upon its surface the soft tread of children and the tottering steps of patriarchs. It rocked in the cradle. It swayed the limbs of age by the chimney corner, and heard, secure within, the roar of those old, unwearied tempests that once surged about its mountain life. All its early struggles and hardships had enabled it to grow tough and hard and beautiful of grain, alike useful and ornamental.

"Sir, you have been to college, I presume?" asked an illiterate but boastful exhorter of a clergyman. "Yes, sir," was the reply. "I am thankful," said the former, "that the Lord opened my mouth without any learning." "A similar event," retorted the clergyman, "happened in Balaam's time."

Why not allow the schoolboy to erase from his list of studies all subjects that appear to him useless? Would he not erase every thing which taxed his pleasure and freedom? Would he not obey the call of his blood, rather than the advice of his teacher? Ignorant men who have made money tell him that the study of geography is useless; his tea will come over the sea to him whether he knows where China is or not; what difference does it make whether verbs agree with their subjects or not? Why waste time learning geometry or algebra? Who keeps accounts by these? Learning spoils a man for business, they tell him; they begrudge the time and money spent in education. They want cheap and rapid transit through college for their children. Veneer will answer every practical purpose for them, instead of solid mahogany, or even paint and pine will do.

It is said that the editors of the Dictionary of American Biography who diligently searched the records of living and dead Americans, found 15,142 names worthy of a place in their six volumes of annals of successful men, and 5326, or more than one-third of them, were college-educated men. One in forty of the college educated attained a success worthy of mention, and but one in 10,000 of those not so educated; so that the college-bred man had two hundred and fifty times the chances for success that others had. Medical records, it is said, show that but five per cent. of the practicing physicians of the United States are college graduates; and yet forty-six per cent. of the physicians who became locally famous enough to be mentioned by those editors came from that small five per cent. of college educated persons. Less than four per cent. of the lawyers were college-bred, yet they furnished more than one-half of all who became successful. Not one per cent. of the business men of the country were college educated, yet that small fraction of college-bred men had seventeen times the chances of success that their fellow men of business had. In brief, the college-educated lawyer has fifty per cent. more chances for success than those not so favored; the college-educated physician, forty-six per cent. more; the author, thirty-seven per cent. more; the statesman, thirty-three per cent.; the clergyman, fifty-eight per cent.; the educator, sixty-one per cent.; the scientist, sixty-three per cent. You should therefore get the best and most complete education that it is possible for you to obtain.

Knowledge, then, is one of the secret keys which unlock the hidden mysteries of a successful life.

"I do not remember," said Beecher, "a book in all the depths of learning, nor a scrap in literature, nor a work in all the schools of art, from which its author has derived a permanent renown, that is not known to have been long and patiently elaborated."

"You are a fool to stick so close to your work all the time," said one of Vanderbilt's young friends; "we are having our fun while we are young, for when will we if not now?" But Cornelius was either earning more money by working overtime, or saving what he had earned, or at home asleep, recruiting for the next day's labor and preparing for a large harvest later. Like all successful men, he made finance a study. When he entered the railroad business, it was estimated that his fortune was thirty-five or forty million dollars.

"The spruce young spark," says Sizer, "who thinks chiefly of his mustache and boots and shiny hat, of getting along nicely and easily during the day, and talking about the theatre, the opera, or a fast horse, ridiculing the faithful young fellow who came to learn the business and make a man of himself, because he will not join in wasting his time in dissipation, will see the day, if his useless life is not earlier blasted by vicious indulgences, when he will be glad to accept a situation from his fellow-clerk whom he now ridicules and affects to despise, when the latter shall stand in the firm, dispensing benefits and acquiring fortune."

"When a man has done his work," says Ruskin, "and nothing can any way be materially altered in his fate, let him forget his toil, and jest with his fate if he will; but what excuse can you find for willfulness of thought at the very time when every crisis of fortune hangs on your decisions? A youth thoughtless, when all the happiness of his home forever depends on the chances or the passions of the hour! A youth thoughtless, when the career of all his days depends on the opportunity of a moment! A youth thoughtless, when his every action is a foundation-stone of future conduct, and every imagination a foundation of life or death! Be thoughtless in any after years, rather than now—though, indeed, there is only one place where a man may be nobly thoughtless, his deathbed. Nothing should ever be left to be done there."

"On to Berlin," was the shout of the French army in July, 1870; but, to the astonishment of the world, the French forces were cut in two and rolled as by a tidal wave into Metz and around Sedan. Soon two French armies and the Emperor surrendered, and German troopers paraded the streets of captured Paris.

But as men thought it out, as Professor Wells tells us, they came to see that it was not France that was beaten, but only Louis Napoleon and a lot of nobles, influential only because they bore titles or were favorites. Louis Napoleon, the feeble bearer of a great name, was emperor because of that name and criminal daring. By a series of happy accidents he had gained credit in the Crimean War, and at Magenta and Solferino. But the unmasking time came in the Franco-Prussian War, as it always comes when sham, artificial toy-men meet genuine self-made men. And such were the German leaders,—William, strong, upright, warlike, "every inch a king;" Von Roon, Minister of War, a master of administrative detail; Bismarck, the master mind of European politics; and, above all, Von Moltke, chief of staff, who hurled armies by telegraph, as he sat at his cabinet, as easily as a master moves chessmen against a stupid opponent.

Said Captain Bingham: "You can have no idea of the wonderful machine that the German army is and how well it is prepared for war. A chart is made out which shows just what must be done in the case of wars with the different nations. And every officer's place in the scheme is laid out beforehand. There is a schedule of trains which will supersede all other schedules the moment war is declared, and this is so arranged that the commander of the army here could telegraph to any officer to take such a train and go to such a place at a moment's notice. When the Franco-Prussian War was declared, Von Moltke was awakened at midnight and told of the fact. He said coolly to the official who aroused him, 'Go to pigeonhole No. —— in my safe and take a paper from it and telegraph as there directed to the different troops of the empire.' He then turned over and went to sleep and awoke at his usual hour in the morning. Every one else in Berlin was excited about the war, but Von Moltke took his morning walk as usual, and a friend who met him said, 'General, you seem to be taking it very easy. Aren't you afraid of the situation? I should think you would be busy.' 'Ah,' replied Von Moltke, 'all of my work for this time has been done long beforehand, and everything that can be done now has been done.'"

"A rare man this Von Moltke!" exclaims Professor Wells; "one who made himself ready for his opportunities beyond all men known to the modern world. Of an impoverished family, he rose very slowly and by his own merit. He yielded to no temptation, vice, or dishonesty, of course, nor to the greater and ever present temptation to idleness, for he constantly worked to the limit of human endurance. He was ready for every emergency, not by accident, but because he made himself ready by painstaking labor, before the opportunity came. His favorite motto was, '*Help yourself and others will help you.*' Hundreds of his age in the Prussian army were of nobler birth, thousands of greater fortune, but he made himself superior to them all by extraordinary fidelity and diligence.

"The greatest master of strategy the world has ever seen was sixty-six years at school to himself before he was ready for his task. Though born with the century, and an army officer at nineteen, he was an old man when, in 1866, as Prussian chief of staff, he crushed Austria at Sadowa and drove her out of Germany. Four years later the silent, modest soldier of seventy, ready for the still greater opportunity, smote France, and changed the map of Europe. Glory and the field-marshal's baton, after fifty-one years of hard work! No wonder Louis Napoleon was beaten by such men as he. All Louis Napoleons have been, and always will be. Opportunity always finds out frauds. It does not make men, but shows the world what they have made of themselves."

Sir Henry Havelock joined the army of India in his twenty-eighth year, and waited till he was sixty-two for the opportunity to show himself fitted to command and skillful to plan. During those four and thirty years of waiting, he was busy preparing himself for that march to Lucknow which was to make him famous as a soldier.

Farragut,

"The viking of our western clime Who made his mast a throne,"

began his naval career as a mere boy, and was sixty-four years old before he had an opportunity to distinguish himself; but when the great test of his life came, the reserve of half a century's preparation made him master of the situation.

Alexander Hamilton said, "Men give me credit for genius. All the genius I have lies just in this: when I have a subject in hand I study it profoundly. Day and night it is before me. I explore it in all its bearings. My mind becomes pervaded with it. Then the effort which I make the people are pleased to call the fruit of genius; it is the fruit of labor and thought." The law of labor is equally binding on genius and mediocrity.

"Fill up the cask! fill up the cask!" said old Dr. Bellamy when asked by a young clergyman for advice about the composition of sermons. "Fill up the cask! and then if you tap it anywhere you will get a good stream. But if you put in but little, it will dribble, dribble, dribble, and you must tap, tap, tap, and then you get but a small stream, after all."

"The merchant is in a dangerous position," says Dr. W. W. Patton, "whose means are in goods trusted out all over the country on long credits, and who in an emergency has no money in the bank upon which to draw. A heavy deposit, subject to a sight-draft, is the only position of strength. And he only is intellectually strong, who has made heavy deposits in the bank of memory, and can draw upon his faculties at any time, according to the necessities of the case."

They say that more life, if not more labor, was spent on the piles beneath the St. Petersburg church of St. Isaac's, to get a foundation, than on all the magnificent marbles and malachite which have since been lodged in it.

Fifty feet of Bunker Hill Monument is under ground, unseen, and unappreciated by the thousands who tread about that historic shaft. The rivers of India run under ground, unseen, unheard, by the millions who tramp above, but are they therefore lost? Ask the golden harvest waving above them if it feels the water flowing beneath? The superstructure of a lifetime cannot stand upon the foundation of a day.

C. H. Parkhurst says that in manhood, as much as in house-building, the foundation keeps asserting itself all the way from the first floor to the roof. The stones laid in the underpinning may be coarse and inelegant, but, even so, each such stone perpetuates itself in silent echo clear up through to the finial. The body is in that respect like an old Stradivarius violin, the ineffable sweetness of whose music is outcome and quotation from the coarse fibre of the case upon which its strings are strung. It is a very pleasant delusion that what we call the higher qualities and energies of a person maintain that self-centered kind of existence that enables them to discard and contemn all dependence upon what is lower and less refined than themselves, but it is a delusion that always wilts in an atmosphere of fact. Climb high as we like our ladder will still require to rest on the ground; and it is probable that the keenest intellectual intuition, and the most delicate throb of passion would, if analysis could be carried so far, be discovered to have its connections with the rather material affair that we know as the body.

Lincoln took the postmastership for the sake of reading all the papers that came to town. He read everything he could lay his hands on; the Bible, Shakespeare, Pilgrim's Progress, Life of Washington and Life of Franklin, Life of Henry Clay, Æsop's Fables; he read them over and over again until he could almost repeat them by heart; but he never read a novel in his life. His education came from the newspapers and from his contact with men and things. After he read a book he would write out an analysis of it. What a grand sight to see this long, lank, backwoods student, lying before the fire in a log cabin without floor or windows, after everybody else was abed, devouring books he had borrowed but could not afford to buy!

"I have been watching the careers of young men by the thousand in this busy city of New York for over thirty years," said Dr. Cuyler, "and I find that the chief difference between the successful and the failures lies in the single element of staying power. Permanent success is oftener won by holding on than by sudden dash, however brilliant. The easily discouraged, who are pushed back by a straw, are all the time dropping to the rear—to perish or to be carried along on the stretcher of charity. They who understand and practice Abraham Lincoln's homely maxim of 'pegging away' have achieved the solidest success."

It is better to deserve success than to merely have it; few deserve it who do not attain it. There is no failure in this country for those whose personal habits are good, and who follow some honest calling industriously, unselfishly, and purely. If one desires to succeed, he must pay the price, work.

No matter how weak a power may be, rational use will make it stronger. No matter how awkward your movements may be, how obtuse your senses, or how crude your thought, or how unregulated your desires, you may by patient discipline acquire, slowly indeed but with infallible certainty, grace and freedom of action, clearness and acuteness of perception, strength and precision of thought, and moderation of desire.

It would go very far to destroy the absurd and pernicious association of genius and idleness, to show that the greatest poets, orators, statesmen, and historians—men of the most imposing and brilliant talents—have actually labored as hard as the makers of dictionaries and arrangers of indexes; and the most obvious reason why they have been superior to other men, is, that they have taken more pains.

Even the great genius, Lord Bacon, left large quantities of material entitled "Sudden thoughts set down for use." John Foster was an indefatigable worker. "He used to hack, split, twist, and pull up by the roots, or practice any other severity on whatever did not please him." Chalmers was asked in London what Foster was doing. "Hard at it" he said, "at the rate of a line a week."

When a young lawyer, Daniel Webster once looked in vain through all the libraries near him, and then ordered at an expense of $50 the necessary books, to obtain authorities and precedents in a case in which his client was a poor blacksmith. He won his case, but, on account of the poverty of his client, only charged $15, thus losing heavily on the books bought, to say nothing of his time. Years after, as he was passing through New York city, he was consulted by Aaron Burr on an important but puzzling case then pending before the Supreme Court. Webster saw in a moment that it was just like the blacksmith's case, an intricate question of title, which he had solved so thoroughly that it was to him simple as the multiplication table. Going back to the time of Charles II., he gave the law and precedents involved with such readiness and accuracy of sequence that Burr asked, in great surprise: "Mr. Webster, have you been consulted before in this case?"

"Most certainly not. I never heard of your case till this evening."

"Very well," said Burr, "proceed." And when he had finished, Webster received a fee that paid him liberally for all the time and trouble he had spent for his early client.

What the age wants is men who have the nerve and the grit to work and wait, whether the world applaud or hiss. It wants a Bancroft, who can spend twenty-six years on the "History of the United States;" a Noah Webster, who can devote thirty-six years to a dictionary; a Gibbon, who can plod for twenty years on the "Decline and Fall of the Roman Empire;" a Mirabeau, who can struggle on for forty years before he has a chance to show his vast reserve, destined to shake an empire; a Farragut, a Von Moltke, who have the persistence to work and wait for half a century for their first great opportunities; a Garfield, burning his lamp fifteen minutes later than a rival student in his academy; a Grant, fighting on in heroic silence, when denounced by his brother generals and politicians everywhere; a Field's untiring perseverance, spending years and a fortune laying a cable when all the world called him a fool; a Michael Angelo, working seven long years decorating the Sistine Chapel with his matchless "Creation" and the "Last Judgment," refusing all remuneration therefor, lest his pencil might catch the taint of avarice; a Titian, spending seven years on the "Last Supper;" a Stephenson, working fifteen years on a locomotive; a Watt, twenty years on a condensing engine; a Lady Franklin, working incessantly for twelve long years to rescue her husband from the polar seas; a Thurlow Weed, walking two miles through the snow with rags tied around his feet for shoes, to borrow the history of the French Revolution, and eagerly devouring it before the sap-bush fire; a Milton, elaborating "Paradise Lost" in a world he could not see, and then selling it for fifteen pounds; a Thackeray, struggling on cheerfully after his "Vanity Fair" was refused by a dozen publishers; a Balzac, toiling and waiting in a lonely garret, whom neither poverty, debt, nor hunger could discourage or intimidate; not daunted by privations, not hindered by discouragements. It wants men who can work and wait.

That is done soon enough which is done well. Soon ripe, soon rotten. He that would enjoy the fruit must not gather the flower. He who is impatient to become his own master is more likely to become his own slave. Better believe yourself a dunce and work away than a genius and be idle. One year of trained thinking is worth more than a whole college course of mental absorption of a vast series of undigested facts. The facility with which the world swallows up the ordinary college graduate who thought he was going to dazzle mankind should bid you pause and reflect. But just as certainly as man was created not to crawl on all fours in the depths of primeval forests, but to develop his mental and moral faculties, just so certainly he needs education, and only by means of it will he become what he ought to become,—man, in the highest sense of the word. Ignorance is not simply the negation of knowledge, it is the misdirection of the mind. "One step in knowledge," says Bulwer, "is one step from sin; one step from sin is one step nearer to Heaven."

The Conquest of Obstacles

Nature, when she adds difficulties, adds brains. —Emerson

Exigencies create the necessary ability to meet and conquer them.—Wendell Phillips

Many men owe the grandeur of their lives to their tremendous difficulties.—Spurgeon

The rugged metal of the mine
Must burn before its surface shine. —Byron

When a man looks through a tear in his own eye, that is a lens which opens reaches in the unknown, and reveals orbs no telescope could do.—Beecher

No man ever worked his way in a dead calm. —John Neal

"Kites rise against, not with, the wind."
Then welcome each rebuff,
That turns earth's smoothness rough,
Each sting, that bids not sit nor stand, but go. —Browning

"What a fine profession ours would be if there were no gibbets!" said one of two highwaymen who chanced to pass a gallows. "Tut, you blockhead," replied the other, "gibbets are the making of us; for, if there were no gibbets, every one would be a highwayman." Just so with every art, trade, or pursuit; it is the difficulties that scare and keep out unworthy competitors.

"Life," says a philosopher, "refuses to be so adjusted as to eliminate from it all strife and conflict and pain. There are a thousand tasks, that, in larger interests than ours, must be done, whether we want them or no. The world refuses to walk upon tiptoe, so that we may be able to sleep. It gets up very early and stays up very late, and all the while there is the conflict of myriads of hammers and saws and axes with the stubborn material that in no other way can be made to serve its use and do its work for man. And then, too, these hammers and axes are not wielded without strain or pang, but swung by the millions of toilers who labor with their cries and groans and tears. Nay, our temple building, whether it be for God or man, exacts its bitter toll, and fills life with cries and blows. The thousand rivalries of our daily business, the fierce animosities when we are beaten, the even fiercer exultation when we have beaten, the crashing blows of disaster, the piercing scream of defeat—these things we have not yet gotten rid of, nor in this life ever will. Why should we wish to get rid of them? We are here, my brother, to be hewed and hammered and planed in God's quarry and on God's anvil for a nobler life to come." Only the muscle that is used is developed.

"Troubles are often the tools by which God fashions us for better things," said Beecher. "Far up the mountain side lies a block of granite, and says to itself, 'How happy am I in my serenity—above the winds, above the trees, almost above the flight of birds! Here I rest, age after age, and nothing disturbs me.'

"Yet what is it? It is only a bare block of granite, jutting out of the cliff, and its happiness is the happiness of death.

"By and by comes the miner, and with strong and repeated strokes he drills a hole in its top, and the rock says, 'What does this mean?' Then the black powder is poured in, and with a blast that makes the mountain echo, the block is blown asunder, and goes crashing down into the valley. 'Ah!' it exclaims as it falls, 'why this rending?' Then come saws to cut and fashion it; and humbled now, and willing to be nothing, it is borne away from the mountain and conveyed to the city. Now it is chiseled and polished, till, at length, finished in beauty, by block and tackle it is raised, with mighty hoistings, high in air, to be the top-stone on some monument of the country's glory."

"It is this scantiness of means, this continual deficiency, this constant hitch, this perpetual struggle to keep the head above water and the wolf from the door, that keeps society from falling to pieces. Let every man have a few more dollars than he wants, and anarchy would follow."

"Do you wish to live without a trial?" asks a modern teacher. "Then you wish to die but half a man. Without trial you cannot guess at your own strength. Men do not learn to swim on a table. They must go into deep water and buffet the waves. Hardship is the native soil of manhood and self-reliance. Trials are rough teachers, but rugged schoolmasters make rugged pupils. A man who goes through life prosperous, and comes to his grave without a wrinkle, is not half a man. Difficulties are God's errands. And when we are sent upon them we should esteem it a proof of God's confidence. We should reach after the highest good."

Suddenly, with much jarring and jolting, an electric car came to a standstill just in front of a heavy truck that was headed in an opposite direction. The huge truck wheels were sliding uselessly round on the car tracks that were wet and slippery from rain. All the urging of the teamster and the straining of the horses were in vain—until the motorman quietly tossed a shovelful of sand on the track under the heavy wheels, and then the truck lumbered on its way. "Friction is a very good thing," remarked a passenger.

There is a beautiful tale of Scandinavian mythology. A hero, under the promise of becoming a demi-god, is bidden in the celestial halls to perform three test-acts of prowess. He is to drain the drinking-horn of Thor. Then he must run a race with a courser so fleet that he fairly spurns the ground under his flying footsteps. Then he must wrestle with a toothless old woman, whose sinewy hands, as wiry as eagle claws in the grapple, make his very flesh to quiver. He is victorious in them all. But as the crown of success is placed upon his temples, he discovers for the first time that he has had for his antagonist the three greatest forces of nature. He raced with thought, he wrestled with old age, he drank the sea. Nature, like the God of nature, wrestles with us as a friend, not an enemy, wanting us to gain the victory, and wrestles with us that we may understand and enjoy her best blessings. Every greatest and highest earthly good has come to us unfolded and enriched by this terrible wrestling with nature.

A curious society still exists in Paris composed of dramatic authors who meet once a month and dine together. Their number has no fixed limit, only every member to be eligible must have been hissed. An eminent dramatist is selected for chairman and holds the post for three months. His election generally follows close upon a splendid failure. Some of the world-famous ones have enjoyed this honor. Dumas, Jr., Zola and Offenbach have all filled the chair and presided at the monthly dinner. These dinners are given on the last Friday of the month, and are said to be extraordinarily hilarious.

"I do believe God wanted a grand poem of that man," said George Macdonald of Milton, "and so blinded him that he might be able to write it."

"Returned with thanks" has made many an author. Failure often leads a man to success by arousing his latent energy, by firing a dormant purpose, by awakening powers which were sleeping. Men of mettle turn disappointments into helps as the oyster turns into pearls the sand which annoys it.

"Let the adverse breath of criticism be to you only what the blast of the storm wind is to the eagle,—a force against him that lifts him higher."

"I do not see," says Emerson, "how any man can afford, for the sake of his nerves and his nap, to spare any action in which he can partake. It is pearls and rubies to his discourse. Drudgery, calamity, exasperation, want, are instructors in eloquence and wisdom. The true scholar grudges every opportunity of action passed by as a loss of power."

"Adversity is a severe instructor," says Edmund Burke, "set over us by one who knows us better than we do ourselves, as He loves us better too. He that wrestles with us strengthens our nerves and sharpens our skill. Our antagonist is our helper. This conflict with difficulty makes us acquainted with our object, and compels us to consider it in all its relations. It will not suffer us to be superficial."

Strong characters, like the palm tree, seem to thrive best when most abused. Men who have stood up bravely under great misfortune for years are often unable to bear prosperity. Their good fortune takes the spring out of their energy, as the torrid zone enervates races accustomed to a vigorous climate. Some people never come to themselves until baffled, rebuffed, thwarted, defeated, crushed, in the opinion of those around them. Trials unlock their virtues; defeat is the threshold of their victory.

"Every man who makes a fortune has been more than once a bankrupt, if the truth were known," said Albion Tourgée. "Grant's failure as a subaltern made him commander-in-chief, and for myself, my failure to accomplish what I set out to do led me to what I never had aspired to."

"What is defeat?" asked Wendell Phillips. "Nothing but education." And a life's disaster may become the landmark from which there has begun a new era, a broader life for man.

"To make his way at the bar," said an eminent jurist, "a young man must live like a hermit and work like a horse. There is nothing that does a young lawyer so much good as to be half starved."

We are the victors of our opponents. They have developed in us the very power by which we overcome them. Without their opposition we could never have braced and anchored and fortified ourselves, as the oak is braced and anchored for its thousand battles with the tempests. Our trials, our sorrows, and our griefs develop us in a similar way.

"Obstacles," says Mitchell, "are great incentives. I lived for whole years upon Virgil and found myself well off." Poverty, Horace tells us, drove him to poetry.

Nothing more unmans a man than to take away from him the spur of necessity, which urges him onward and upward to the goal of his ambition. Man is naturally lazy, and wealth induces indolence. The great object of life is development, the unfolding and drawing out of our powers, and whatever tempts us to a life of indolence or inaction, or to seek pleasure merely, whatever furnishes us a crutch when we can develop our muscles better by walking, all helps, guides, props, whatever tempts to a life of inaction, in whatever guise it may come, is a curse. I always pity the boy or girl with inherited wealth, for the temptation to hide their talents in a napkin, undeveloped, is very, very great. It is not natural for them to walk when they can ride, to go alone when they can be helped.

Quentin Matsys was a blacksmith at Antwerp. When in his twentieth year he wished to marry the daughter of a painter. The father refused his consent. "Wert thou a painter," said he, "she should be thine; but a blacksmith—never!" "*I will be* a painter," said the young man. He applied to his new art with so much perseverance that in a short time he produced pictures which gave a promise of the highest excellence. He gained for his reward the fair hand for which he sighed, and rose ere long to a high rank in his profession.

Take two acorns from the same tree, as nearly alike as possible; plant one on a hill by itself, and the other in the dense forest, and watch them grow. The oak standing alone is exposed to every storm. Its roots reach out in every direction, clutching the rocks and piercing deep into the earth. Every rootlet lends itself to steady the growing giant, as if in anticipation of fierce conflict with the elements. Sometimes its upward growth seems checked for years, but all the while it has been expending its energy in pushing a root across a large rock to gain a firmer anchorage. Then it shoots proudly aloft again, prepared to defy the hurricane. The gales which sport so rudely with its wide branches find more than their match, and only serve still further to toughen every minutest fibre from pith to bark.

The acorn planted in the deep forest shoots up a weak, slender sapling. Shielded by its neighbors, it feels no need of spreading its roots far and wide for support.

Take two boys, as nearly alike as possible. Place one in the country away from the hothouse culture and refinements of the city, with only the district school, the Sunday school, and a few books. Remove wealth and props of every kind; and, if he has the right kind of material in him, he will thrive. Every obstacle overcome lends him strength for the next conflict. If he falls, he rises with more determination than before. Like a rubber ball, the harder the obstacle he meets the higher he rebounds. Obstacles and opposition are but apparatus of the gymnasium in which the fibres of his manhood are developed. He compels respect and recognition from those who have ridiculed his poverty. Put the other boy in a Vanderbilt family. Give him French and German nurses; gratify every wish. Place him under the tutelage of great masters and send him to Harvard. Give him thousands a year for spending money, and let him travel extensively.

The two meet. The city lad is ashamed of his country brother. The plain, threadbare clothes, hard hands, tawny face, and awkward manner of the country boy make sorry contrast with the genteel appearance of the other. The poor boy bemoans his hard lot, regrets that he has "no chance in life," and envies the city youth. He thinks that it is a cruel Providence that places such a wide gulf between them. They meet again as men, but how changed! It is as easy to distinguish the sturdy, self-made man from the one who has been propped up all his life by wealth, position, and family influence, as it is for the shipbuilder to tell the difference between the plank from the rugged mountain oak and one from the sapling of the forest. If you think there is no difference, place each plank in the bottom of a ship, and test them in a hurricane at sea.

The athlete does not carry the gymnasium away with him, but he carries the skill and muscle which give him his reputation.

The lessons you learn at school will give you strength and skill in after life, and power, just in proportion to the accuracy, the clearness of perception with which you learn your lessons. The school was your gymnasium. You do not carry away the Greek and Latin text-books, the geometry and algebra into your occupations any more than the athlete carries the apparatus of the gymnasium, but you carry away the skill and the power if you have been painstaking, accurate and faithful.

"It is in me, and it *shall* come out!" And it did. For Richard Brinsley Sheridan became the most brilliant, eloquent and amazing statesman of his day. Yet if his first efforts had been but moderately successful, he might have been content with mere mediocrity. It was his defeats that nerved him to strive for eminence and win it. But it took hard, persistent work in his case to secure it, just as it did in that of so many others.

Byron was stung into a determination to go to the top by a scathing criticism of his first book, "Hours of Idleness," published when he was but nineteen years of age. Macaulay said, "There is scarce an instance in history of so sudden a rise to so dizzy an eminence as Byron reached." In a few years he stood by the side of such men as Scott, Southey and Campbell. Many an orator like "stuttering Jack Curran," or "Orator Mum," as he was once called, has been spurred into eloquence by ridicule and abuse.

Where the sky is gray and the climate unkindly, where the soil yields nothing save to the diligent hand, and life itself cannot be supported without incessant toil, man has reached his highest range of physical and intellectual development.

The most beautiful and the strongest animals, as a rule, have come from the same narrow belt of latitude which has produced the heroes of the world.

The most beautiful as well as the strongest characters are not developed in warm climates, where man finds his bread ready made on trees, and where exertion is a great effort, but rather in a trying climate and on a stubborn soil. It is no chance that returns to the Hindoo ryot a penny and to the American laborer a dollar for his daily toil; that makes Mexico with her mineral wealth poor, and New England with its granite and ice rich. It is rugged necessity, it is the struggle to obtain, it is poverty the priceless spur, that develops the stamina of manhood, and calls the race out of barbarism. Labor found the world a wilderness and has made it a garden.

The law of adaptation by which conditions affect an organism is simple and well known. It is that which callouses the palm of the oarsman, strengthens the waist of the wrestler, fits the back to its burden. It inexorably compels the organism to adapt itself to its conditions, to like them, and so to survive them.

As soon as young eagles can fly the old birds tumble them out and tear the down and feathers from their nest. The rude and rough experience of the eaglet fits him to become the bold king of birds, fierce and expert in pursuing his prey.

Benjamin Franklin ran away and George Law was turned out of doors. Thrown upon their own resources, they early acquired the energy and skill to overcome difficulties.

Boys who are bound out, crowded out, kicked out, usually "turn out," while those who do not have these disadvantages frequently fail to "come out."

From an aimless, idle and useless brain, emergencies often call out powers and virtues before unknown and unsuspected. How often we see a young man develop astounding ability and energy after the death of a parent or the loss of a fortune, or after some other calamity has knocked the props and crutches from under him. The prison has roused the slumbering fire in many a noble mind. "Robinson Crusoe" was written in prison. The "Pilgrim's Progress" appeared in Bedford Jail. The "Life and Times" of Baxter, Eliot's "Monarchia of Man," and Penn's "No Cross, No Crown," were written by prisoners. Sir Walter Raleigh wrote "The History of the World" during his imprisonment of thirteen years. Luther translated the Bible while confined in the Castle of Wartburg. For twenty years Dante worked in exile, and even under sentence of death. His works were burned in public after his death; but genius will not burn.

Adversity exasperates fools, dejects cowards, draws out the faculties of the wise and industrious, puts the modest to the necessity of trying their skill, awes the opulent, and makes the idle industrious. Neither do uninterrupted success and prosperity qualify men for usefulness and happiness. The storms of adversity, like those of the ocean, rouse the faculties, and excite the invention, prudence, skill and fortitude of the voyager. The martyrs of ancient times, in bracing their minds to outward calamities, acquired a loftiness of purpose and a moral heroism worth a lifetime of softness and security. A man upon whom continuous sunshine falls is like the earth in August: he becomes parched and dry and hard and close-grained. Men have drawn from adversity the elements of greatness. If you have the blues, go and see the poorest and sickest families within your knowledge. The darker the setting, the brighter the diamond. Don't run about and tell acquaintances that you have been unfortunate; people do not like to have unfortunate men for acquaintances.

This is the crutch age. "Helps" and "aids" are advertised everywhere. We have institutes, colleges, universities, teachers, books, libraries, newspapers, magazines. Our thinking is done for us. Our problems are all worked out in "explanations" and "keys." Our boys are too often tutored through college with very little study. "Short roads" and "abridged methods" are characteristic of the century. Ingenious methods are used everywhere to get the drudgery out of the college course. Newspapers give us our politics, and preachers our religion. Self-help and self-reliance are getting old fashioned. Nature, as if conscious of delayed blessings, has rushed to man's relief with her wondrous forces, and undertakes to do the world's drudgery and emancipate him from Eden's curse.

Dead In Earnest

It is the live coal that kindles others, not the dead. What made Demosthenes the greatest of all orators was that he appeared the most entirely possessed by the feelings he wished to inspire. The effect produced by Charles Fox, who by the exaggerations of party spirit, was often compared to Demosthenes, seems to have arisen wholly from this earnestness, which made up for the want of almost every grace, both of manner and style. —Anon

Twelve poor men taken out of boats and creeks, without any help of learning, should conquer the world to the cross. —Stephen Carnock

For his heart was in his work, and the heart Giveth grace unto every art.—Longfellow

He did it with all his heart and prospered. —II. Chronicles

The only conclusive evidence of a man's sincerity is that he gives himself for a principle. Words, money, all things else are comparatively easy to give away; but when a man makes a gift of his daily life and practice, it is plain that the truth, whatever it may be, has taken possession of him. —Lowell

"The emotions," says Whipple, "may all be included in the single word 'enthusiasm,' or that impulsive force which liberates the mental power from the ice of timidity as spring loosens the streams from the grasp of winter, and sends them forth in a rejoicing rush. The mind of youth, when impelled by this original strength and enthusiasm of Nature, is keen, eager, inquisitive, intense, audacious, rapidly assimilating facts into faculties and knowledge into power, and above all teeming with that joyous fullness of creative life which radiates thoughts as inspirations, and magnetizes as well as informs."

"Columbus, my hero," exclaims Carlyle, "royalist sea-king of all! It is no friendly environment this of thine, in the waste, deep waters; around thee mutinous discouraged souls, behind thee disgrace and ruin, before thee the unpenetrated veil of night. Brother, these wild water-mountains, bounding from their deep bases (ten miles deep, I am told), are not there on thy behalf! Meseems *they* have other work than floating thee forward:—and the huge winds, that sweep from Ursa Major to the tropics and equator, dancing their giant-waltz through the kingdoms of chaos and immensity, they care little about filling rightly or filling wrongly the small shoulder-of-mutton sails in this cockle skiff of thine! Thou art not among articulate-speaking friends, my brother; thou art among immeasurable dumb monsters, tumbling, howling wide as the world here. Secret, far-off, invisible to all hearts but thine, there lies a help in them: see how thou wilt get at that. Patiently thou wilt wait till the mad southwester spend itself, saving thyself by dexterous science of defence the while: valiantly, with swift decision, wilt thou strike in, when the favoring east wind, the possible, springs up. Mutiny of men thou wilt sternly repress; weakness, despondency, thou wilt cheerily encourage: thou wilt swallow down complaint, unreason, weariness, weakness of others and thyself;—how much wilt thou swallow down? There shall be a depth of silence in thee, deeper than this sea, which is but ten miles deep: a silence unsoundable; known to God only. Thou shalt be a great man. Yes, my world-soldier, thou of the world marine-service,—thou wilt have to be greater than this tumultuous unmeasured world here round thee is: thou, in thy strong soul, as with wrestler's arms, shall embrace it, harness it down; and make it bear thee on,—to new Americas, or whither God wills!"

With what concentration of purpose did Washington put the whole weight of his character into the scales of our cause in the Revolution! With what earnest singleness of aim did Lincoln in the cabinet, Grant in the field, throw his whole soul into the contest of our civil war?

The power of Phillips Brooks, at which men wondered, lay in his tremendous earnestness.

"No matter what your work is," says Emerson, "let it be yours; no matter if you are a tinker or preacher, blacksmith or president, let what you are doing be organic, let it be in your bones, and you open the door by which the affluence of heaven and earth shall stream into you." Again, he says: "God will not have His works made manifest by cowards. A man is relieved and gay when he has put his heart into his work and done his best; but what he has said or done otherwise, shall give him no peace. It is a deliverance which does not deliver. In the attempt, his genius deserts him; no muse befriends; no invention, no hope."

"I do not know how it is with others when speaking on an important question," said Henry Clay; "but on such occasions I seem to be unconscious of the external world. Wholly engrossed by the subject before me, I lose all sense of personal identity, of time, or of surrounding objects."

"I have been so busy for twenty years trying to save the souls of other people," said Livingstone, "that I had forgotten that I have one of my own until a savage auditor asked me if I felt the influence of the religion I was advocating."

"Well, I've worked hard enough for it," said Malibran when a critic expressed his admiration of her D in alt, reached by running up three octaves from low D; "I've been chasing it for a month. I pursued it everywhere,—when I was dressing, when I was doing my hair; and at last I found it on the toe of a shoe that I was putting on."

"People smile at the enthusiasm of youth," said Charles Kingsley; "that enthusiasm which they themselves secretly look back at with a sigh, perhaps unconscious that it is partly their own fault that they ever lost it."

"Should I die this minute," said Nelson at an important crisis, "want of frigates would be found written on my heart."

Said Dr. Arnold, the celebrated instructor: "I feel more and more the need of intercourse with men who take life in earnest. It is painful to me to be always on the surface of things. Not that I wish for much of what is called religious conversation. That is often apt to be on the surface. But I want a sign which one catches by a sort of masonry, that a man knows what he is about in life. When I find this it opens my heart with as fresh a sympathy as when I was twenty years younger."

Archimedes, the greatest geometer of antiquity, was consulted by the king in regard to a gold crown suspected of being fraudulently alloyed with silver. While considering the best method of detecting any fraud, he plunged into a full bathing tub; and, with the thought that the water that overflowed must be equal in weight to his body, he discovered the method of obtaining the bulk of the crown compared with an equally heavy mass of pure gold. Excited by the discovery, he ran through the streets undressed, crying, "I have found it."

Equally celebrated is his remark, "Give me where to stand and I will move the world."

His only remark to the Roman soldier who entered his room while engaged in geometrical study, was, "Don't step on my circle."

Refusing to follow the soldier to Marcellus, who had captured the city, he was killed on the spot. He is said to have remarked, "My head, but not my circle."

"Every great and commanding moment in the annals of the world," says Emerson, "is the triumph of some enthusiasm. The victories of the Arabs after Mahomet, who, in a few years, from a small and mean beginning, established a larger empire than that of Rome, is an example. They did they knew not what. The naked Derar, horsed on an idea, was found an overmatch for a troop of cavalry. The women fought like men and conquered the Roman men. They were miserably equipped, miserably fed. They were temperance troops. There was neither brandy nor flesh needed to feed them. They conquered Asia and Africa and Spain on barley. The Caliph Omar's walking-stick struck more terror into those who saw it than another man's sword."

Horace Vernet's enthusiasm and devotion to the one idea of his life knew no bounds. He had himself lashed to the mast in a terrible gale on the Mediterranean when all others on board were seized with terror, and with great delight sketched the towering waves which threatened every minute to swallow the vessel. Several writers tell the story that a great artist, Giotto, about to paint the crucifixion, induced a poor man to let him bind him upon a cross in order that he might get a better idea of the terrible scene that he was about to put upon the canvas. He promised faithfully that he would release his model in an hour, but to the latter's horror the painter seized a dagger and plunged it into his heart; and, while the blood was streaming from the ghastly wound, painted his death agony.

Beecher was a very dull boy and was the last member of the family of whom anything was expected. He had a weak memory, and disliked study. He shunned society and wanted to go to sea. Even when he went to college many of his classmates stood ahead of him, who have fallen into oblivion. But when he was converted his whole life changed: he was full of enthusiasm, hopefulness and zeal. Nothing was too menial for him to undertake to carry his purpose. He chopped wood, built the fire in his little church in Lawrenceburg, Ind., of only eighteen members, cleaned the lamps, swept the floor and washed the windows. He built the fire, baked, washed, when his wife was ill. The pent-up enthusiasm of his ambitious life burst the barriers of his inhospitable surroundings until he blossomed out into America's greatest pulpit orator.

When Handel was a little boy he bought a clavichord, hid it in the attic, and went there at night to play upon it, muffling the strings with small pieces of fine woolen cloth so that the sounds should not wake the family. Michael Angelo neglected school to copy drawings which he dared not carry home. Murillo filled the margin of his school-book with drawings. Dryden read Polybius before he was ten years old. Le Brum, when a boy, drew with a piece of charcoal on the walls of the house. Pope wrote excellent verses at fourteen. Blaise Pascal, the French mathematician, composed at sixteen a tract on the conic sections.

Professor Agassiz was so enthusiastic in his work and so loved the fishes, the fowl and the cattle that it is said these creatures would die for him to give him their skeletons. His father wanted him to fit for commercial life, but the fish haunted him day and night.

Confucius said that "he was so eager in the pursuit of knowledge that he forgot his food;" and that, "in the joy of its attainment, he forgot his sorrows;" and that "he did not even perceive that old age was coming on."

"That boy tries to make himself useful," said an employer of the errand boy, George W. Childs. It is this trying to be useful and helpful that promotes us in life.

Once, when Mr. Harvey, an accomplished mathematician, was in a bookseller's shop, he saw a poor lad of mean appearance enter and write something on a slip of paper and give it to the proprietor. On inquiry he found this was a poor deaf boy, Kitto, who afterward became one of the most noted Biblical scholars in the world, and who wrote his first book in the poor-house. He had come to borrow a book. When a lad he had fallen backward from a ladder thirty-five feet upon the pavement with a load of slates that he was carrying to the roof. The poor lad was so thirsty for books that he would borrow from booksellers who would loan them to him out of pity, read them and return them.

The *Youth's Companion* says that Mr. Edison in his new biography—his "Life and Inventions"—describes the accidental method by which he discovered the principle of the phonograph. There is a kind of accident that happens only to a certain kind of man.

"I was singing to the mouthpiece of a telephone," Mr. Edison says, "when the vibrations of the voice sent the fine steel point into my finger. That set me to thinking. If I could record the actions of the point, and send the point over the same surface afterward, I saw no reason why the thing would not talk.

"I tried the experiment first on a slip of telegraph paper and found that the point made an alphabet. I shouted the words 'Halloo! Halloo!' into the mouthpiece, ran the paper back over the steel point, and heard a faint 'Halloo! Halloo!' in return.

"I determined to make a machine that would work accurately, and gave my assistants instructions, telling them what I had discovered. They laughed at me. That's the whole story. The phonograph is the result of the pricking of a finger."

It is one thing to hit upon an idea, however, and another thing to carry it out to perfection. The machine would talk, but, like many young children, it had difficulty with certain sounds—in the present case with aspirants and sibilants. Mr. Edison's biographers say, but the statement is somewhat exaggerated:

"He has frequently spent from fifteen to twenty hours daily, for six or seven months on a stretch, dinning the word 'Spezia,' for example, into the stubborn surface of the wax. 'Spezia,' roared the inventor, 'Pezia' lisped the phonograph in tones of ladylike reserve, and so on through thousands of graded repetitions till the desired results were obtained.

"The primary education of the phonograph was comical in the extreme. To hear those grave and reverend signors, rich in scientific honors, patiently reiterating:

Mary had a little lamb, A little lamb, *lamb*, **lamb**,

and elaborating that point with anxious gravity, was to receive a practical demonstration of the eternal unfitness of things."

Milton, when blind, old and poor, showed a royal cheerfulness and never "bated one jot of heart or hope, but steered right onward."

Dickens' characters seemed to possess him, and haunt him day and night until properly portrayed in his stories.

At a time when it was considered dangerous to society in Europe for the common people to read books and listen to lectures on any but religious subjects, Charles Knight determined to enlighten the masses by cheap literature. He believed that a paper could be instructive and not be dull, cheap without being wicked. He started the *Penny Magazine*, which acquired a circulation of 200,000 the first year. Knight projected the *Penny Cyclopedia*, the *Library of Entertaining Knowledge, Half-Hours With the Best Authors*, and other useful books at a low price. His whole adult life was spent in the work of elevating the common people by cheap, yet wholesome, publications. He died in poverty, but grateful people have erected a noble monument over his ashes.

Demosthenes roused the torpid spirits of his countrymen to a vigorous effort to preserve their independence against the designs of an ambitious and artful prince, and Philip had just reason to say he was more afraid of that man than of all the fleets and armies of the Athenians.

Horace Greeley was a hampered genius who never had a chance to show himself until he started the *Tribune*, into which he poured his whole individuality, life and soul.

Emerson lost the first years of his life trying to be somebody else. He finally came to himself and said: "If a single man plant himself indomitably on his instincts, and there abide, the whole world will come round to him in the end." "Though we travel the world over to find the beautiful we must carry it with us or we find it not." "The man that stands by himself the universe stands by him also." "Take Michael Angelo's course, 'to confide in one's self and be something of worth and value.'" "None of us will ever accomplish anything excellent or commanding except when he listens to this whisper which is heard by him alone."

Many unknown writers would make fame and fortune if, like Bunyan and Milton and Dickens and George Eliot and Scott and Emerson, they would write their own lives in their MSS., if they would write about things they have seen, that they have felt, that they have known. It is life thoughts that stir and convince, that move and persuade, that carry their very iron particles into the blood. The real heaven has never been outdone by the ideal.

Neither poverty nor misfortune could keep Linnæus from his botany.

The English and Austrian armies called Napoleon the one-hundred-thousand-man. His presence was considered equal to that force in battle.

The lesson he teaches is that which vigor always teaches—that there is always room for it. To what heaps of cowardly doubts is not that man's life an answer.

To Be Great, Concentrate

Let every one ascertain his special business and calling, and then stick to it. —Franklin

"He who follows two hares is sure to catch neither."
None sends his arrow to the mark in view, Whose hand is feeble, or his aim untrue. —Cowper

He who wishes to fulfill his mission must be a man of one idea, that is, of one great overmastering purpose, overshadowing all his aims, and guiding and controlling his entire life. —Bate

The shortest way to do anything is to do only one thing at a time. —Cecil

The power of concentration is one of the most valuable of intellectual attainments. —Horace Mann

The power of a man increases steadily by continuance in one direction.—Emerson

Careful attention to one thing often proves superior to genius and art.—Cicero

"It puffed like a locomotive," said a boy of the donkey engine; "it whistled like the steam-cars, but it didn't go anywhere."
The world is full of donkey-engines, of people who can whistle and puff and pull, but they don't go anywhere, they have no definite aim, no controlling purpose.
The great secret of Napoleon's power lay in his marvelous ability to concentrate his forces upon a single point. After finding the weak place in the enemy's ranks he would mass his men and hurl them upon the enemy like an avalanche until he made a breach. What a lesson of the power of concentration there is in that man's life! He was such a master of himself that he could concentrate his powers upon the smallest detail as well as upon an empire.
When Napoleon had anything to say he always went straight to his mark. He had a purpose in everything he did; there was no dilly-dallying nor shilly-shallying; he knew what he wanted to say, and said it. It was the same with all his plans; what he wanted to do, he did. He always hit the bull's eye. His great success in war was due largely to his definiteness of aim. He knew what he wanted to do, and did it. He was like a great burning glass, concentrating the rays of the sun upon a single spot; he burned a hole wherever he went.
The sun's rays scattered do no execution, but concentrated in a burning glass, they melt solid granite; yes, a diamond, even. There are plenty of men

who have ability enough, the rays of their faculties taken separately are all right; but they are powerless to collect them, to concentrate them upon a single object. They lack the burning glass of a purpose, to focalize upon one spot the separate rays of their ability. Versatile men, universal geniuses, are usually weak, because they have no power to concentrate the rays of their ability, to focalize them upon one point, until they burn a hole in whatever they undertake.

This power to bring all of one's scattered forces into one focal point makes all the difference between success and failure. The sun might blaze out upon the earth forever without burning a hole in it or setting anything on fire; whereas a very few of these rays concentrated in a burning glass would, as stated, transform a diamond into vapor.

Sir James Mackintosh was a man of marvelous ability. He excited in everybody who knew him great expectations, but there was no purpose in his life to act as a burning glass to collect the brilliant rays of his intellect, by which he might have dazzled the world. Most men have ability enough, if they could only focalize it into one grand, central, all-absorbing purpose, to accomplish great things.

"To encourage me in my efforts to cultivate the power of attention," said a friend of John C. Calhoun, "he stated that to this end he had early subjected his mind to such a rigid course of discipline, and had persisted without faltering until he had acquired a perfect control over it; that he could now confine it to any subject as long as he pleased, without wandering even for a moment; that it was his uniform habit, when he set out alone to walk or ride, to select a subject for reflection, and that he never suffered his attention to wander from it until he was satisfied with its examination."

"My friend laughs at me because I have but one idea," said a learned American chemist; "but I have learned that if I wish ever to make a breach in a wall, I must play my guns continually upon one point."

"It is his will that has made him what he is," said an intimate friend of Philip D. Armour, the Chicago millionaire. "He fixes his eye on something ahead, and no matter what rises upon the right or the left he never sees it. He goes straight in pursuit of the object ahead, and overtakes it at last. He never gives up what he undertakes."

While Horace Greeley would devote a column of the New York *Tribune* to an article, Thurlow Weed would treat the same subject in a few words in the Albany *Evening Journal*, and put the argument into such shape as to carry far more conviction.

"If you would be pungent," says Southey, "be brief; for it is with words as with sunbeams—the more they are condensed the deeper they burn."

"The only valuable kind of study," said Sydney Smith, "is to read so heartily that dinner-time comes two hours before you expected it; to sit with your Livy before you and hear the geese cackling that saved the Capitol, and to see with your own eyes the Carthaginian sutlers gathering up the rings of the Roman knights after the battle of Cannæ, and heaping them into bushels, and to be so intimately present at the actions you are reading of, that when anybody knocks at the door it will take you two or three seconds to determine whether you are in your own study or on the plains of Lombardy, looking at Hannibal's weather-beaten face and admiring the splendor of his single eye."

"Never study on speculation," says Waters; "all such study is vain. Form a plan; have an object; then work for it; learn all you can about it, and you will be sure to succeed. What I mean by studying on speculation is that aimless learning of things because they may be useful some day; which is like the conduct of the woman who bought at auction a brass door-plate with the name of Thompson on it, thinking it might be useful some day!"

"I resolved, when I began to read law," said Edward Sugden, afterward Lord St. Leonard, "to make everything I acquired perfectly my own, and never go on to a second reading till I had entirely accomplished the first. Many of the competitors read as much in a day as I did in a week; but at the end of twelve months my knowledge was as fresh as on the day it was acquired, while theirs had glided away from their recollection."

"Very often," says Sidney Smith, "the modern precept of education is, 'Be ignorant of nothing.' But my advice is, have the courage to be ignorant of a great number of things, that you may avoid the calamity of being ignorant of all things."

"Lord, help me to take fewer things into my hands, and to do them well," is a prayer recommended by Paxton Hood to an overworked man.

"Many persons seeing me so much engaged in active life," said Edward Bulwer Lytton, "and as much about the world as if I had never been a student, have said to me, 'When do you get time to write all your books? How on earth do you contrive to do so much work?' I shall surprise you by the answer I made. The answer is this—I contrive to do so much work by never doing too much at a time. A man to get through work well must not overwork himself; or, if he do too much to-day, the reaction of fatigue will come, and he will be obliged to do too little to-morrow. Now, since I began really and earnestly to study, which was not till I had left college, and was actually in the world, I may perhaps say that I have gone through as large a course of general reading as most men of my time. I have traveled much and I have seen much; I have mixed much in politics, and in the various business of life; and in addition to all this, I have published somewhere about sixty volumes, some upon subjects requiring much special research. And what time do you think, as a general rule, I have devoted to study, to reading, and writing? Not more than three hours a day; and, when Parliament is sitting, not always that. But then, during these three hours, I have given my whole attention to what I was about."

"The things that are crowded out of a life are the test of that life. Not what we would like, but what we long for and strive for with all our might we attain."

"One great cause of failure of young men in business," says Carnegie, "is lack of concentration. They are prone to seek outside investments. The cause of many a surprising failure lies in so doing. Every dollar of capital and credit, every business-thought, should be concentrated upon the one business upon which a man has embarked. He should never scatter his shot. It is a poor business which will not yield better returns for increased capital than any outside investment. No man or set of men or corporation can manage a business-man's capital as well as he can manage it himself. The rule, 'Do not put all your eggs in one basket,' does not apply to a man's life-work. Put all your eggs in one basket and then watch that basket, is the true doctrine—the most valuable rule of all."

"A man must not only desire to be right," said Beecher, "he must *be* right. You may say, 'I wish to send this ball so as to kill the lion crouching yonder, ready to spring upon me. My wishes are all right, and I hope Providence will direct the ball.' Providence won't. You must do it; and if you do not, you are a dead man."

The ruling idea of Milton's life and the key to his mental history is his resolve to produce a great poem. Not that the aspiration in itself is singular, for it is probably shared in by every poet in his turn. As every clever schoolboy is destined by himself or his friends to become Lord-Chancellor, and every private in the French army carries in his haversack the baton of a marshal, so it is a necessary ingredient of the dream of Parnassus that it should embody itself in a form of surpassing brilliance. What distinguishes Milton from the crowd of youthful literary aspirants, *audax juventa*, is his constancy of resolve. He not only nourished through manhood the dream of youth, keeping under the importunate instincts which carry off most ambitions in middle life into the pursuit of place, profit, honor—the thorns which spring up and smother the wheat—but carried out his dream in its integrity in old age. He formed himself for this achievement and no other. Study at home, travel abroad, the arena of political controversy, the public service, the practice of the domestic virtues, were so many parts of the schooling which was to make a poet.

Bismarck adopted it as the aim of his public life "to snatch Germany from Austrian oppression," and to gather round Prussia, in a North German Confederation, all the states whose tone of thought, religion, manners and interest "were in harmony with those of Prussia." "To attain this end," he once said in conversation, "I would brave all dangers—exile, the scaffold itself. What matter if they hang me, provided the rope with which I am hung binds this new Germany firmly to the Prussian throne?"

It is related of Greeley that, when he was writing his "American Conflict," he found it necessary to conceal himself somewhere, to prevent constant interruptions. He accordingly took a room in the Bible house, where he worked from ten in the morning till five in the afternoon, and then appeared in the sanctum, seemingly as fresh as ever.

Cooper Institute is the evening school which Peter Cooper, as long ago as 1810, resolved to found some day, when he was looking about as an apprentice for a place where he could go to school evenings. Through all his career in various branches of business he never lost sight of this object; and, as his wealth increased, he was pleased that it brought nearer the realization of his dream.

"See a great lawyer like Rufus Choate," says Dr. Storrs, "in a case where his convictions are strong and his feelings are enlisted. He saw long ago, as he glanced over the box, that five of those in it were sympathetic with him; as he went on he became equally certain of seven; the number now has risen to ten; but two are still left whom he feels that he has not persuaded or mastered.

Upon them he now concentrates his power, summing up the facts, setting forth anew and more forcibly the principles, urging upon them his view of the case with a more and more intense action of his mind upon theirs, until one only is left. Like the blow of a hammer, continually repeated until the iron bar crumbles beneath it, his whole force comes with ceaseless percussion on that one mind till it has yielded, and accepts the conviction on which the pleader's purpose is fixed. Men say afterward, 'He surpassed himself.' It was only because the singleness of his aim gave unity, intensity, and overpowering energy to the mind."

"The foreman of the jury, however," said Whipple, "was a hard-hearted, practical man, a model of business intellect and integrity, but with an incapacity of understanding any intellect or conscience radically differing from his own. Mr. Choate's argument, as far as the facts and the law were concerned, was through in an hour. Still he went on speaking. Hour after hour passed, and yet he continued to speak with constantly increasing eloquence, repeating and recapitulating, without any seeming reason, facts which he had already stated and arguments which he had already urged. The truth was, as I gradually learned, that he was engaged in a hand-to-hand—or rather in a brain-to-brain and a heart-to-heart—contest with the foreman, whose resistance he was determined to break down, but who confronted him for three hours with defiance observable in every rigid line of his honest countenance. 'You fool!' was the burden of the advocate's ingenious argument. 'You rascal!' was the phrase legibly printed on the foreman's incredulous face. But at last the features of the foreman began to relax, and at the end the stern lines melted into acquiescence with the opinion of the advocate, who had been storming at the defences of his mind, his heart, and his conscience for five hours, and had now entered as victor. The verdict was 'Not guilty.'"

"He who would do some great thing in this short life must apply himself to the work with such a concentration of his forces as, to idle spectators, who live only to amuse themselves, looks like insanity."

It is generally thought that when a man is said to be dissipated in his habits he must be a drinking man, or a gambler, or licentious, or all three; but dissipation is of two kinds, coarse and refined. A man can dissipate or scatter all of his mental energies and physical power by indulging in too many respectable diversions, as easily as in habits of a viler nature. Property and its cares make some men dissipated; too many friends make others. The exactions of "society," the balls, parties, receptions, and various entertainments constantly being given and attended by the *beau monde*, constitute a most wasting species of dissipation. Others, again, fritter away all their time and strength in political agitations, or in controversies and gossip; others in idling with music or some other one of the fine arts; others in feasting or fasting, as their dispositions and feelings incline. But the man of concentration of purpose is never a dissipated man in any sense, good or bad. He has no time to devote to useless trifling of any kind, but puts in as many strokes of faithful work as possible toward the attainment of some definite good.

At Once

Note the sublime precision that leads the earth over a circuit of 500,000,000 miles back to the solstice at the appointed moment without the loss of one second—no, not the millionth part of a second—for ages and ages of which it traveled that imperial road. —Edward Everett

Despatch is the soul of business. —Chesterfield

Unfaithfulness in the keeping of an appointment is an act of clear dishonesty. You may as well borrow a person's money as his time. —Horace Mann

By the street of by-and-by one arrives at the house of never. —Cervantes

The greatest thief this world has ever produced is procrastination, and he is still at large. —H. W. Shaw

"Oh, how I do appreciate a boy who is always on time!" says H. C. Bowen. "How quickly you learn to depend on him, and how soon you find yourself intrusting him with weightier matters! The boy who has acquired a reputation for punctuality has made the first contribution to the capital that in after years makes his success a certainty!"

"Nothing commends a young man so much to his employers," says John Stuart Blackie, "as accuracy and punctuality in the conduct of his business. And no wonder. On each man's exactitude depends the comfortable and easy going of his machine. If the clock goes fitfully nobody knows the time of day; and, if your task is a link in the chain of another man's work, you are his clock, and he ought to be able to rely on you."

"The whole period of youth," said Ruskin, "is one essentially of formation, edification, instruction. There is not an hour of it but is trembling with destinies—not a moment of which, once passed, the appointed work can ever be done again, or the neglected blow struck on the cold iron."

"To-morrow, didst thou say?" asked Cotton. "Go to—I will not hear of it. To-morrow! 't is a sharper who stakes his penury against thy plenty—who takes thy ready cash and pays thee naught but wishes, hopes and promises, the currency of idiots. *To-morrow*! it is a period nowhere to be found in all the hoary registers of time, unless perchance in the fool's calendar. Wisdom disclaims the word, nor holds society with those that own it. 'Tis fancy's child, and folly is its father; wrought of such stuffs as dreams are; and baseless as the fantastic visions of the evening." Oh, how many a wreck on the road to success could say: "I have spent all my life in the pursuit of to-morrow, being assured that to-morrow has some vast benefit or other in store for me."

"I give it as my deliberate and solemn conviction," said Dr. Fitch, "that the individual who is tardy in meeting an appointment will never be respected or successful in life."

"If a man has no regard for the time of other men," said Horace Greeley, "why should he have for their money? What is the difference between taking a man's hour and taking his five dollars? There are many men to whom each hour of the business day is worth more than five dollars."

A man who keeps his time will keep his word; in truth, he cannot keep his word unless he *does* keep his time.

When the Duchess of Sutherland came late, keeping the court waiting, the queen, who was always vexed by tardiness, presented her with her own watch, saying, "I am afraid your's does not keep good time."

"Then you must get a new watch, or I another secretary," replied Washington, when his secretary excused the lateness of his attendance by saying that his watch was too slow.

"I have generally found that a man who is good at an excuse is good for nothing else," said Franklin to a servant who was always late, but always ready with an excuse.

One of the best things about school and college life is that the bell which strikes the hour for rising, for recitations, or for lectures, teaches habits of promptness. Every young man should have a watch which is a good timekeeper; one that is *nearly* right encourages bad habits, and is an expensive investment at any price. Wear threadbare clothes if you must, but never carry an inaccurate watch.

"Five minutes behind time" has ruined many a man and many a firm.

"He who rises late," says Fuller, "must trot all day, and shall scarcely overtake his business at night."

Some people are too late for everything but ruin; when a nobleman apologized to George III. for being late, and said, "better late than never," the king replied, "No, I say, *better never than late.*"

"Better late than never" is not half so good a maxim as "Better never late."

If Samuel Budgett was even a minute late at an appointment he would apologize; he was as punctual as a chronometer. Punctuality is contagious. Napoleon infused promptness into his officers every minute. What power there is in promptness to take the drudgery out of a disagreeable task.

"A singular mischance has happened to some of our friends," said Hamilton. "At the instant when He ushered them into existence, God gave them work to do, and He also gave them a competency of time; so much that if they began at the right moment and wrought with sufficient vigor, their time and their work would end together. But a good many years ago a strange misfortune befell them. A fragment of their allotted time was lost. They cannot tell what became of it, but sure enough, it has dropped out of existence; for just like two measuring lines laid alongside the one an inch shorter than the other, their work and their time run parallel, but the work is always ten minutes in advance of the time. They are not irregular. They are never too soon. Their letters are posted the very minute after the mail is closed. They arrive at the wharf just in time to see the steamboat off, they come in sight of the terminus precisely as the station gates are closing. They do not break any engagement nor neglect any duty; but they systematically go about it too late, and usually too late by about the same fatal interval."

Of Tours, the wealthy New Orleans ship-owner, it is said that he was as methodical and regular as a clock, and that his neighbors were in the habit of judging of the time of the day by his movements.

"How," asked a man of Sir Walter Raleigh, "do you accomplish so much and in so short a time?" "When I have anything do, I go and do it," was the reply. The man who always acts promptly, even if he makes occasional mistakes, will succeed when a procrastinator will fail—even if he have the better judgment.

When asked how he got through so much work, Lord Chesterfield replied: "Because I never put off till morrow what I can do to-day."

Dewitt, pensionary of Holland, answered the same question: "Nothing is more easy; never do but one thing at a time, and never put off until to-morrow what can be done to-day."

Walter Scott was a very punctual man. This was the secret of his enormous achievements. He made it a rule to answer all letters the day they were received. He rose at five. By breakfast time he had broken the neck of the day's work, as he used to say. Writing to a youth who had obtained a situation and asked him for advice, he gave this counsel: "Beware of stumbling over a propensity which easily besets you from not having your time fully employed—I mean what the women call dawdling. Do instantly whatever is to be done, and take the hours of recreation after business, never before it."

Frederick the Great had a maxim: "Time is the only treasure of which it is proper to be avaricious."

Leibnitz declared that "the loss of an hour is the loss of a part of life."

Napoleon, who knew the value of time, remarked that it was the quarter hours that won battles. The value of minutes has been often recognized, and any person watching a railway clerk handing out tickets and change during the last few minutes available must have been struck with how much could be done in these short periods of time.

At the appointed hour the train starts and by and by is carrying passengers at the rate of sixty miles an hour. In a second you are carried twenty-nine yards. In one twenty-ninth of a second you pass over one yard. Now, one yard is quite an appreciable distance, but one twenty-ninth of a second is a period which cannot be appreciated.

The father of the Webster brothers, before going away to be gone for a week, gave his boys a stint to cut a field of corn, telling them that after it was done, if they had any time left, they might do what they pleased. The boys looked the field over on Monday morning and concluded they could do all the work in three days, so they decided to play the first three days. Thursday morning they went to the field, but it looked so much larger than it did on Monday morning, that they decided they could not possibly do it in three days, and rather than not do it all, they would not touch it. When the angry father returned, he called Ezekiel to him and asked him why they had not harvested the corn. "What have you been doing?" said the stern father. "Nothing, father." "And what have you been doing, Daniel?" "Helping Zeke, sir."

How many boys, and men, too, waste hours and days "helping Zeke!"

"Remember the world was created in six days," said Napoleon to one of his officers. "Ask for whatever you please except time."

Railroads and steamboats have been wonderful educators in promptness. No matter who is late they leave right on the minute.

It is interesting to watch people at a great railroad station, running, hurrying, trying to make up time, for they well know when the time arrives the train will leave.

Factories, shops, stores, banks, everything opens and closes on the minute. The higher the state of civilization the prompter is everything done. In countries without railroads, as in Eastern countries, everything is behind time. Everybody is indolent and lazy.

The world knows that the prompt man's bills and notes will be paid on the day they are due, and will trust him. People will give him credit, for they know they can depend upon him. But lack of promptness will shake confidence almost as quickly as downright dishonesty. The man who has a habit of dawdling or listlessness will show it in everything he does. He is late at meals, late at work, dawdles on the street, loses his train, misses his appointments, and dawdles at his store until the banks are closed. Everybody he meets suffers more or less from his malady, for dawdling becomes practically a disease.

"You will never find time for anything," said Charles Buxton; "if you want time you must make it."

The best work we ever do is that which we do now, and can never repeat. "Too late," is the curse of the unsuccessful, who forget that "one to-day is worth two to-morrows."

Time accepts no sacrifice; it admits of neither redemption nor atonement. *It is the true avenger.* Your enemy may become your friend,—your injurer may do you justice,—but Time is inexorable, and has no mercy.

Then stay the present instant, dear Horatio:
Imprint the marks of wisdom on its wings.
'Tis of more worth than kingdoms! far more precious
Than all the crimson treasures of life's fountain.
O! let it not elude thy grasp; but, like
The good old patriarch upon record,
Hold the fleet angel fast until he bless thee. —Nathaniel Cotton

Thoroughness

Doing well depends upon doing completely. —Persian Proverb

He who does well will always have patrons enough. —Plautus

If a man can write a better book, preach a better sermon, or make a better mouse-trap than his neighbor, though he build his house in the woods, the world will make a beaten path to his door. —Emerson

I hate a thing done by halves. If it be right, do it boldly; if it be wrong, leave it undone. —Gilpin

No two things differ more than Hurry and Dispatch. Hurry is the mark of a weak mind, Dispatch of a strong one. Like a turnstile, he (the weak man) is in everybody's way, but stops nobody; he talks a great deal, but says very little; looks into everything, but sees nothing; and has a hundred irons in the fire, but very few of them are hot, and with those few that are he only burns his fingers. —Colton

"Make me as good a hammer as you know how," said a carpenter to the blacksmith in a New York village before the first railroad was built; "six of us have come to work on the new church, and I've left mine at home." "As good a one as I know how?" asked David Maydole, doubtfully, "but perhaps you don't want to pay for as good a one as I know how to make." "Yes, I do," said the carpenter, "I want a good hammer."

It was indeed a good hammer that he received, the best, probably, that had ever been made. By means of a longer hole than usual, David had wedged the handle in its place so that the head could not fly off, a wonderful improvement in the eyes of the carpenter, who boasted of his prize to his companions. They all came to the shop next day, and each ordered just such a hammer. When the contractor saw the tools, he ordered two for himself, asking that they be made a little better than those for his men. "I can't make any better ones," said Maydole; "when I make a thing, I make it as well as I can, no matter whom it is for."

The storekeeper soon ordered two dozen, a supply unheard of in his previous business career. A New York dealer in tools came to the village to sell his wares, and bought all the storekeeper had, and left a standing order for all the blacksmith could make. David might have grown very wealthy by making goods of the standard already attained; but throughout his long and successful life he never ceased to study still further to perfect his hammers in the minutest detail. They were usually sold without any warrant of excellence, the word "Maydole" stamped on the head being universally considered a guaranty of the best article the world could produce. Character is power, and is the best advertisement in the world.

"Yes," said he one day to the late James Parton, who told this story, "I have made hammers in this little village for twenty-eight years." "Well," replied the great historian, "by this time you ought to make a pretty good hammer."

"No, I can't," was the reply, "I can't make a pretty good hammer. I make the best hammer that's made. My only care is to make a perfect hammer. If folks don't want to pay me what they're worth, they're welcome to buy cheaper ones somewhere else. My wants are few, and I'm ready any time to go back to my blacksmith's shop, where I worked forty years ago, before I thought of making hammers. Then I had a boy to blow by bellows, now I have one hundred and fifteen men. Do you see them over there watching the heads cook over the charcoal furnace, as your cook, if she knows what she is about, watches the chops broiling? Each of them is hammered out of a piece of iron, and is tempered under the inspection of an experienced man. Every handle is seasoned three years, or until there is no shrink left in it. Once I thought I could use machinery in manufacturing them; now I know that a perfect tool can't be made by machinery, and every bit of the work is done by hand."

"In telling this little story," said Parton, "I have told thousands of stories. Take the word 'hammer' out of it, and put 'glue' in its place, and you have the history of Peter Cooper. By putting in other words, you can make the true history of every great business in the world which has lasted thirty years."

"We have no secret," said Manager Daniel J. Morrill, of the Cambria Iron Works, employing seven thousand men, at Johnstown, Pa. "We always try to beat our last batch of rails. That is all the secret we've got, and we don't care who knows it."

"I don't try to see how cheap a machine I can produce, but how good a machine," said the late John C. Whitin, of Northbridge, Mass., to a customer who complained of the high price of some cotton machinery. Business men soon learned what this meant; and when there was occasion to advertise any machinery for sale, New England cotton manufacturers were accustomed to state the number of years it had been in use and add, as an all-sufficient guaranty of Northbridge products, "Whitin make." Put thoroughness into your work: it pays.

"The accurate boy is always the favored one," said President Tuttle. If a carpenter must stand at his journeyman's elbow to be sure his work is right, or if a cashier must run over his bookkeeper's columns, he might as well do the work himself as employ another to do it in that way.

"Mr. Girard, can you not assist me by giving me a little work?" asked one John Smith, who had formerly worked for the great banker and attracted attention by his activity.

"Assistance—work—ah? You want work?" "Yes sir; it's a long time since I've had anything to do."

"Very well, I shall give you some. You see dem stone yondare?" "Yes, sir." "Very well; you shall fetch and put them in this place; you see?" "Yes sir." "And when you done, come to me at my bank."

Smith finished his task, reported to Mr. Girard, and asked for more work. "Ah, ha, oui. You want more work? Very well; you shall go place dem stone where you got him. Understandez? You take him back." "Yes, sir."

Again Smith performed the work and waited on Mr. Girard for payment. "Ah, ha, you all finish?" "Yes, sir." "Very well; how much money shall I give you?" "One dollar, sir." "Dat is honest. You take no advantage. Dare is your dollar." "Can I do anything else for you?" "Oui, come here when you get up to-morrow. You shall have more work."

Smith was punctual, but for the third time, and yet again for the fourth, he was ordered to "take dem stone back again." When he called for his pay in the evening Stephen Girard spoke very cordially. "Ah, Monsieur Smit, you shall be my man; you mind your own business and do it, ask no questions, you do not interfere. You got one vife?" "Yes, sir." "Ah, dat is bad. Von vife is bad. Any little chicks?" "Yes, sir, five living."

"Five? Dat is good; I like five. I like you, Monsieur Smit; you like to work; you mind your business. Now I do something for your five little chicks. There: take these five pieces of paper for your five little chicks; you shall work for them; you shall mind your own business, and your little chicks shall never want five more." In a few years Mr. Smith became one of the wealthiest and most respected merchants of Philadelphia.

It is difficult to estimate the great influence upon a life of the early formed habit of doing everything to a finish, not leaving it half done, or pretty nearly done, but completely done. Nature finishes every little leaf, even to every little rib, its edges and stem, as exactly and perfectly as though it were the only leaf to be made that year. Even the flower that blooms in the mountain dell, where no human eye will ever behold it, is finished with the same perfection and exactness of form and outline, with the same delicate shade of color, with the same completeness of beauty, as though it was made for royalty in the queen's garden. "Perfection to the finish" is a motto which every youth should adopt.

"How did you attain such excellence in your profession?" was asked of Sir Joshua Reynolds. "By observing one simple rule, namely, to make each picture the best," he replied.

The discipline of being exact is uplifting. Progress is never more rapid than it is when we are studying to be accurate. The effort educates all the powers. Arthur Helps says: "I do not know that there is anything except it be humility, which is so valuable, as an incident of education, as accuracy: and accuracy can be taught. Direct lies told to the world are as dust in the balance when weighed against the falsehoods of inaccuracy."

Too many youths enter upon their business in a languid, half-hearted way, and do their work in a slipshod manner. The consequence is that they inspire neither admiration nor confidence on the part of their superiors, and cut off almost every chance of success. There is a loose, perfunctory method of doing one's work that never merits advance, and very rarely wins it. Instead of buckling to their task with all the force they possess, they merely touch it with the tips of their fingers, their rule apparently being, the maximum of ease with the minimum of work. The principle of Strafford, the great minister of Charles I., is indicated by his motto, the one word "Thorough." It was said of King Hezekiah, "In every work that he began, he did it with all his heart and prospered."

The stone-cutter goes to work on a stone and most patiently shapes it. He carves that bit of fern, putting all his skill and taste into it. And by-and-by the master says, "Well done," and takes it away and gives him another block and tells him to work on that. And so he works on that from the rising of the sun till the going down of the same, and he only knows that he is earning his bread. And he continues to put all his skill and taste into his work. He has no idea what use will be made of these few stones which he has been carving, until afterward, when, one day, walking along the street, and looking up at the front of the Art Gallery, he sees the stones upon which he has worked. He did not know what they were for, but the architect did. And as he stands looking at his work on that structure which is the beauty of the whole street, he says: "I am glad I did it well." And every day as he passes that way, he says to himself exultingly, "I did it well." He did not draw the design, nor plan the building, and he knew nothing of what use was to be made of his work: but he took pains in cutting those stems; and when he saw they were a part of that magnificent structure, his soul rejoiced.

Work that is not finished, is not work at all; it is merely a botch. We often see this defect of incompleteness in a child, which increases in youth. All about the house, everywhere, there are half-finished things. It is true that children often become tired of things which they begin with enthusiasm; but there is a great difference in children about finishing what they undertake. A boy, for instance, will start out in the morning with great enthusiasm to dig his garden over; but, after a few minutes, his enthusiasm has evaporated, and he wants to go fishing. He soon becomes tired of this, and thinks he will make a boat. No sooner does he get a saw and knife and a few pieces of board about him than he makes up his mind that really what he wanted to do, after all, was to play ball, and this, in turn, must give way to something else.

One watch, set right, will do to set many by; but, on the other hand, one that goes wrong may be the means of misleading a whole neighborhood. The same may be said of the example we individually set to those around us.

"Whatever I have tried to do in life," said Dickens, "I have tried with all my heart to do well. What I have devoted myself to, I have devoted myself to completely."

It is no disgrace to be a shoemaker, but it is a disgrace for a shoemaker to make bad shoes.

A traveler, recently returned from Jerusalem, found, in conversation with Humboldt, that the latter was as conversant with the streets and houses of Jerusalem as he was himself. On being asked how long it was since he had visited it, the aged philosopher replied: "I have never been there; but I expected to go sixty years since, and I prepared myself."

So noted for excellency was everything bearing the brand of George Washington, that a barrel of flour marked "George Washington, Mount Vernon," was exempted from the customary inspection in the West India ports.

Pascal, the most wonderful mathematical genius of his time, whose work on conic sections, at sixteen, Descartes refused to believe could be produced at that age, is considered to have fixed the French language, as Luther did the German, by his writings. None of his provincial letters, with the exception of the last three, was more than eight quarto pages in length, yet he devoted twenty days to the writing of a single letter, and one of them was written no less than thirteen times.

The night the Tasmania was wrecked, the captain had given the course north by west, sixty-seven degrees. He had taken account of eddies and currents. The second officer, overlooking these, ordered the helmsman to make it north by west, fifty-seven degrees, but to bring the ship around so gently that the captain wouldn't know it. Hence her destruction.

Rev. Mr. Maley, of the Ohio Conference of the Methodist Church, had the habit of greatly exaggerating anything he talked about. His brethren at conference told him that this habit was growing on him, and rendering him unpopular in the ministry. Mr. Maley heard them patiently, and then said: "Brethren, I am aware of the truth of all you have said, and have shed barrels of tears over it."

There is a great difference between going just right and a little wrong.

Trifles

In the elder days of Art
Builders wrought with greatest care
Each minute and unseen part,
For the gods see everywhere. —Longfellow

Think naught a trifle, though it small appear,
Small sands the mountain, moments make the year,
And trifles, life. —Young

The smallest hair throws its shadow. —Goethe

He that despiseth small things shall fall little by little. —Ecclesiastes

It is the little rift within the lute,
That by and by will make the music mute,
And ever widening slowly silence all. —Tennyson

"A pebble in the streamlet scant
Has turned the course of many a river:
A dewdrop on the baby plant
Has warped the giant oak forever."

It is the close observation of little things which is the
secret of success in business, in art, in science, and in every
pursuit of life. —Smiles

"Only!—But then the onlys make up the mighty all."

"My rule of conduct has been that whatever is worth doing at all is worth doing well," said Nicolas Poussin, the great French painter. When asked the reason why he had become so eminent in a land of famous artists he replied, "Because I have neglected nothing."

"Do little things now," says a Persian proverb; "so shall big things come to thee by and by asking to be done." God will take care of the great things if we do not neglect the little ones.

A gentleman advertised for a boy to assist him in his office, and nearly fifty applicants presented themselves to him. Out of the whole number he in a short time selected one and dismissed the rest. "I should like to know," said a friend, "on what ground you selected that boy, who had not a single recommendation?" "You are mistaken," said the gentleman, "he had a great many. He wiped his feet when he came in, and closed the door after him, showing that he was careful. He gave up his seat instantly to that lame old man, showing that he was kind and thoughtful. He took off his cap when he came in, and answered my questions promptly and respectfully, showing that he was polite and gentlemanly. He picked up the book which I had purposely laid upon the floor, and replaced it on the table, while all the rest stepped over it, or shoved it aside; and he waited quietly for his turn, instead of pushing and crowding, showing that he was honest and orderly. When I talked to him, I noticed that his clothes were carefully brushed, his hair in nice order, and his teeth as white as milk; and when he wrote his name, I noticed that his finger-nails were clean, instead of being tipped with jet, like that handsome little fellow's, in the blue jacket. Don't you call those letters of recommendation? I do; and I would give more for what I can tell about a boy by using my eyes ten minutes, than for all the fine letters he can bring me."

"Least of all seeds, greatest of all harvests," seems to be one of the great laws of nature. All life comes from microscopic beginnings. In nature there is nothing small. The microscope reveals as great a world below as the telescope above. All of nature's laws govern the smallest atoms, and a single drop of water is a miniature ocean.

"I cannot see that you have made any progress since my last visit," said a gentleman to Michael Angelo. "But," said the sculptor, "I have retouched this part, polished that, softened that feature, brought out that muscle, given some expression to this lip, more energy to that limb, etc." "But they are trifles!" exclaimed the visitor. "It may be so," replied the great artist, "but trifles make perfection, and perfection is no trifle." That infinite patience which made Michael Angelo spend a week in bringing out a muscle in a statue with more vital fidelity to truth, or Gerhard Dow a day in giving the right effect to a dewdrop on a cabbage leaf, makes all the difference between success and failure.

"Of what use is it?" people asked with a sneer, when Franklin told of his discovery that lightning and electricity are identical. "What is the use of a child?" replied Franklin; "it may become a man."

In the earliest days of cotton spinning, the small fibres would stick to the bobbins, and make it necessary to stop and clear the machinery. Although this loss of time reduced the earnings of the operatives, the father of Robert Peel noticed that one of his spinners always drew full pay, as his machine never stopped. "How is this, Dick?" asked Mr. Peel one day; "the on-looker tells me your bobbins are always clean." "Ay, that they be," replied Dick Ferguson. "How do you manage it, Dick?" "Why, you see, Meester Peel," said the workman, "it is sort o' secret! If I tow'd ye, yo'd be as wise as I am." "That's so," said Mr. Peel, smiling; "but I'd give you something to know. Could you make all the looms work as smoothly as yours?" "Ivery one of 'em, meester," replied Dick. "Well, what shall I give you for your secret?" asked Mr. Peel, and Dick replied, "Gi' me a quart of ale every day as I'm in the mills, and I'll tell thee all about it." "Agreed," said Mr. Peel, and Dick whispered very cautiously in his ear, "Chalk your bobbins!" That was the whole secret, and Mr. Peel soon shot ahead of all his competitors, for he made machines that would chalk their own bobbins. Dick was handsomely rewarded with money instead of beer. His little idea has saved the world millions of dollars.

The totality of a life at any moment is the product mainly of little things. Trifling choices, insignificant exercises of the will, unimportant acts often repeated,—things seemingly of small account,—these are the thousand tiny sculptors that are carving away constantly at the rude block of our life, giving it shape and feature. Indeed the formation of character is much like the work of an artist in stone. The sculptor takes a rough, unshapen mass of marble, and with strong, rapid strokes of mallet and chisel quickly brings into view the rude outline of his design; but after the outline appears then come hours, days, perhaps even years, of patient, minute labor. A novice might see no change in the statue from one day to another; for though the chisel touches the stone a thousand times, it touches as lightly as the fall of a rain-drop, but each touch leaves a mark.

The smallest thing becomes respectable when regarded as the commencement of what has advanced or is advancing into magnificence. The crude settlement of Romulus would have remained an insignificant circumstance and might have justly sunk into oblivion, if Rome had not at length commanded the world.

Beecher says that men, in their property, are afraid of conflagrations and lightning strokes; but if they were building a wharf in Panama, a million madrepores, so small that only the microscope could detect them, would begin to bore the piles down under the water. There would be neither noise nor foam; but in a little while, if a child did but touch the post, over it would fall as if a saw had cut it through.

Men think, with regard to their conduct, that, if they were to lift themselves up gigantically and commit some crashing sin, they should never be able to hold up their heads; but they will harbor in their souls little sins, which are piercing and eating them away to inevitable ruin.

Lichens, of themselves of little value, prepare the way for important vegetation. They deposit, in dying, an acid which wears away the rock and prepares the mould necessary for the nourishment of superior plants.

It was but a tiny rivulet trickling down the embankment that started the terrible Johnstown flood and swept thousands into eternity. One noble heroic act has elevated a nation. Franklin's whole career was changed by a torn copy of Cotton Mather's Essays to Do Good. Taking up a stone to throw at a turtle was the turning point in Theodore Parker's life. As he raised the stone something within him said, "Don't do it," and he didn't. He went home and asked his mother what it was in him that said "don't." She told him it was conscience. Small things become great when a great soul sees them. A child, when asked why a certain tree grew crooked, answered, "Somebody trod upon it when it was a little fellow."

By gnawing through a dike, even a rat may drown a nation. A little boy in Holland saw water trickling from a small hole near the bottom of a dike. He realized that the leak would rapidly become larger if the water was not checked, so he held his hand over the hole for hours on a dark and dismal night until he could attract the attention of passers-by. His name is still held in grateful remembrance in Holland.

We may tell which way the wind blew before the Deluge by marking the ripple and cupping of the rain in the petrified sand now preserved forever. We tell the very path by which gigantic creatures, whom man never saw, walked to the river's edge to find their food.

The tears of Virgilia and Volumnia saved Rome from the Volscians when nothing else could move the vengeful heart of Coriolanus.

Not even Helen of Troy, it is said, was beautiful enough to spare the tip of her nose; and if Cleopatra's had been an inch shorter Mark Antony would never have become infatuated with her wonderful charms, and the blemish would have changed the history of the world. Anne Boleyn's fascinating smile split the great Church of Rome in twain, and gave a nation an altered destiny. Napoleon, who feared not to attack the proudest monarchs in their capitals, shrank from the political influence of one independent woman in private life, Madame de Staël.

It was a little thing for a cow to kick over a lantern left in a shanty, but it laid Chicago in ashes, and rendered homeless a hundred thousand people.

The discovery of glass was due to a mere accident—the building of a fire on the sand; and the bayonet, first made at Bayonne, in France, owes its existence to the fact that a Basque regiment, being hard pressed by the enemy, one of the soldiers suggested that, as their ammunition was exhausted, they should fix their long knives into the barrels of their muskets, which was done, and the first bayonet-charge was made.

A jest led to a war between two great nations. The presence of a comma in a deed, lost to the owner of an estate five thousand dollars a month for eight months. The battle of Corunna was fought and Sir John Moore's life sacrificed, in 1809, through a dragoon stopping to drink while bearing despatches.

"You do no work," said the scissors to the rivet. "Where would your work be," said the rivet to the scissors, "if I didn't keep you together?"

Every day is a little life; and our whole life but a day repeated. Those that dare lose a day are dangerously prodigal; those that dare misspend it, desperate. What is the happiness of your life made up of? Little courtesies, little kindnesses, pleasant words, genial smiles, a friendly letter, good wishes, and good deeds. One in a million—once in a lifetime—may do a heroic action.

We call the large majority of human lives *obscure*. Presumptuous that we are! How know we what lives a single thought retained from the dust of nameless graves may have lighted to renown?

Courage

Quit yourselves like men. —1 Samuel IV. 9

Cowards have no luck —Elizabeth Kulman

He has not learned the lesson of life who does not every day surmount a fear. —Emerson

To dare is better than to doubt,
For doubt is always grieving;
'Tis faith that finds the riddles out;
The prize is for believing. —Henry Burton

Walk boldly and wisely in that light thou hast; There is a hand above will help thee on. —Bailey's Festus

"Have hope! Though clouds environ now,
And gladness hides her face in scorn,
Put thou the shadow from thy brow—
No night but hath its morn."

"Our enemies are before us," exclaimed the Spartans at Thermopylæ. "And we are before them," was the cool reply of Leonidas. "Deliver your arms," came the message from Xerxes. "Come and take them," was the answer Leonidas sent back. A Persian soldier said: "You will not be able to see the sun for flying javelins and arrows." "Then we will fight in the shade," replied a Lacedemonian. What wonder that a handful of such men checked the march of the greatest host that ever trod the earth.

"The hero," says Emerson, "is the man who is immovably centred."

Darius the Great sent ambassadors to the Athenians, to demand earth and water, which denoted submission. The Athenians threw them into a ditch and told them, there was earth and water enough.

"Bring back the colors," shouted a captain at the battle of the Alma, when an ensign maintained his ground in front, although the men were retreating. "No," cried the ensign, "bring up the men to the colors." "To dare, and again to dare, and without end to dare," was Danton's noble defiance to the enemies of France.

Shakespeare says: "He is not worthy of the honeycomb that shuns the hives because the bees have stings."

"It is a bad omen," said Eric the Red, when his horse slipped and fell on the way to his ship, moored on the coast of Greenland, in readiness for a voyage of discovery. "Ill-fortune would be mine should I dare venture now upon the sea." So he returned to his house; but his young son Leif decided to go, and with a crew of thirty-five men, sailed southward in search of the unknown shore upon which Captain Biarni had been driven by a storm, while sailing in another Viking ship two or three years before. The first land that they saw was probably Labrador, a barren, rugged plain. Leif called this country Heluland, or the land of flat stones. Sailing onward many days, he came to a low, level coast thickly covered with woods, on account of which he called the country Markland, probably the modern Nova Scotia. Sailing onward, they came to an island which they named Vinland, on account of the abundance of delicious wild grapes in the woods. This was in the year 1000. Here where the city of Newport, R. I., stands, they spent many months, and then returned to Greenland with their vessel loaded with grapes and strange kinds of wood. The voyage was successful, and no doubt Eric was sorry he had been frightened by the bad omen.

"Not every vessel that sails from Tarshish will bring back the Gold of Ophir. But shall it therefore rot in the harbor? No! Give its sails to the wind!"

Men who have dared have moved the world, often before reaching the prime of life. It is astonishing what daring to begin and perseverance have enabled even youths to achieve. Alexander, who ascended the throne at twenty, had conquered the whole known world before dying at thirty-three. Julius Cæsar captured eight hundred cities, conquered three hundred nations, and defeated three million men, became a great orator and one of the greatest statesmen known, and still was a young man. Washington was appointed adjutant-general at nineteen, was sent at twenty-one as an ambassador to treat with the French, and won his first battle as a colonel at twenty-two. Lafayette was made general of the whole French army at twenty. Charlemagne was master of France and Germany at thirty. Condé was only twenty-two when he conquered at Rocroi. Galileo was but eighteen when he saw the principle of the pendulum in the swinging lamp in the cathedral at Pisa. Peel was in Parliament at twenty-one. Gladstone was in Parliament before he was twenty-two, and at twenty-four he was a Lord of the Treasury. Elizabeth Barrett Browning was proficient in Greek and Latin at twelve; De Quincey at eleven. Robert Browning wrote at eleven poetry of no mean order. Cowley, who sleeps in Westminster Abbey, published a volume of poems at fifteen. N. P. Willis won lasting fame as a poet before leaving college. Macaulay was a celebrated author before he was twenty-three. Luther was but twenty-nine when he nailed his famous thesis to the door of the bishop and defied the pope. Nelson was a lieutenant in the British navy before he was twenty. He was but forty-seven when he received his death wound at Trafalgar. Charles the Twelfth was only nineteen when he gained the battle of Narva; at thirty-six Cortes was the conqueror of Mexico; at thirty-two Clive had established the British power in India. Hannibal, the greatest of military commanders, was only thirty when, at Cannæ, he dealt an almost annihilating blow at the Republic of Rome; and Napoleon was only twenty-seven when, on the plains of Italy, he out-generaled and defeated, one after another, the veteran marshals of Austria.

Equal courage and resolution are often shown by men who have passed the allotted limit of life. Victor Hugo and Wellington were both in their prime after they had reached the age of threescore years and ten. George Bancroft wrote some of his best historical work when he was eighty-five. Gladstone ruled England with a strong hand at eighty-four, and was a marvel of literary and scholarly ability.

"Your Grace has not the organ of animal courage largely developed," said a phrenologist, who was examining Wellington's head. "You are right," replied the Iron Duke, "and but for my sense of duty I should have retreated in my first fight." That first fight, on an Indian field, was one of the most terrible on record.

Grant never knew when he was beaten. When told that he was surrounded by the enemy at Belmont, he quietly replied: "Well, then, we must cut our way out."

When General Jackson was a judge and was holding court in a small settlement, a border ruffian, a murderer and desperado, came into the court-room with brutal violence and interrupted the court. The judge ordered him to be arrested. The officer did not dare approach him. "Call a posse," said the judge, "and arrest him." But they also shrank with fear from the ruffian. "Call me, then," said Jackson; "this court is adjourned for five minutes." He left the bench, walked straight up to the man, and with his eagle eye actually cowed the ruffian, who dropped his weapons, afterward saying: "There was something in his eye I could not resist."

Lincoln never shrank from espousing an unpopular cause when he believed it to be right. At the time when it almost cost a young lawyer his bread and butter to defend the fugitive slave, and when other lawyers had refused, Lincoln would always plead the cause of the unfortunate whenever an opportunity presented. "Go to Lincoln," people would say, when these bounded fugitives were seeking protection; "he's not afraid of any cause, if it's right."

Abraham Lincoln's boyhood was one long struggle with poverty, with little education and no influential friends. When at last he had begun the practice of law it required no little daring to cast his fortune with the weaker side in politics, and thus imperil what small reputation he had gained. Only the most sublime moral courage could have sustained him as President to hold his ground against hostile criticism and a long train of disaster; to issue the Emancipation Proclamation; to support Grant and Stanton against the clamor of the politicians and the press; and through it all to do the right as God gave him to see the right.

"Doubt indulged becomes doubt realized." To determine to do anything is half the battle. "To think a thing is impossible is to make it so." "Courage is victory, timidity is defeat."

Don't waste time dreaming of obstacles you may never encounter, or in crossing bridges you have not reached. Don't fool with a nettle! Grasp with firmness if you would rob it of its sting. To half will and to hang forever in the balance is to lose your grip on life.

Execute your resolutions immediately. Thoughts are but dreams till their effects be tried. Does competition trouble you? work away; what is your competitor but a man? *Conquer your place in the world*, for all things serve a brave soul. Combat difficulty manfully; sustain misfortune bravely; endure poverty nobly; encounter disappointment courageously. The influence of the brave man is a magnetism which creates an epidemic of noble zeal in all about him. Every day sends to the grave obscure men, who have only remained in obscurity because their timidity has prevented them from making a first effort; and who, if they could have been induced to begin, would in all probability have gone great lengths in the career of usefulness and fame. "No great deed is done," says George Eliot, "by falterers who ask for certainty."

A mouse that dwelt near the abode of a great magician was kept in such constant distress by its fear of a cat that the magician, taking pity on it, turned it into a cat itself. Immediately it began to suffer from its fear of a dog, so the magician turned it into a dog. Then it began to suffer from fear of a tiger, and the magician turned it into a tiger. Then it began to suffer from its fear of huntsmen, and the magician, in disgust, said, "Be a mouse again. As you have only the heart of a mouse it is impossible to help you by giving you the body of a nobler animal." And the poor creature again became a mouse.

Young Commodore Oliver H. Perry, not twenty-eight years old, was intrusted with the plan to gain control of Lake Erie. With great energy Perry directed the construction of nine ships, carrying fifty-four guns, and conquered Commodore Barclay, a veteran of European navies, with six vessels, carrying sixty-three guns. Perry had no experience in naval battles before this.

To believe a business impossible is the way to make it so. Feasible projects often miscarry through despondency, and are strangled at birth by a cowardly imagination. A ship on a lee shore stands out to sea to escape shipwreck. Shrink and you will be despised.

One of Napoleon's drummer boys won the battle of Arcola. Napoleon's little army of fourteen thousand men had fought fifty thousand Austrians for seventy-two hours; the Austrians' position enabled them to sweep the bridge of Arcola, which the French had gained and which they must hold to win the battle. The drummer boy, on the shoulders of his sergeant (who swam across the river with him), beat the drum all the way across the river, and when on the opposite end of the bridge he beat his drum so vigorously that the Austrians, remembering the terrible French onslaught of the day before, fled in terror, thinking the French army was advancing upon them. Napoleon dated his great confidence in himself from this drum. This boy's heroic act was represented in stone on the front of the Pantheon of Paris.

Two days before the battle of Jena Napoleon said: "My lads, you must not fear death: when soldiers brave death they drive him into the enemy's ranks."

Arago says, in his autobiography, that when he was puzzled and discouraged with difficulties he met with in his early studies in mathematics some words he found on the waste leaf of his text-book caught his attention and interested him. He found it to be a short letter from D'Alembert to a young person, disheartened like himself, and read: "Go on, sir, go on. The difficulties you meet with will resolve themselves as you advance. Proceed and light will dawn and shine with increasing clearness on your path." "That maxim," he said, "was my greatest master in mathematics."

Overtaken near a rocky coast by a sudden storm of great violence, the captain of a French brig gave orders to put out to sea; but in spite of all the efforts of the crew they could not steer clear of the rocks, and after struggling for a whole day they felt a violent shock, accompanied by a horrible crash. The boats were lowered, but only to be swept away by the waves. As a last resort the captain proposed that some sailors should swim ashore with a rope, but not a man would volunteer.

"Captain," said the little twelve-year-old cabin boy, Jacques, timidly, "You don't wish to expose the lives of good sailors like these; it does not matter what becomes of a little cabin boy. Give me a ball of strong string, which will unroll as I go on; fasten one end around my body, and I promise you that within an hour the rope shall be well fastened to the shore or I will perish in the attempt."

Before anyone could stop him he leaped overboard. His head was soon seen like a black point rising above the waves and then it disappeared in the distance and mist, and but for the occasional pull upon the ball of cord all would have thought him dead. At length it fell as if slackened and the sailors looked at one another in silence, when a quick, violent pull, followed by a second and a third, told that Jacques had reached the shore. A strong rope was fastened to the cord and pulled to the shore, and by its aid many of the sailors were rescued.

In 1833 Miss Prudence Crandall, a Quaker schoolmistress of Canterbury, Conn., opened her school to negro children as well as to whites. The whole place was thrown into uproar; town meetings were called to denounce her; the most vindictive and inhuman measures were taken to isolate the school from the support of the townspeople; stores and churches were closed against teacher and pupils; public conveyances were denied them; physicians would not attend them; Miss Crandall's own friends dared not visit her; the house was assailed with rotten eggs and stones and finally set on fire. Yet the cause was righteous and the opposition proved vain and fruitless. Public opinion is often radically wrong.

Staunch old Admiral Farragut—he of the true heart and the iron will—said to another officer of the navy, "Dupont, do you know why you didn't get into Charleston with your ironclads?" "Oh, it was because the channel was so crooked." "No, Dupont, it was not that." "Well, the rebel fire was perfectly horrible." "Yes, but it wasn't that." "What was it, then?" "*It was because you didn't believe you could go in.*"

"I have tried Lord Howe on most important occasions. He never asked me *how* he was to execute any service entrusted to his charge, but always went straight forward and *did it*." So answered Sir Edward Hawke, when his appointment of Howe for some peculiarly responsible duty was criticized on the ground that Howe was the junior admiral in the fleet.

There is a tradition among the Indians that Manitou was traveling in the invisible world and came upon a hedge of thorns, then saw wild beasts glare upon him from the thicket, and after awhile stood before an impassable river. As he determined to proceed, the thorns turned out phantoms, the wild beasts powerless ghosts, and the river only a shadow. When we march on obstacles disappear. Many distinguished foreign and American statesmen were present at a fashionable dinner party where wine was freely poured, but Schuyler Colfax, then Vice-President of the United States, declined to drink from a proffered cup. "Colfax does not drink," sneered a Senator who had already taken too much. "You are right," said the Vice-President, "I dare not."

A Western party recently invited the surviving Union and Confederate officers to give an account of the bravest act observed by each during the Civil War. Colonel Thomas W. Higginson said that at a dinner at Beaufort, S. C., where wine flowed freely and ribald jests were bandied, Dr. Miner, a slight, boyish fellow who did not drink, was told that he could not go until he had drunk a toast, told a story, or sung a song. He replied: "I cannot sing, but I will give a toast, although I must drink it in water. It is 'Our Mothers.'" The men were so affected and ashamed that some took him by the hand and thanked him for displaying courage greater than that required to walk up to the mouth of a cannon.

When Grant was in Houston several years ago, he was given a rousing reception. Naturally hospitable, and naturally inclined to like a man of Grant's make-up, the Houstonites determined to go beyond any other Southern city in the way of a banquet and other manifestations of their good-will and hospitality. They made great preparations for the dinner, the committee taking great pains to have the finest wines that could be procured for the table at night. When the time came to serve the wine, the head-waiter went first to Grant. Without a word the general quietly turned down all the glasses at his plate. This movement was a great surprise to the Texans, but they were equal to the occasion. Without a single word being spoken, every man along the line of the long tables turned his glasses down, and there was not a drop of wine taken that night.

Don't be like Uriah Heep, begging everybody's pardon for taking the liberty of being in the world. There is nothing attractive in timidity, nothing lovable in fear. Both are deformities and are repulsive. Manly courage is dignified and graceful. The worst manners in the world are those of persons conscious "of being beneath their position, and trying to conceal it or make up for it by style." It takes courage for a young man to stand firmly erect while others are bowing and fawning for praise and power. It takes courage to wear threadbare clothes while your comrades dress in broadcloth. It takes courage to remain in honest poverty when others grow rich by fraud. It takes courage to say "No" squarely when those around you say "Yes." It takes courage to do your duty in silence and obscurity while others prosper and grow famous although neglecting sacred obligations. It takes courage to unmask your true self, to show your blemishes to a condemning world, and to pass for what you really are.

Will Power

In the moral world there is nothing impossible if we can bring a thorough will to do it. —W. Humboldt

It is firmness that makes the gods on our side. —Voltaire

Stand firm, don't flutter. —Franklin

People do not lack strength they lack will. —Victor Hugo

Perpetual pushing and assurance put a difficulty out of countenance and make a seeming difficulty give way. —Jeremy Collier

When a firm, decisive spirit is recognized, it is curious to see how the space clears around a man and leaves him room and freedom. —John Foster

"Do you know," asked Balzac's father, "that in literature a man must be either a king or a beggar?" "Very well," replied his son, "*I will be a king*." After ten years of struggle with hardship and poverty, he won success as an author.

"Why do you repair that magistrate's bench with such great care?" asked a bystander of a carpenter who was taking unusual pains. "Because I wish to make it easy against the time when I come to sit on it myself," replied the other. He did sit on that bench as a magistrate a few years later.

"*I will be marshal of France and a great general*," exclaimed a young French officer as he paced his room with hands tightly clenched. He became a successful general and a marshal of France.

"There is so much power in faith," says Bulwer, "even when faith is applied but to things human and earthly, that let a man but be firmly persuaded that he is born to do some day, what at the moment seems impossible, and it is fifty to one but what he does it before he dies."

There is about as much chance of idleness and incapacity winning real success, or a high position in life, as there would be in producing a Paradise Lost by shaking up promiscuously the separate words of Webster's Dictionary, and letting them fall at random on the floor. Fortune smiles upon those who roll up their sleeves and put their shoulders to the wheel; upon men who are not afraid of dreary, dry, irksome drudgery, men of nerve and grit who do not turn aside for dirt and detail.

"Is there one whom difficulties dishearten?" asked John Hunter. "He will do little. Is there one who will conquer? That kind of a man never fails."

"Circumstances," says Milton, "have rarely favored famous men. They have fought their way to triumph through all sorts of opposing obstacles."

"We have a half belief," said Emerson, "that the person is possible who can counterpoise all other persons. We believe that there may be a man *who is a match for events*,—one who never found his match,—against whom other men being dashed are broken,—one who can give you any odds and beat you."

The simple truth is that a will strong enough to keep a man continually striving for things not wholly beyond his powers will carry him in time very far toward his chosen goal.

At nineteen Bayard Taylor walked to Philadelphia, thirty miles, to find a publisher for fifteen of his poems. He wanted to see them printed in a book; but no publisher would undertake it. He returned to his home whistling, however, showing that his courage and resolution had not abated.

In Europe he was often forced to live on twenty cents a day for weeks on account of his poverty. He returned to London with only thirty cents left. He tried to sell a poem of twelve hundred lines, which he had in his knapsack, but no publisher wanted it. Of that time he wrote: "My situation was about as hopeless as it is possible to conceive." But his will defied circumstances and he rose above them. For two years he lived on two hundred and fifty dollars a year in London, earning every dollar of it with his pen.

His untimely death in 1879, at fifty-four, when Minister to Berlin, was lamented by the learned and great of all countries.

We are told of a young New York inventor who about twenty years ago spent every dollar he was worth in an experiment, which, if successful, would introduce his invention to public notice and insure his fortune, and, what he valued more, his usefulness. The next morning the daily papers heaped unsparing ridicule upon him. Hope for the future seemed vain. He looked around the shabby room where his wife, a delicate little woman, was preparing breakfast. He was without a penny. He seemed like a fool in his own eyes; all these years of hard work were wasted. He went into his chamber, sat down, and buried his face in his hands.

At length, with a fiery heat flashing through his body, he stood erect. "It *shall* succeed!" he said, shutting his teeth. His wife was crying over the papers when he went back. "They are very cruel," she said. "They don't understand." "I'll make them understand," he replied cheerfully. "It was a fight for six years," he said afterward. "Poverty, sickness and contempt followed me. I had nothing left but the *dogged determination* that it should succeed." It did succeed. The invention was a great and useful one. The inventor is now a prosperous and happy man.

Napoleon was a terrible example of what the power of will can accomplish. He always threw his whole force of body and mind direct upon his work. Imbecile rulers and the nations they governed went down before him in succession. He was told that the Alps stood in the way of his armies,—"There shall be no Alps," he said, and the road across the Simplon was constructed, through a district formerly almost inaccessible. "Impossible," said he, "is a word only to be found in the dictionary of fools." He was a man who toiled terribly; sometimes employing and exhausting four secretaries at a time. He spared no one, not even himself. His influence inspired other men, and put a new life into them. "I made my generals out of mud," he said.

To think we are able is almost to be so—to determine upon attainment, is frequently attainment itself. Thus, earnest resolution has often seemed to have about it almost a savor of omnipotence. The strength of Suwarrow's character lay in his power of willing, and, like most resolute persons, he preached it up as a system.

Before Pizarro, D'Almagro and De Luque obtained any associates or arms or soldiers, and with a very imperfect knowledge of the country or the powers they were to encounter, they celebrated a solemn mass in one of the great churches, dedicating themselves to the conquest of Peru. The people expressed their contempt at such a monstrous project, and were shocked at such sacrilege. But these decided men continued the service and afterward retired for their great preparation with an entire insensibility to the expressions of contempt. Their firmness was absolutely invincible. The world has deplored the results of this expedition, but there is a great lesson for us in the firmness of decision of its leaders. Such firmness would keep to its course and retain its purpose unshaken amidst the ruins of the world.

At the battle of Marengo the French army was supposed to be defeated; but, while Bonaparte and his staff were considering their next move, Dessaix suggested that there was yet time to retrieve their disaster, as it was only about the middle of the afternoon. Napoleon rallied his men, renewed the fight, and won a great victory over the Austrians, though the unfortunate Dessaix lost his own life on that field.

What has chance ever done in the world? Has it built any cities? Has it invented any telephones, any telegraphs? Has it built any steamships, established any universities, any asylums, any hospitals? Was there any chance in Cæsar's crossing the Rubicon? What had chance to do with Napoleon's career, with Wellington's, or Grant's, or Von Moltke's? Every battle was won before it was begun. What had luck to do with Thermopylæ, Trafalgar, Gettysburg? Our successes we ascribe to ourselves; our failures to destiny.

A vacillating man, no matter what his abilities, is invariably pushed to the wall in the race of life by a determined will. It is he who resolves to succeed, and who at every fresh rebuff begins resolutely again, that reaches the goal. The shores of fortune are covered with the stranded wrecks of men of brilliant ability, but who have wanted courage, faith and decision, and have therefore perished in sight of more resolute but less capable adventurers, who succeeded in making port. Hundreds of men go to their graves in obscurity, who have been obscure only because they lacked the pluck to make a first effort, and who, could they only have resolved to begin, would have astonished the world by their achievements and successes. The fact is, as Sydney Smith has well said, that in order to do anything in this world that is worth doing, we must not stand shivering on the bank, and thinking of the cold and the danger, but jump in and scramble through as well as we can.

Is not this a grand privilege of man, immortal man, that though he may not be able to stir a finger; that though a moth may crush him; that merely by a righteous will, he is raised above the stars; that by it he originates a good in the universe, which the universe could not annihilate; a good which can defy extinction, though all created energies of intelligence or matter were combined against it?

A man whose moral nature is ascendant is not the subject, but the superior of circumstances. He is free; nay, more, he is a king; and though this sovereignty may have been won by many desperate battles, once on the throne, and holding the sceptre with a firm grasp, he has a royalty of which neither time nor accident can strip him.

What can you do with a man who has an invincible purpose in him; who never knows when he is beaten; and who, when his legs are shot off, will fight on the stumps? Difficulties and opposition do not daunt him. He thrives upon persecution; it only stimulates him to more determined endeavor. Give a man the alphabet and an iron will, and who shall place bounds to his achievements! Imprison a Galileo for his discoveries in science, and he will experiment with the straw in his cell. Deprive Euler of his eyesight, and he but studies harder upon mental problems, thus developing marvelous powers of mathematical calculation. Lock up the poor Bedford tinker in jail, and he will write the finest allegory in the world, or will leave his imperishable thoughts upon the walls of his cell. Burn the body of Wycliffe and throw the ashes into the Severn; but they will be swept to the ocean, which will carry them, permeated with his principles, to all lands. *The world always listens to a man with a will in him.* You might as well snub the sun as such men as Bismarck and Grant.

Hope would storm the castle of despair; it gives courage when despondency would give up the battle of life. He is the best doctor who can implant *hope* and courage in the human soul. So he is the greatest man who can inspire us to the grandest achievements.

"Our remedies oft in ourselves do lie,
Which we ascribe to heaven; the fated sky
Gives us free scope; and only backward pulls
Our slow designs when we ourselves are dull."
"How much I could do if I only tried."

Guard Your Weak Point

He that is slow to anger is better than the mighty: and he that ruleth his spirit than he that taketh a city. —Bible

The first and best of victories is for a man to conquer himself: to be conquered by himself is, of all things, the most shameful and vile. —Plato

The worst education which teaches self-denial is better than the best which teaches everything else and not that. —John Sterling

Most powerful is he who has himself in his own power. —Seneca

The energy which issues in growth, or assimilates knowledge, must originate in self and be self-directed. —Thomas J. Morgan

The foes with which they waged their strife
Were passion, self and sin;
The victories that laureled life,
Were fought and won within. —Edward H. Dewart

"I'll sign it after awhile," a drunkard would reply, when repeatedly urged by his wife to sign the pledge; "but I don't like to break off at once, the best way is to get used to a thing." "Very well, old man," said his wife, "see if you don't fall into a hole one of these days, with no one to help you out."

Not long after, when intoxicated, he did fall into a shallow well, but his shouts for help were fortunately heard by his wife. "Didn't I tell you so?" she asked. "It's lucky I was in hearing or you might have drowned." He took hold of the bucket and she tugged at the windlass; but when he was near the top her grasp slipped and down he went into the water again. This was repeated until he screamed: "Look here, you're doing that on purpose, I know you are." "Well, now, I am," admitted the wife. "Don't you remember telling me it's best to get used to a thing by degrees? I'm afraid if I bring you up sudden, you would not find it wholesome." Finding that his case was becoming desperate, he promised to sign the pledge at once. His wife raised him out immediately, but warned him that if ever he became intoxicated and fell into the well again, she would leave him there.

A man captured a young tiger and resolved to make a pet of it. It grew up like a kitten, fond and gentle. There was no evidence of its savage, bloodthirsty nature, and it seemed perfectly harmless. But one day while the master was playing with his pet, the rough tongue upon his hand started the blood from a scratch. The moment the beast tasted blood, his ferocious tiger nature was roused, and he rushed upon his master to tear him to pieces. Sometimes the appetite for drink, which was thought to be buried years ago, is roused by the taste or the smell of "the devil in solution," and the wretched victim finds himself a helpless slave to the passion which he thought dead.

When a young man, Hugh Miller once drank the two glasses of whiskey which fell to his share at the usual treat of drink of the masons with whom he worked. On reaching home he tried to read Bacon's Essays, his favorite book, but he could not distinguish the letters or comprehend the meaning. "The condition into which I had brought myself was, I felt, one of degradation," said he. "I had sunk, by my own act, for the time, to a lower level of intelligence than that on which it was my privilege to be placed; and though the state could have been no very favorable one for forming a resolution, I in that hour determined that I should never again sacrifice my capacity of intellectual enjoyment to a drinking usage; and with God's help I was enabled to hold by the determination."

In a certain manufacturing town an employer one Saturday paid to his workmen $700 in crisp new bills that had been secretly marked. On Monday $450 of those identical bills were deposited in the bank by the saloon-keepers. When the fact was made known, the workmen were so startled by it that they helped to make the place a no-license town. The times would not be so "hard" for the workmen if the saloons did not take in so much of their wages. If they would organize a strike against the saloons, they would find the result to be better than an increase of wages, and to include an increase of savings.

How often we might read the following sign over the threshold of a youthful life: "For sale, grand opportunities, for a song;" "golden chances for beer;" "magnificent opportunities exchanged for a little sensual enjoyment;" "for exchange, a beautiful home, devoted wife, lovely children, for drink;" "for sale, cheap, all the magnificent possibilities of a brilliant life, a competence, for one chance in a thousand at the gambling table;" "for exchange, bright prospects, a brilliant outlook, a cultivated intelligence, a college education, a skilled hand, an observant eye, valuable experience, great tact, all exchanged for rum, for a muddled brain, a bewildered intellect, a shattered nervous system, poisoned blood, a diseased body, for fatty degeneration of the heart, for Bright's disease, for a drunkard's liver."

With almost palsied hand, at a temperance meeting, John B. Gough signed the pledge. For six days and nights in a wretched garret, without a mouthful of food, with scarcely a moment's sleep, he fought the fearful battle with appetite. Weak, famished, almost dying, he crawled into the sunlight; but he had conquered the demon which had almost killed him. Gough used to describe the struggles of a man who tried to leave off using tobacco. He threw away what he had, and said that was the end of it; but no, it was only the beginning of it. He would chew camomile, gentian, tooth-picks, but it was of no use. He bought another plug of tobacco and put it in his pocket. He wanted a chew awfully, but he looked at it and said, "You are a *weed*, and I am a *man*. I'll master you if I die for it;" and he did, while carrying it in his pocket daily.

There was an abbot that desired a piece of ground that lay conveniently for him. The owner refused to sell; yet with much persuasion he was contented to let it. The abbot hired it and covenanted only to farm it for one crop. He had his bargain, and sowed it with acorns—a crop that lasted three hundred years. So Satan asks to get possession of our souls by asking us to permit some small sin to enter, some one wrong that seems of no great account. But when once he has entered and planted the seeds and beginnings of evil, he holds his ground.

"Teach self-denial and make its practice pleasurable," says Walter Scott, "and you create for the world a destiny more sublime than ever issued from the brain of the wildest dreamer."

Thomas A. Edison was once asked why he was a total abstainer. He said, "I thought I had a better use for my head."

Byron could write poetry easily, for it was merely indulging his natural propensity; but to curb his temper, soothe his discontent, and control his animal appetites was a very different thing. At all events, it seemed so great to him that he never seriously attempted self-conquest. Let every youth who would not be shipwrecked on life's voyage cultivate this one great virtue, "self-control." There is nothing so important to a youth starting out in life as a thoroughly trained and cultivated will; everything depends upon it. If he has it, he will succeed; if he does not have it, he will fail.

"The first and best of victories," says Plato, "is for a man to conquer himself; to be conquered by himself is, of all things, the most shameful and vile."

"Silence," says Zimmerman, "is the safest response for all the contradiction that arises from impertinence, vulgarity, or envy."

"He is a fool who cannot be angry," says English, "but he is a wise man who will not."

Seneca, one of the greatest of the ancient philosophers, said that "we should every night call ourselves to account. What infirmity have I mastered to-day? what passion opposed? what temptation resisted? what virtue acquired?" and then he follows with the profound truth that "our vices will abate of themselves if they be brought every day to the shrift." If you cannot at first control your anger, learn to control your tongue, which, like fire, is a good servant, but a hard master.

It does no good to get angry. Some sins have a seeming compensation or apology, a present gratification of some sort, but anger has none. A man feels no better for it. It is really a torment, and when the storm of passion has cleared away, it leaves one to see that he has been a fool. And he has made himself a fool in the eyes of others too.

The wife of Socrates, Xanthippe, was a woman of a most fantastical and furious spirit. At one time, having vented all the reproaches upon Socrates her fury could suggest, he went out and sat before the door. His calm and unconcerned behavior but irritated her so much the more; and, in the excess of her rage, she ran upstairs and emptied a vessel upon his head, at which he only laughed and said that "so much thunder must needs produce a shower." Alcibiades, his friend, talking with him about his wife, told him he wondered how he could bear such an everlasting scold in the same house with him. He replied, "I have so accustomed myself to expect it, that it now offends me no more than the noise of carriages in the street."

It is said of Socrates, that whether he was teaching the rules of an exact morality, whether he was answering his corrupt judges, or was receiving sentence of death, or swallowing the poison, he was still the same man; that is to say, calm, quiet, undisturbed, intrepid—in a word, wise to the last.

"It is not enough to have great qualities," says La Rochefoucauld; "we should also have the management of them." No man can call himself educated until every voluntary muscle obeys his will.

"You ask whether it would not be manly to resent a great injury," said Eardley Wilmot; "I answer that it would be manly to resent it, but it would be Godlike to forgive it."

"He who, with strong passions, remains chaste; he who, keenly sensitive, with manly power of indignation in him, can be provoked, and yet restrain himself and forgive—these are strong men, the spiritual heroes."

To feel provoked or exasperated at a trifle, when the nerves are exhausted, is, perhaps, natural to us in our imperfect state. But why put into the shape of speech the annoyance which, once uttered, is remembered; which may burn like a blistering wound, or rankle like a poisoned arrow? If a child be crying or a friend capricious, or a servant unreasonable, be careful what you say. Do not speak while you feel the impulse of anger, for you will be almost certain to say too much, to say more than your cooler judgment will approve, and to speak in a way that you will regret. Be silent until the "sweet by and by," when you will be calm, rested, and self-controlled.

But self-respect must be accompanied by self-conquest, or our strong feelings may prove but runaway horses. He who would command others must first learn to obey, and he who would command his own powers must learn to be submissive to the still small voice within. Discipline the passions, curb pride and impatience, restrain all hasty impulses. Deny yourself the gratification of any desire not sanctioned by reason. Shame and its consequent degradation follow the loss of our own good opinion rather than the esteem of others. Too many yield in the perpetual conflict between temptation to gratify the coarser appetites and aspiration for the good, the true, and the beautiful. Voices unheard by those around us whisper "Don't," but too often self-respect is lost, the will lies prostrate, and the debauch goes on. Such battles must be fought by all; be ours the victory born of self-control, aided by that Heaven which always helps him who prays while putting his own shoulder to the wheel.

No man had a better heart or more thoroughly hated oppression than Edmund Burke. He possessed neither experience in affairs, nor a tranquil judgment, nor the rule over his own spirit, so that his genius, under the impulse of his bewildering passions, wrought much evil to his country and to Europe, even while he rendered noble service to the cause of commercial freedom, to Ireland, and to America.

Burns could not resist the temptation to utter his clever sarcasms at another's expense, and one of his biographers has said that he made a hundred enemies for every ten jokes he made. But Burns could no more control his appetite than his tongue.

"Thus thoughtless follies laid him low
And stained his name."

Xanthus, the philosopher, told his servant that on the morrow he was going to have some friends to dine, and asked him to get the best thing he could find in the market. The philosopher and his guests sat down the next day at the table. They had nothing but tongue—four or five courses of tongue—tongue cooked in this way, and tongue cooked in that way, and the philosopher lost his patience, and said to his servant, "Didn't I tell you to get the best thing in the market?" He said, "I did get the best thing in the market. Isn't the tongue the organ of sociality, the organ of eloquence, the organ of kindness, the organ of worship?" Then Xanthus said, "To-morrow I want you to get the worst thing in the market." And on the morrow the philosopher sat at the table, and there was nothing there but tongue—four or five courses of tongue—tongue in this shape, and tongue in that shape—and the philosopher again lost his patience, and said, "Didn't I tell you to get the worst thing in the market?" The servant replied, "I did; for isn't the tongue the organ of blasphemy, the organ of defamation, the organ of lying?"

"I can reform my people," said Peter the Great, "but I cannot reform myself." He forbade all Russians to wear beards, and to quell the insurrection which resulted, he had 8000 revolters beheaded. With a hatchet he began the ghastly work. He had his own son beheaded.

He who cannot resist temptation is not a man. He is wanting in the highest attributes of humanity. The honor and nobleness of the old "knight-errantry" consisted in defending the innocence of men and protecting the chastity of women against the assaults of others. But the truer and nobler knighthood protects the property and the character, the innocence and the chastity of others against one's self. We should all be posted upon our weak points, for after all there are many emergencies in life when these weak points, not our strong ones, will measure our manhood and our strength. Many a woman whom a mouse would frighten out of her wits would not shrink from assisting in terrible surgical operations in our city or war hospitals, and many an officer and soldier who would walk up to the cannon's mouth without a tremor in battle, would not dare to say his soul was his own in a society parlor. Many a great statesman has quailed before the ringer of scorn of a fellow-Congressman, and has been completely cowed by a hiss from the gallery or a ridiculing paragraph in a newspaper. We all have tender spots, weak spots, and a man can never know his strength who does not study his weaknesses.

"Violent passions and ardent feelings are seldom found united with complete self-command; but when they are they form the strongest possible character, for there is all the power of clear thought and cool judgment impelled by the resistless energy of feeling. This combination Washington possessed; for in his impetuosity there was no foolish rashness, and in his passion no injustice. Besides, whatever violence there might be within, the explosion seldom came to the surface, and when it did it was arrested at once by the stern mandate of his will. He never lost the mastery of himself in any emergency, and in 'ruling his spirit' showed himself greater than in 'taking a city.'

"It is one of the astonishing things in his life that, amid the perfect chaos of feeling into which he was thrown,—amid the distracted counsels and still more distracted affairs that surrounded him,—he never once lost the perfect equilibrium of his own mind. The contagion of fear and doubt and despair could not touch him. He did not seem susceptible to the common influences which affect men. His soul poised on its own centre, reposed calmly there through all the storms that beat for seven years on his noble breast. The ingratitude and folly of those who should have been his allies, the insults of his foes, and the frowns of fortune never provoked him into a rash act, or deluded him into a single error."

Horace Mann says that there must be a time when the vista of the future, with all its possibilities of glory and of shame, first opens to the vision of youth. Then is he summoned to make his choice between truth and treachery; between honor and dishonor; between purity and profligacy; between moral life and moral death. And as he doubts or balances between the heavenward or hellward course; as he struggles to rise or consents to fall; is there in all the universe of God a spectacle of higher exultation or of deeper pathos? Within him are the appetites of a brute and the attributes of an angel; and when these meet in council to make up the roll of his destiny and seal his fate, shall the beast hound out the seraph? Shall the young man, now conscious of the largeness of his sphere and of the sovereignty of his choice, wed the low ambitions of the world, and seek, with their emptiness, to fill his immortal desires? Because he has a few animal wants that must be supplied, shall he become all animal,—an epicure and an inebriate,—and blasphemously make it the first doctrine of his catechism,—"the Chief End of Man?"—to glorify his stomach and enjoy it? Because it is the law of self-preservation that he shall provide for himself, and the law of religion that he shall provide for his family, when he has one, must he, therefore, cut away all the bonds of humanity that bind him to his race, forswear charity, crush down every prompting of benevolence, and if he can have the palace and equipage of the prince, and the table of a sybarite, become a blind man, and a deaf man, and a dumb man, when he walks the streets where hunger moans and nakedness shivers?

The strong man is the one who ever keeps himself under strict discipline, who never once allows the lower to usurp the place of the higher in him; who makes his passions his servants and never allows them to be his master; who is ever led by his mind and not by his inclinations. He drills and disciplines his desires and keeps the roots of his life under ground, and never allows them to interfere with his character. He is never the slave of his inclinations, nor the sport of impulse. He is the commander of himself and heads his ship due north even in the wildest tempests of passion. He is never the slave of his strongest desire.

A noted teacher has said that the propensities and habits are as teachable as Latin and Greek, while they are infinitely more essential to happiness. We are very largely the creatures of our wills. By constantly looking on the bright side of things, by viewing everything hopefully, by setting the face as a flint every hour of every day toward all that is harmonious and beautiful in life, and refusing to listen to the discord or to look at the ugly side of life, by constantly directing the thought toward what is noble, grand and true, we can soon form habits which will develop into a beautiful character, a harmonious and well-rounded life. We are creatures of habit, and by knowing the laws of its formation we can, in a little while, build up a network of habit about us, which will protect us from most of the ugly, selfish and degrading things of life. In fact, the only real happiness and unalloyed satisfaction we get out of life, is the product of self-control. It is the great guardian of all the virtues, without which none of them is safe. It is the sentinel, which stands on guard at the door of life, to admit friends and exclude enemies.

"I call that mind free," says Channing, "which jealously guards its intellectual rights and powers, which calls no man master, which does not content itself with a passive or hereditary faith, which opens itself to light whencesoever it may come, which receives new truth as an angel from heaven, which, whilst consulting others, inquires still more of the oracle within; itself, and uses instructions from abroad, not to supersede, but to quicken and exalt its own energies. I call that mind free which is not passively framed by outward circumstances, which is not swept away by the torrent of events, which is not the creature of accidental impulse, but which bends events to its own improvement, and acts from an inward spring, from immutable principles which it has deliberately espoused. I call that mind free which protects itself against the usurpations of society, which does not cower to human opinion, which feels itself accountable to a higher tribunal than man's, which respects a higher law than fashion, which respects itself too much to be the slave or tool of the many or the few. I call that mind free which through confidence in God and in the power of virtue has cast off all fear but that of wrong-doing, which no menace or peril can enthrall, which is calm in the midst of tumults, and possesses itself though all else be lost. I call that mind free which resists the bondage of habit, which does not mechanically repeat itself and copy the past, which does not live on its old virtues, which does not enslave itself to precise rules, but which forgets what is behind, listens for new and higher monitions of conscience, and rejoices to pour itself forth in fresh and higher exertions. I call that mind free which is jealous of its own freedom, which guards itself from being merged in others, which guards its empire over itself as nobler than the empire of the world."

Stick

Patience is the courage of the conqueror; it is the virtue,
par excellence, of Man against Destiny, of the One against
the World, and of the Soul against Matter. Therefore this is
the courage of the Gospel; and its importance, in a social
view—its importance to races and institutions—cannot be too
earnestly inculcated. —Bulwer

Perpetual pushing and assurance put a difficulty out of countenance, and
make a seeming impossibility give way. —Jeremy Collier

To bear is to conquer fate. —Campbell

The nerve that never relaxes, the eye that never blenches, the thought that
never wanders,—these are the masters of victory. —Burke

Let us, then, be up and doing,
With a heart for any fate;
Still achieving, still pursuing,
Learn to labor and to wait. —Longfellow

"How long did it take you to learn to play?" asked a young man of Geradini.
"Twelve hours a day for twenty years," replied the great violinist. Layman
Beecher's father, when asked how long it took him to write his celebrated
sermon on the "Government of God," replied, "About forty years."

"If you will study a year I will teach you to sing well," said an Italian music
teacher to a pupil who wished to know what can be hoped for with study; "if
two years, you may excel. If you will practice the scale constantly for three
years, I will make you the best tenor in Italy; if for four years, you may have
the world at your feet."

Perceiving that Caffarelli had a fine tenor voice and unusual talent, a
teacher offered to give him a thorough musical education free of charge,
provided the pupil would promise never to complain of the course of
instruction given. The first year the master gave nothing but the scales,
compelling the youth to practice them over and over again. The second year
it was the same, the third, and the fourth, the conditions of the bargain being
the only reply to any question in relation to a change from such monotonous
drill. The fifth year the teacher introduced chromatics and thorough bass, and,
at its close, when Caffarelli looked for something more brilliant and
interesting, the master said: "Go, my son, I can teach you nothing more. You
are the first singer of Italy and of the world." The *mastery* of scales and
diatonics gave him power to sing anything.

"Keep at the helm," said President Porter; "steer your own ship, and
remember that the great art of commanding is to take a fair share of the work.

Strike out. Assume your own position. Put potatoes in a cart, over a rough road, and the small ones go to the bottom."

"Never depend upon your genius," said John Ruskin, in the words of Joshua Reynolds; "if you have talent, industry will improve it; if you have none, industry will supply the deficiency."

"The only merit to which I lay claim," said Hugh Miller, "is that of patient research—a merit in which whoever wills may rival or surpass me; and this humble faculty of patience when rightly developed may lead to more extraordinary development of ideas than even genius itself."

Titian, the greatest master of color the world has seen, used to say: "White, red and black, these are all the colors that a painter needs, but he must know how to use them." It took fifty years of constant, hard practice to bring him to his full mastery.

"How much grows everywhere if we do but wait!" exclaims Carlyle. "Not a difficulty but can transfigure itself into a triumph; not even a deformity, but if our own soul have imprinted worth on it, will grow dear to us."

Persistency is characteristic of all men who have accomplished anything great. They may lack in some other particular, have many weaknesses, or eccentricities, but the quality of persistence is never absent in a successful man. No matter what opposition he meets or what discouragements overtake him, he is always persistent. Drudgery cannot disgust him, obstacles cannot discourage him, labor cannot weary him. He will persist, no matter what comes or what goes; it is a part of his nature. He could almost as easily stop breathing.

It is not so much brilliancy of intellect or fertility of resource as persistency of effort, constancy of purpose, that makes a great man. Persistency always gives confidence. Everybody believes in the man who persists. He may meet misfortunes, sorrows and reverses, but everybody believes that he will ultimately triumph because they know there is no keeping him down. "Does he keep at it, is he persistent?" is the question which the world asks of a man.

Even the man with small ability will often succeed if he has the quality of persistence, where a genius without persistence would fail.

"How hard I worked at that tremendous shorthand, and all improvement appertaining to it," said Dickens. "I will only add to what I have already written of my perseverance at this time of my life, and of a patient and continuous energy which then began to be matured within me, and which I know to be the strong point of my character, if it have any strength at all, that there, on looking back, I find the source of my success."

"I am sorry to say that I don't think this is in your line," said Woodfall the reporter, after Sheridan had made his first speech in Parliament. "You had better have stuck to your former pursuits." With head on his hand Sheridan mused for a time, then looked up and said, "It is in me, and it shall come out of me." From the same man came that harangue against Warren Hastings which the orator Fox called the best speech ever made in the House of Commons.

"The man who is perpetually hesitating which of two things he will do first," said William Wirt, "will do neither." The man who resolves, but suffers his resolution to be changed by the first counter-suggestion of a friend—who fluctuates from opinion to opinion, from plan to plan, and veers like a weather-cock to every point of the compass, with every breath of caprice that blows, can never accomplish anything great or useful. Instead of being progressive in anything, he will be at best stationary, and, more probably, retrograde in all.

Great writers have ever been noted for their tenacity of purpose. Their works have not been flung off from minds aglow with genius, but have been elaborated and elaborated into grace and beauty, until every trace of their efforts has been obliterated. Bishop Butler worked twenty years incessantly on his "Analogy," and even then was so dissatisfied that he wanted to burn it. Rousseau says he obtained the ease and grace of his style only by ceaseless inquietude, by endless blotches and erasures. Virgil worked eleven years on the Æneid. The note-books of great men like Hawthorne and Emerson are tell-tales of enormous drudgery, of the years put into a book which may be read in an hour. Montesquieu was twenty-five years writing his "Esprit de Louis," yet you can read it in sixty minutes. Adam Smith spent ten years on his "Wealth of Nations." A rival playwright once laughed at Euripides for spending three days on three lines, when he had written five hundred lines. "But your five hundred lines in three days will be dead and forgotten, while my three lines will live forever," replied Euripides.

Sir Fowell Buxton thought he could do as well as others, if he devoted twice as much time and labor as they did. Ordinary means and extraordinary application have done most of the great things in the world.

Defoe offered the manuscript of Robinson Crusoe to many booksellers and all but one refused it. Addison's first play, Rosamond, was hissed off the stage, but the editor of the Spectator and Tattler was made of stern stuff and was determined that the world should listen to him, and it did.

David Livingstone said: "Those who have never carried a book through the press can form no idea of the amount of toil it involves. The process has increased my respect for authors a thousand-fold. I think I would rather cross the African continent again than undertake to write another book."

"For the statistics of the negro population of South America alone," says Robert Dale Owen, "I examined more than a hundred and fifty volumes."

Another author tells us that he wrote paragraphs and whole pages of his book as many as fifty times.

It is said of one of Longfellow's poems that it was written in four weeks, but that he spent six months in correcting and cutting it down. Bulwer declared that he had rewritten some of his briefer productions as many as eight or nine times before their publication. One of Tennyson's pieces was rewritten fifty times. John Owen was twenty years on his "Commentary on the Epistle to the Hebrews;" Gibbon on his "Decline and Fall," twenty years; and Adam Clark, on his "Commentary," twenty-six years. Carlyle spent fifteen years on his "Frederick the Great."

A great deal of time is consumed in reading before some books are prepared. George Eliot read 1000 books before she wrote "Daniel Deronda." Allison read 2000 before he completed his history. It is said of another that he read 20,000 and wrote only two books.

Virgil spent several years on the Georgics, which could be printed in two columns of an ordinary newspaper.

"Generally speaking," said Sydney Smith, "the life of all truly great men has been a life of intense and incessant labor. They have commonly passed the first half of life in the gross darkness of indigent humility,—overlooked, mistaken, condemned by weaker men,—thinking while others slept, reading while others rioted, feeling something within them that told them they should not always be kept down among the dregs of the world. And then, when their time has come, and some little accident has given them their first occasion, they have burst out into the light and glory of public life, rich with the spoils of time, and mighty in all the labors and struggles of the mind."

Malibran said: "If I neglect my practice a day, I see the difference in my execution; if for two days, my friends see it; and if for a week, all the world knows my failure." Constant, persistent struggle she found to be the price of her marvelous power.

"If I am building a mountain," said Confucius, "and stop before the last basketful of earth is placed on the summit, I have failed."

"Young gentlemen," said Francis Wayland, "remember that nothing can stand day's work."

America will never produce any great art until our resources are developed and we get more time. As a people we have not yet learned the art of patience. We do not know how to wait. Think of an American artist spending seven, eight, ten, and even twelve years on a single painting as did Titian, Michael Angelo and many of the other old masters. Think of an American sculptor spending years and years upon a single masterpiece, as did the Greeks and Romans. We have not yet learned the secret of working and waiting.

"The single element in all the progressive movements of my pencil," said the great David Wilkie, "was persevering industry."

The kind of ability which most men rank highest is that which enables its possessor to do what he undertakes, and attain the object of his ambition or desire.

"The reader of a newspaper does not see the first insertion of an ordinary advertisement," says a French writer. "The second insertion he sees, but does not read; the third insertion he reads; the fourth insertion he looks at the price; the fifth insertion he speaks of it to his wife; the sixth insertion he is ready to purchase, and the seventh insertion he purchases."

The large fees which make us envy the great lawyer or doctor are not remuneration for the few minutes' labor of giving advice, but for the mental stores gathered during the precious spare moments of many a year while others were sleeping or enjoying holidays. A client will frequently object to paying fifty dollars for an opinion written in five minutes, but such an opinion could be written only by one who has read a hundred law books. If the lawyer had not previously read those books, but should keep a client waiting until he could read them with care, there would be fewer complaints that fees of this kind are not earned.

We are told that perseverance built the pyramids on Egypt's plains, erected the gorgeous temple at Jerusalem, inclosed in adamant the Chinese Empire, scaled the stormy, cloud-capped Alps, opened a highway through the watery wilderness of the Atlantic, leveled the forests of the new world, and reared in its stead a community of States and nations. Perseverance has wrought from the marble block the exquisite creations of genius, painted on canvas the gorgeous mimicry of nature, and engraved on a metallic surface the viewless substance of the shadow. Perseverance has put in motion millions of spindles, winged as many flying shuttles, harnessed thousands of iron steeds to as many freighted cars, and sent them flying from town to town and nation to nation; tunneled mountains of granite, and annihilated space with the lightning's speed. Perseverance has whitened the waters of the world with the sails of a hundred nations, navigated every sea and explored every land. Perseverance has reduced nature in her thousand forms to as many sciences, taught her laws, prophesied her future movements, measured her untrodden spaces, counted her myriad hosts of worlds, and computed their distances, dimensions, and velocities.

"Whoever is resolved to excel in painting, or, indeed, in any other art," said Reynolds, "must bring all his mind to bear upon that one object from the moment that he rises till he goes to bed."

"If you work hard two weeks without selling a book," wrote a publisher to an agent, "you will make a success of it."

"Know thy work and do it," said Carlyle; "and work at it like a Hercules. One monster there is in the world—an idle man."

Save

If you want to test a young man and ascertain whether nature made him for a king or a subject, give him a thousand dollars and see what he will do with it. If he is born to conquer and command, he will put it quietly away till he is ready to use it as opportunity offers. If he is born to serve, he will immediately begin to spend it in gratifying his ruling propensity. —Parton

The man who builds, and lacks wherewith to pay,
Provides a home from which to run away. —Young

Buy what thou hast no need of, and ere long thou shalt sell thy necessaries.
For age and want save while you may:
No morning sun lasts a whole day. —Franklin

Whatever be your talents, whatever be your prospects, never speculate away on a chance of a palace that which you may need as a provision against the workhouse. —Bulwer

"What do you do with all these books?" "Oh, that library is my 'one cigar a day,'" was the response. "What do you mean?" "Mean! Just this: when you bothered me so about being a man, and learning to smoke, I'd just been reading about a young fellow who bought books with money that others would have spent in smoke, and I thought I'd try and do the same. You remember, I said I should allow myself one cigar a day." "Yes." "Well, I never smoked. I just put by the price of a five-cent cigar every day, and as the money accumulated I bought books—the books you see there." "Do you mean to say that those books cost no more than that? Why there are dollars' worth of them." "Yes, I know there are. I had six years more of my apprenticeship to serve when you persuaded me to 'be a man.' I put by the money I have told you of, which of course at five cents a day amounted to $18.25 a year or $109.50 in six years. I keep those books by themselves, as a result of my apprenticeship cigar-money; and if you'd done as I did, you would by this time have saved many, many more dollars than that, and been in business besides."

If a man will begin at the age of twenty and lay by twenty-six cents every working day, investing at 7 per cent. compound interest, he will have thirty-two thousand dollars when he is seventy years old. Twenty cents a day is no unusual expenditure for beer or cigars, yet in fifty years it would easily amount to twenty thousand dollars. Even a saving of one dollar a week from the date of one's majority would give him one thousand dollars for each of the last ten of the allotted years of life. "What maintains one vice would bring up two children."

Who does not feel honored by his relationship to Dr. Franklin, whether as a townsman or a countryman, or even as belonging to the same race? Who does not feel a sort of personal complacency in that frugality of his youth which laid the foundation for so much competence and generosity in his mature age; in that wise discrimination of his outlays, which held the culture of the soul in absolute supremacy over the pleasures of the sense; and in that consummate mastership of the great art of living, which has carried his practical wisdom into every cottage in Christendom, and made his name immortal? And yet, how few there are among us who would not disparage, nay, ridicule and contemn a young man who should follow Franklin's example.

Washington examined the minutest expenditures of his family, even when President of the United States. He understood that without economy none can be rich, and with it none need be poor.

Napoleon examined his domestic bills himself, detected overcharges and errors.

Unfortunately Congress can pass no law that will remedy the vice of living beyond one's means.

"We are ruined," says Colton, "not by what we really want, but by what we think we do. Therefore never go abroad in search of your wants; if they be real wants, they will come home in search of you; for he that buys what he does not want will soon want what he cannot buy."

"I hope that there will not be another sale," exclaimed Horace Walpole, "for I have not an inch of room nor a farthing left." A woman once bought an old door-plate with "Thompson" on it because she thought it might come in handy some time. The habit of buying what you don't need because it is cheap encourages extravagance. "Many have been ruined by buying good pennyworths."

Barnum tells the story of one of his acquaintances, whose wife would have a new and elegant sofa, which in the end cost him thirty thousand dollars. When the sofa reached the house it was found necessary to get chairs "to match," then sideboards, carpets, and tables, "to correspond" with them, and so on through the entire stock of furniture, when at last it was found that the house itself was quite too small and old-fashioned for the furniture, and a new one was built "to correspond" with the sofa and *et ceteras*: "thus," added my friend, "running up an outlay of $30,000 caused by that single sofa, and saddling on me in the shape of servants, equipage, and the necessary expenses attendant on keeping up a fine 'establishment' a yearly outlay of eleven thousand dollars, and a habit of extravagance which was a constant menace to my prosperity."

Cicero said: "Not to have a mania for buying, is to possess a revenue." Many are carried away by the habit of bargain-buying. "Here's something wonderfully cheap; let's buy it." "Have you any use for it?" "No, not at present; but it is sure to come in useful, some time."

"Annual income," says Macawber, "twenty pounds; annual expenditure, nineteen six, result—happiness. Annual income, twenty pounds; annual expenditure, twenty pounds ought and six, result—misery."

"Hunger, rags, cold, hard work, contempt, suspicion, unjust reproach, are disagreeable," says Horace Greeley; "but debt is infinitely worse than them all."

"If I had but fifty cents a week to live on," said Greeley, "I'd buy a peck of corn and parch it before I'd owe any man a dollar."

To find out uses for the persons or things which are now wasted in life is to be the glorious work of the men of the next generation, and that which will contribute most to their enrichment.

Economizing "in spots" or by freaks is no economy at all; it must be done by management.

Let us learn the meaning of economy. Economy is a high, humane office, a sacrament, when its aim is great; when it is the prudence of simple tastes, when it is practiced for freedom, or love or devotion. Much of the economy we see in houses is of a base origin, and is best kept out of sight. Parched corn eaten to-day that I may have roast fowl for my dinner on Sunday, is a baseness, but parched corn and a house with one apartment, that I may be free of all perturbations, that I may be serene and docile to what the mind shall speak, and girt and road-ready for the lowest mission of knowledge or good will, is frugality for gods and heroes.

Like many other boys P. T. Barnum picked up pennies driving oxen for his father, but unlike many other boys he would invest these earnings in knick-knacks which he would sell to others on every holiday, thus increasing his pennies to dollars.

The eccentric John Randolph once sprang from his seat in the House of Representatives, and exclaimed in his piercing voice, "Mr. Speaker, I have found it." And then, in the stillness which followed this strange outburst, he added, "I have found the Philosopher's stone: it is *Pay as you go.*"

In France, all classes, the men as well as the women, study the economy of cookery and practice it; and there, as many travelers affirm, the people live at one-third the expense of Englishmen or Americans. There they know how to make savory messes out of remnants that others would throw away. There they cook no more for each day than is required for that day. With them the art ranks with the fine arts, and a great cook is as much honored and respected as a sculptor or a painter. The consequence is, as ex-Secretary McCullough thinks, a French village of 1000 inhabitants could be supported luxuriously on the waste of one of our large American hotels, and he believes that the entire population of France could be supported on the food which is literally wasted in the United States. Professor Blot, who resided for some years in the United States, remarks, pathetically, that here, "where the markets rival the best markets of Europe, it is really a pity to live as many do live. There are thousands of families in moderately good circumstances who have never eaten a loaf of really good bread, nor tasted a well-cooked steak, nor sat down to a properly prepared meal."

There are many who think that economy consists in saving cheese parings and candle ends, in cutting off two pence from the laundress' bill, and doing all sorts of little, mean, dirty things. Economy is not meanness. The misfortune is also that this class of persons let their economy apply only in one direction. They fancy they are so wonderfully economical in saving a half-penny, where they ought to spend two-pence, that they think they can afford to squander in other directions. *Punch*, in speaking of this "one idea" class of people, says, "They are like a man who bought a penny herring for his family's dinner, and then hired a coach and four to take it home." I never knew a man to succeed by practicing this kind of economy. True economy consists in always making the income exceed the out-go. Wear the old clothes a little longer, if necessary; dispense with the new pair of gloves, live on plainer food if need be. So that under all circumstances, unless some unforeseen accident occurs, there will be a margin in favor of the income. A penny here and a dollar there placed at interest go on accumulating, and in this way the desired result is obtained.

"I wish I could write all across the sky in letters of gold," says Rev. William Marsh, "the one word, savings bank."

Boston savings banks have $130,000,000 on deposit, mostly saved in driblets. Josiah Quincy used to say that the servant girls built most of the palaces on Beacon street.

"Nature uses a grinding economy," says Emerson, "working up all that is wasted to-day into to-morrow's creation; not a superfluous grain of sand for all the ostentation she makes of expense and public works. She flung us out in her plenty, but we cannot shed a hair or a paring of a nail but instantly she snatches at the shred and appropriates it to her general stock. Last summer's flowers and foliage decayed in autumn only to enrich the earth this year for other forms of beauty. Nature will not even wait for our friends to see us, unless we die at home. The moment the breath has left the body she begins to take us to pieces, that the parts may be used again for other creations."

"So apportion your wants that your means may exceed them," says Bulwer. "With one hundred pounds a year I may need no man's help; I may at least have 'my crust of bread and liberty.' But with £5000 a year I may dread a ring at my bell; I may have my tyrannical master in servants whose wages I cannot pay; my exile may be at the fiat of the first long-suffering man who enters a judgment against me; for the flesh that lies nearest my heart some Shylock may be dusting his scales and whetting his knife. Every man is needy who spends more than he has; no man is needy who spends less. I may so ill manage, that with £5000 a year I purchase the worst evils of poverty—terror and shame; I may so well manage my money, that with £100 a year I purchase the best blessings of wealth: safety and respect."

Live Upward

"Do what thou dost as if the stake were heaven,
And this thy last deed ere the judgment day."
If you wish to reach the highest begin at the lowest. —Publius Syrus

What is a man,
If his chief good, and market of his time,
Be but to sleep, and feed? A beast, no more.
Sure He, that made us with such large discourse,
Looking before, and after, gave us not
That capability and godlike Reason
To rust in us unused. —Shakespeare

Ambition is the spur that makes man struggle with destiny. It is heaven's own incentive to make purpose great and achievement greater. —Anonymous

"Not failure, but low aim, is crime."
"Endeavor to be first in thy calling, whatever it may be; neither let anyone go before thee in well doing."
O may I join the choir invisible
Of those immortal dead who live again
In minds made better by their presence; live
In pulses stirred to generosity,
In deeds of daring rectitude, in scorn
For miserable aims that end with self,
In thoughts sublime that pierce the night like stars,
And with their mild persistence urge man's search
To vaster issues. —George Eliot

"Alexander, Cæsar, Charlemagne and myself have founded empires," said Napoleon to Montholon at St. Helena; "but upon what did we rest the creations of our genius? Upon force. Jesus Christ alone founded his empire on love, and at this moment millions of men would die for Him. I die before my time and my body will be given back to worms. Such is the fate of him who has been called the great Napoleon. What an abyss between my deep misery and the eternal kingdom of Christ, which is proclaimed, loved and adored, and which is extended over the whole earth. Call you this dying? Is it not rather living? The death of Christ is the death of a God."
"No true man can live a half life," says Phillips Brooks, "when he has genuinely learned that it is a half life. The other half, the higher half, must haunt him."
"Ideality," says Horace Mann, "is only the *avant courier* of the mind; and where that in a healthy and normal state goes I hold it to be a prophecy that realization can follow."

"If the certainty of future fame bore Milton rejoicing through his blindness, or cheered Galileo in his dungeon," writes Bulwer, "what stronger and holier support shall not be given to him who has loved mankind as his brothers and devoted his labors to their cause?—who has not sought, but relinquished, his own renown?—who has braved the present censures of men for their future benefit, and trampled upon glory in the energy of benevolence? Will there not be for him something more powerful than fame to comfort his sufferings and to sustain his hopes?"

"If I live," wrote Rufus Choate in his diary in September, 1844, "all blockheads which are shaken at certain mental peculiarities shall know and feel a reasoner, a lawyer and a man of business."

I have read that none of the humbler races have the muscle by which man turns his eye upward, though I am not anatomist enough to be sure of the fact.

"Show me a contented slave," says Burke, "and I will show you a degraded man."

"They truly are faithful," says one writer, "who devote their entire lives to amendment."

General Grant said of the Chinese Wall: "I believe that the labor expended on this wall could have built every railroad in the United States, every canal and highway, and most, if not all, our cities."

"The real benefactors of mankind," says Emerson, "are the men and women who can raise their fellow beings out of the world of corn and money, who make them forget their bank account by interesting them in their higher selves; who can raise mere money-getters into the intellectual realm, where they will cease to measure greatness and happiness by dollars and cents; who can make men forget their stomachs and feast on being's banquet."

"Men are not so much mistaken in desiring to advance themselves," said Beecher, "as in judging what will be an advance, and what the right method of obtaining it. An ambition which has conscience in it will always be a laborious and faithful engineer, and will build the road and bridge the chasms between itself and eminent success by the most faithful and minute performances of duty. The liberty to go higher than we are is given only when we have fulfilled amply the duty of our present sphere. Thus men are to rise upon their performances and not upon their discontent. And this is the secret and golden meaning of the command to be *content* in whatever sphere we are placed. It is not to be the content of indifference, of indolence, of unambitious stupidity, but the content of industrious fidelity. When men are building the foundations of vast structures they must needs labor far below the surface, and in disagreeable conditions. But every course of stone which they lay raises them higher; and at length, when they reach the surface, they have laid such solid work under them that they need not fear now to carry up their walls, through towering stories, till they overlook the whole neighborhood. A man proves himself fit to go higher who shows that he is faithful where he is. A man that will not do well in his present place, because he longs to be higher, is fit neither to be where he is nor yet above it; he is already too high and should be put lower."

Do that which is assigned thee and thou canst not hope too much, or dare too much. What a man does, that he has. In himself is his might. Don't waste life on doubts and fears. Spend yourself on the work before you, well assured that the performance of this hour's duties will be the best preparation for the hours or ages that follow it.

Tradition says that when Solomon received the gift of an emerald vase from the Queen of Sheba he filled it with an elixir which he only knew how to prepare, one drop of which would prolong life indefinitely. A dying criminal begged for a drop of the precious fluid, but Solomon refused to prolong a wicked life. When good men asked for it they were refused, or failed to obtain it when promised, as the king would forget or prefer not to open the vase to get but a single drop. When at last the king became ill, and bade his servants bring the vase, he found that the contents had all evaporated. So it is often with our hope, our faith, our ambition, our aspiration.

A man cannot aspire if he looks down. God has not created us with aspirations and longings for heights to which we cannot climb. Live upward. The unattained still beckons us toward the summit of life's mountains, into the atmosphere where great souls live and breathe and have their being. Even hope is but a promise of the possibility of its own fulfillment. Life should be lived in earnest. It is no idle game, no farce to amuse and be forgotten. It is a stern reality, fuller of duties than the sky of stars. You cannot have too much of that yearning which we call aspiration, for, even though you do not attain your ideal, the efforts you make will bring nothing but blessing; while he who fails of attaining mere worldly goals is too often eaten up with the canker-worm of disappointed ambition. To all will come a time when the love of glory will be seen to be but a splendid delusion, riches empty, rank vain, power dependent, and all outward advantages without inward peace a mere mockery of wretchedness. The wisest men have taken care to uproot selfish ambition from their breasts. Shakespeare considered it so near a vice as to need extenuating circumstances to make it a virtue.

Who has not noticed the power of love in an awkward, crabbed, shiftless, lazy man? He becomes gentle, chaste in language, energetic. Love brings out the poetry in him. It is only an idea, a sentiment, and yet what magic it has wrought. Nothing we can see has touched the man, yet he is entirely transformed.

Not less does ambition completely transform a human being, for a woman thirsting for fame can work where a man equally resolute would faint. He despises ease and sloth, welcomes toil and hardship, and shakes even kingdoms to gratify his master passion. Mere ambition has impelled many a man to a life of eminence and usefulness; its higher manifestation, aspiration, has led him beyond the stars. If the aim be right the life in its details cannot be far wrong. Your heart must inspire what your hands execute, or the work will be poorly done. The hand cannot reach higher than does the heart.

But do not strive to reach impossible goals. It is wholly in your power to develop yourself, but not necessarily so to make yourself a king. How many Presidents of the United States or Prime Ministers of England are chosen within the working lifetime of a man? What if a thousand young men resolve to become President or Prime Minister? While such prizes are within your reach, remember that your will must be tremendous and your qualifications of the highest order, or you cannot hope to secure them. Too many are deluded by ambition beyond their power of attainment, or tortured by aspirations totally disproportionate to their capacity for execution. You may, indeed, confidently hope to become eminent in usefulness and power, but only as you build upon a broad foundation of self-culture; while, as a rule, specialists in ambition as in science are apt to become narrow and one-sided. Darwin was very fond of poetry and music when young, but after devoting his life to science, he was surprised to find Shakespeare tedious. He said that, if he were to live his life again, he would read poetry and hear music every day, so as not to lose the power of appreciating such things.

God asks no man whether he will accept life. That is not the choice. You *must* take it. The only choice is *how*.

"When I found I was black," said Dumas, "I resolved to live as if I were white, and so force men to look below my skin."

In the collection of the Massachusetts Historical Society is a prospectus used by Longfellow in canvassing, on one of the blank leaves of which are the skeleton stanzas of "Excelsior," which he was evidently evolving as he trudged from house to house.

"Disregarding the honors that most men value and looking to the truth," said Plato, "I shall endeavor in reality to live as virtuously as I can; and, when I die, to die so. And I invite all other men to the utmost of my power; and you, too, I invite to this contest, which, I affirm, surpasses all contests here."

"Did you ever hear of a man who had striven all his life faithfully and singly toward an object, and in no measure obtained it?" asked Thoreau. "If a man constantly aspires, is he not elevated? Did ever a man try heroism, magnanimity, truth, sincerity, and find that there was no advantage in them,—that it was a vain endeavor?"

"O if the stone can only have some vision of the temple of which it is to be a part forever," exclaimed Phillips Brooks, "what patience must fill it as it feels the blows of the hammer, and knows that success for it is simply to let itself be wrought into what shape the master wills."

Man never reaches heights above his habitual thought. It is not enough now and then to mount on wings of ecstasy into the infinite. We must habitually dwell there. The great man is he who abides easily on heights to which others rise occasionally and with difficulty. Don't let the maxims of a low prudence daily dinned into your ears lower the tone of your high ambition or check your aspirations. Hope lifts us step by step up the mysterious ladder, the top of which no eye hath ever seen. Though we do not find what hope promised, yet we are stronger for the climbing, and we get a broader outlook upon life which repays the effort. Indeed, if we do not follow where hope beckons, we gradually slide down the ladder in despair. Strive ever to be at the top of your condition. A high standard is absolutely necessary.

"Sand"

I shall show the cinders of my spirits
Through the ashes of my chance. —Shakespeare

Perseverance is a virtue
That wins each god-like act, and plucks success
E'en from the spear-proof crest of rugged danger. —William Harvard

Never say "Fail" again. —Richelieu

It is the one neck nearer that wins the race and shows the blood; the one pull more of the oar that proves the "beefiness of the fellow," as Oxford men say; it is the one march more that wins the campaign; the five minutes' more persistent courage that wins the fight. Though your force be less than another's, you equal and out-master your opponent if you continue it longer and concentrate it more. —Smiles

"I know no such unquestionable badge and ensign of a sovereign mind as that tenacity of purpose which, through all changes of companions, or parties, or fortunes, changes never, bates no jot of heart or hope, but wearies out opposition and arrives at its port."

"Well done, Tommy Brooks!" exclaimed his teacher in pleased surprise when the dunce of the school spoke his piece without omitting a single word. The other boys had laughed when he rose, for they expected a bad failure. But when the rest of the class had tried, the teacher said Tommy had done the best of all, and gave him the prize.

"And now tell me," said she, "how you learned the poem so well."

"Please, ma'am, it was the snail on the wall that taught me how to do it," said Tommy. At this the other pupils laughed aloud, but the teacher said: "You need not laugh, boys, for we may learn much from such things as snails. How did the snail teach you, Tommy?"

"I saw it crawl up the wall little by little," replied the boy. "It did not stop nor turn back, but went on, and on; and I thought I would do the same with the poem. So I learned it little by little, and did not give up. By the time the snail reached the top of the wall, I had learned the whole poem."

"I may here impart the secret of what is called good and bad luck," said Addison. "There are men who, supposing Providence to have an implacable spite against them, bemoan in the poverty of old age the misfortunes of their lives. Luck forever runs against them, and for others. One with a good profession lost his luck in the river, where he idled away his time a-fishing. Another with a good trade perpetually burnt up his luck by his hot temper, which provoked all his employes to leave him. Another with a lucrative business lost his luck by amazing diligence at everything but his own business. Another who steadily followed his trade, as steadily followed the bottle. Another who was honest and constant to his work, erred by his perpetual misjudgment,—he lacked discretion. Hundreds lose their luck by indulging sanguine expectations, by trusting fraudulent men, and by dishonest gains. A man never has good luck who has a bad wife. I never knew an early-rising, hard-working, prudent man, careful of his earnings and strictly honest, who complained of his bad luck. A good character, good habits, and iron industry are impregnable to the assaults of the ill luck that fools are dreaming of. But when I see a tatterdemalion creeping out of a grocery late in the forenoon with his hands stuck into his pockets, the rim of his hat turned up, and the crown knocked in, I know he has had bad luck,—for the worst of all luck is to be a sluggard, a knave, or a tippler."

"You have a difficult subject," said Anthony Trollope at Niagara Falls, to an artist who had attempted to draw the spray of the waters. "All subjects are difficult," was the reply, "to a man who desires to do well." "But yours, I fear, is impossible," said Trollope. "You have no right to say so till I have finished my picture," protested the artist.

"Tell Louisa to stick to her teaching; she can never succeed as a writer." When her father delivered the rejected manuscript of a story sent to James T. Fields, editor of the *Atlantic Monthly*, with the above message, Miss Alcott said, "Tell him I *will* succeed as a writer, and some day I shall write for the *Atlantic*." Not long after she sent an article to the *Atlantic* and received a check for $50. With the money she said she bought "a second hand carpet for the parlor, a bonnet for her sister, shoes and stockings for herself." Her father was calling upon Longfellow some time after this, when Longfellow took the *Atlantic*, and said, "I want to read to you Emerson's fine poem upon Thoreau's flute." Mr. Alcott interrupted him with delight and said, "My daughter Louisa wrote that."

"Men talk as if victory were something fortunate," says Emerson. "*Work is victory. Wherever work is done victory is obtained. There is no chance and no blanks.* You want but one verdict; if you have your own, you are secure of the rest. But if witnesses are wanted, witnesses are near."

"Young gentlemen," said Francis Wayland, "remember that nothing can stand day's work."

Alexander the Great exclaimed to his soldiers, disaffected after a long campaign, "Go home and tell them that you left Alexander to conquer the world alone."

"We discount only our own bills, and not those of private persons," said the cashier of the Bank of England, when a large bill was offered drawn by Anselm Rothschild of Frankfort, on Nathan Rothschild of London. "Private persons!" exclaimed Nathan, when told of the cashier's remark; "I will make these gentlemen see what sort of private persons we are." Three weeks later he presented a five-pound note at the bank at the opening of the office. The teller counted out five sovereigns, looking surprised that Baron Rothschild should have troubled himself about such a trifle. The baron examined the coins one by one, weighing them in the balance, as he said "the law gave him the right to do," put them into a little canvas bag, and offered a second, then a third, fourth, fiftieth, thousandth note. When a bag was full he handed it to a clerk in waiting, and proceeded to fill another. In seven hours he had changed £21,000, and, with nine employes of his house similarly engaged, had occupied the tellers so busily in changing $1,050,000 worth of notes that no one else could receive attention. The bankers laughed, but the next morning Rothschild appeared with his nine clerks and several drays to carry away the gold, remarking, "These gentlemen refuse to pay my bills; I have sworn not to keep theirs. They can pay at their leisure, only I notify them that I have enough to employ them for two months." The smiles faded from the features of the bank officials, as they thought of a draft of $55,000,000 in gold which they did not hold. Next morning notice was given in the newspapers that the Bank of England would pay Rothschild's bills as well as its own.

"Well," said Barnum to a friend in 1841, "I am going to buy the American Museum." "Buy it!" exclaimed the astonished friend, who knew that the showman had not a dollar; "what do you intend buying it with?" "Brass," was the prompt reply, "for silver and gold have I none."

Every one interested in public entertainments in New York knew Barnum, and knew the condition of his pocket; but Francis Olmstead, who owned the Museum building, consulted numerous references all telling of "a good showman, who would do as he agreed," and accepted a proposition to give security for the purchaser. Mr. Olmstead was to appoint a money-taker at the door, and credit Barnum toward the purchase with all above expenses and an allowance of fifty dollars per month to support his wife and three children. Mrs. Barnum gladly assented to the arrangement, and offered, if need be, to cut down the household expenses to a little more than a dollar a day. Some six months later Mr. Olmstead happened to enter the ticket office at noon, and found Barnum eating for dinner a few slices of bread and some corned beef. "Is this the way you eat your dinner?" he asked.

"I have not eaten a warm dinner since I bought the Museum, except on the Sabbath; and I intend never to eat another until I get out of debt." "Ah! you are safe, and will pay for the Museum before the year is out," said Mr. Olmstead, slapping the young man approvingly on the shoulder. He was right, for in less than a year Barnum had paid every cent out of the profits of the establishment.

A noted philosopher said: "The favors of fortune are like steep rocks; only eagles and creeping things mount to the summit." Lord Campbell, who became Chief Justice and Lord Chancellor of England and amassed a large fortune, began life as a drudge in a printing office. A little observation shows us that, as a rule, the men who accomplish the most in the world are the most useful, and sensible members of society, the men who are depended upon most in emergencies, the men of backbone and stamina, the bone and sinew of their communities; the men who can always be relied upon, who are healthiest and happiest, are, as a rule, of ordinary mental calibre and medium capacity. But with persistent and untiring industry, these are they, after all, who carry the burdens and reap the prizes of life. It is the men and women who keep everlastingly at it, who do not believe themselves geniuses, but who know that if they ever accomplish anything great, they must do it by common drudgery and persistent industry and with an unwavering aim in one pursuit. Those who believe themselves geniuses are apt to scatter their efforts and thus fritter away their great energies without accomplishing anything in proportion to their high promise. Often the men who promise the most pay the least.

Mrs. Frank Leslie often refers to the time she lived in her carpetless attic while striving to pay her husband's obligations. She has fought her way successfully through nine lawsuits, and has paid the entire debt. She manages her ten publications entirely herself, signs all checks and money-orders, makes all contracts, looks over all proofs, and approves the make-up of everything before it goes to press. She has developed great business ability, which no one dreamed she possessed.

A little boy was asked how he learned to skate. "Oh, by getting up every time I fell down," he replied.

The boy Thorwaldsen, whose father died in the poorhouse, and whose education was so scanty that he had to write his letters over many times before they could be posted, by his indomitable perseverance, tenacity and grit, fascinated the world with the genius which neither his discouraging father, poverty, nor hardship could repress.

"It is all very well," said Charles J. Fox, "to tell me that a young man has distinguished himself by a brilliant first speech. He may go on, or he may be satisfied with his first triumph; but show me a young man who has not succeeded at first, and nevertheless has gone on, and I will back that young man to do better than most of those who have succeeded at the first trial."

It was the last three days of the first voyage of Columbus that told. All his years of struggle and study would have availed nothing if he had yielded to the mutiny. It was all in those three days. But what days!

"Often defeated in battle," said Macaulay of Alexander the Great, "he was always successful in war." He might have said the same of Washington, and, with appropriate changes, of all who win great triumphs of any kind.

One of the greatest preachers of modern times, Lacordaire, failed again and again. Everybody said he would never make a preacher, but he was determined to succeed, and in two years from his humiliating failures he was preaching in Notre Dame to immense congregations.

Orange Judd was a remarkable example of success through grit. He earned corn by working for farmers, carried it on his back to mill, brought back the meal to his room, cooked it himself, milked cows for his pint of milk per day, and lived on mush and milk for months together. He worked his way through Wesleyan University, and took a three years' post-graduate course at Yale.

Oh, the triumphs of this indomitable spirit of the conqueror! This it was that enabled Franklin to dine on a small loaf in the printing-office with a book in his hand. It helped Locke to live on bread and water in a Dutch garret. It enabled Gideon Lee to go barefoot in the snow, half starved and thinly clad. It sustained Lincoln and Garfield on their hard journeys from the log cabin to the White House.

The very reputation of being strong-willed, plucky, and indefatigable is of priceless value. It often cowes enemies and dispels at the start opposition to one's undertakings which would otherwise be formidable.

"When you get into a tight place and everything goes against you, till it seems as if you could not hold on a minute longer," said Harriet Beecher

Stowe, "never give up then, for that's just the place and time that the tide'll turn."

"Never despair," says Burke, "but if you do, work on in despair."

Once when Marshal Ney was going into battle, looking down at his knees which were smiting together, he said, "You may well shake; you would shake worse yet if you knew where I am going to take you."

"Go it, William!" an old boxer was overheard saying to himself in the midst of a fight; "at him again!—never say 'die'!"

A striking incident is related of the early experience of George Law, who, in his day, was one of the most conspicuous financiers and capitalists of New York City. When he was a young man he went to New York, poor and friendless. One day he was walking along the streets, hungry, not knowing where his next meal would come from, and passed a new building in course of erection. Through some accident one of the hod carriers fell from the structure and dropped dead at his feet. Young Law, in his desperation, applied for the job to take the dead man's place, and the place was given him. He went to work, and this was how one of the wealthiest and shrewdest New York business men got his start.

See young Disraeli, sprung from a hated and persecuted race; without opportunity, pushing his way up through the middle classes, up through the upper classes, until he stands self-poised upon the topmost round of political and social power. Scoffed, ridiculed, rebuffed, hissed from the House of Commons, he simply says, "The time will come when you will hear me." The time did come, and the boy with no chance swayed the sceptre of England for a quarter of a century.

If impossibilities ever exist, popularly speaking, they ought to have been found somewhere between the birth and the death of Kitto, that deaf pauper and master of Oriental learning. But Kitto did not find them there. In the presence of his decision and imperial energy they melted away. Kitto begged his father to take him out of the poorhouse, even if he had to subsist like the Hottentots. He told him that he would sell his books and pawn his handkerchief, by which he thought he could raise about twelve shillings. He said he could live upon blackberries, nuts and field turnips, and was willing to sleep on a hayrick. Here was real grit. What were impossibilities to such a resolute will? Patrick Henry voiced that decision which characterized the great men of the Revolution when he said, "Is life so dear, or peace so sweet, as to be purchased at the price of chains and slavery? Forbid it, Almighty God! I know not what course others may take; but as for me, give me liberty or give me death!"

Look at Garrison reading this advertisement in a Southern paper: "Five thousand dollars will be paid for the head of W. L. Garrison by the Governor of Georgia." Behold him again; a broadcloth mob is leading him through the streets of Boston by a rope. He is hurried to jail. See him return calmly and unflinchingly to his work, beginning at the point at which he was interrupted. Note this heading in the *Liberator*, the type of which he set himself in an attic on State Street, in Boston: "I am in earnest, I will not equivocate, I will not excuse, I will not retreat a single inch, and I will be heard." Was Garrison heard? Ask a race set free largely by his efforts. Even the gallows erected in front of his own door did not daunt him. He held the ear of an unwilling world with that burning word "freedom," which was destined never to cease its vibrations until it had breathed its sweet secret to the last slave.

At a time when abolitionists were dangerously unpopular, a crowd of brawny Cape Cod fishermen had made such riotous demonstrations that all the speakers announced, except Stephen Foster and Lucy Stone, had fled from an open-air platform. "You had better run, Stephen," said she; "they are coming." "But who will take care of you?" asked Foster. "This gentleman will take care of me," she replied, calmly laying her hand within the arm of a burly rioter with a club, who had just sprung upon the platform. "Wh—what did you say?" stammered the astonished rowdy, as he looked at the little woman; "yes, I'll take care of you, and no one shall touch a hair of your head." With this he forced a way for her through the crowd, and, at her earnest request, placed her upon a stump and stood guard with his club while she delivered an address so effective that the audience offered no further violence, and even took up a collection of twenty dollars to repay Mr. Foster for the damage his clothes had received when the riot was at its height.

"Luck is ever waiting for something to turn up," says Cobden; "labor, with keen eyes and strong will, will turn up something. Luck lies in bed, and wishes the postman would bring him the news of a legacy; labor turns out at six o'clock, and with busy pen or ringing hammer lays the foundation of a competence. Luck whines; labor whistles. Luck relies on chance; labor, on character."

There is no luck, for all practical purposes, to him who is not striving, and whose senses are not all eagerly attent. What are called accidental discoveries are almost invariably made by those who are looking for something. A man incurs about as much risk of being struck by lightning as by accidental luck. There is, perhaps, an element of luck in the amount of success which crowns the efforts of different men; but even here it will usually be found that the sagacity with which the efforts are directed and the energy with which they are prosecuted measure pretty accurately the luck contained in the results achieved. Apparent exceptions will be found to relate almost wholly to single undertakings, while in the long run the rule will hold good. Two pearl-divers, equally expert, dive together and work with equal energy. One brings up a pearl, while the other returns empty-handed. But let both persevere and at the end of five, ten or twenty years it will be found that they succeeded almost in exact proportion to their skill and industry.

Lincoln, being asked by an anxious visitor what he would do after three or four years if the rebellion was not subdued, replied: "Oh, there is no alternative but to keep pegging away."

"It is in me and it shall come out," said Sheridan, when told that he would never make an orator, as he had failed in his first speech in Parliament. He became known as one of the foremost orators of his day.

It takes great courage to fight a lost cause when there is no hope even of victory. To contest every inch of ground with as much persistency and enthusiasm as if we were assured of victory; this is true courage.

The world admires the man who never flinches from unexpected difficulties, who calmly, patiently, and courageously grapples with his fate; who dies, if need be, at his post.

President Chadbourne put grit in place of his lost lung, and worked thirty-five years after his funeral had been planned.

Henry Fawcett put grit in place of eyesight, and became the greatest Postmaster-General England ever had.

Prescott also put grit in place of eyesight, and became one of America's greatest historians. Francis Parkman put grit in place of health and eyesight, and became the greatest historian of America in his line. Thousands of men have put grit in place of health, eyes, ears, hands, legs, and yet have achieved marvelous success. Indeed, most of the great things of the world have been accomplished by grit and pluck. You cannot keep a man down who has these qualities. He will make stepping-stones out of his stumbling-blocks, and lift himself to success.

Grit and pluck are not always exhibited only by poor boys who have no chance, for there are many notable examples of pluck, persistence and real grit among youth in good circumstances, who never have to fight their way to their own loaf. Mr. Mifflin, who has recently become the head of the celebrated publishing firm of Houghton, Mifflin & Co., is a notable example of persistency, push and grit. After graduating at Harvard and traveling abroad, he was determined, although not obliged to work for a living, to get a position at the Riverside Press in Cambridge. He called upon the late Mr. Houghton and asked him for a situation. Mr. Houghton told him that he had no opening, and that, even if he had, he did not believe that a graduate from Harvard who had money and who had traveled abroad would ever be willing to begin at the bottom and do the necessary drudgery, for boy's pay. Mr. Mifflin protested that he was not afraid of hard work, and that he was willing to do anything and take any sort of a position, if he could only learn the business. But Mr. Houghton would not give him any encouragement. Again and again Mr. Mifflin came to the Riverside Press, and pressed his suit, but to no purpose. Mr. Mifflin persuaded his father to intercede for him, but Mr. Houghton succeeded in convincing him that it would be very unwise for his son to attempt it. But young Mifflin was determined not to give up. Finally, Mr. Houghton, out of admiration for his persistence and pluck, made a place for him, which had been occupied by a boy, for $5 a week.

Young Mifflin took hold of the work with such earnestness, and showed so much pluck and determination, that Mr. Houghton soon called him into the office and raised his pay to $9 a week from the time he began. Although the young man lived in Boston, he was always at the Riverside Press in Cambridge early in the morning, and would frequently remain after all the others had gone. Mr. Houghton happened to go in late one night, after everybody had gone, as he supposed, and was surprised to find Mr. Mifflin there, taking one of the presses apart. Of course such a young man would be advanced. These are the boys who become the heads of firms.

It is victory after victory with the soldier, lesson after lesson with the scholar, blow after blow with the laborer, crop after crop with the farmer, picture after picture with the painter, and mile after mile with the traveler, that secures what all so much Desire—*success*.

Stick to the thing and carry it through. Believe you were made for the place you fill, and that no one else can fill it as well. Put forth your whole energies. Be awake, electrify yourself; go forth to the task. Only once learn to carry a thing through in all its completeness and proportion, and you will become a hero. You will think better of yourself; others will think better of you. The world in its very heart admires the stern, determined doer.

Above Rubies

The best way to settle the quarrel between capital and labor is by allopathic doses of Peter-Cooperism. —Talmage

In the sublimest flights of the soul, rectitude is never surmounted, love is never outgrown. —Emerson

"One ruddy drop of manly blood the surging sea outweighs."
Virtue alone out-builds the pyramids:
Her monuments shall last when Egypt's fall. —Young

He believed that he was born, not for himself, but for the whole world.—Lucan

Wherever man goes to dwell, his character goes with him. —African Proverb

The spirit of a single mind
Makes that of multitudes take one direction,
As roll the waters to the breathing wind. —Byron

"No, say what you have to say in her presence, too," said King Cleomenes of Sparta, when his visitor Anistagoras asked him to send away his little daughter Gorgo, ten years old, knowing how much harder it is to persuade a man to do wrong when his child is at his side. So Gorgo sat at her father's feet, and listened while the stranger offered more and more money if Cleomenes would aid him to become king in a neighboring country. She did not understand the matter, but when she saw her father look troubled and hesitate, she took hold of his hand and said, "Papa, come away—come, or this strange man will make you do wrong." The king went away with the child, and saved himself and his country from dishonor. Character is power, even in a child. When grown to womanhood, Gorgo was married to the hero Leonidas. One day a messenger brought a tablet sent by a friend who was a prisoner in Persia. But the closest scrutiny failed to reveal a single word or line on the white waxen surface, and the king and all his noblemen concluded that it was sent as a jest. "Let me take it," said Queen Gorgo; and, after looking it all over, she exclaimed, "There must be some writing underneath the wax!" They scraped away the wax and found a warning to Leonidas from the Grecian prisoner, saying that Xerxes was coming with his immense host to conquer all Greece. Acting on this warning, Leonidas and the other kings assembled their armies and checked the mighty host of Xerxes, which is said to have shaken the earth as it marched.

"I fear John Knox's prayers more than an army of ten thousand men," said Mary, Queen of Scotland.

"The man behind the sermon," said William M. Evarts, "is the secret of John Hall's power." In fact if there is not a man with a character behind it nothing about it is of the slightest consequence.

Thackeray says, "Nature has written a letter of credit upon some men's faces which is honored wherever presented. You can not help trusting such men; their very presence gives confidence. There is a 'promise to pay' in their very faces which gives confidence, and you prefer it to another man's indorsement." *Character is credit.*

In the great monetary panic of 1857, a meeting was called of the various bank presidents of New York City. When asked what percentage of specie had been drawn during the day, some replied fifty per cent., some even as high as seventy-five per cent., but Moses Taylor of the City Bank said: "We had in the bank this morning, $400,000; this evening, $470,000." While other banks were badly "run," the confidence in the City Bank under Mr. Taylor's management was such that people had deposited in that institution what they had drawn from other banks. Character gives confidence.

"There is no such thing as a small country," said Victor Hugo. "The greatness of a people is no more affected by the number of its inhabitants than the greatness of an individual is measured by his height."

"It is the nature of party in England," said John Russell, "to ask the assistance of men of genius, but to follow the guidance of men of character."

"A handful of good life," says George Herbert, "is worth a bushel of learning."

"I have read," Emerson says, "that they who listened to Lord Chatham felt that there was something finer in the man than anything which he said." It has been complained of Carlyle that when he has told all his facts about Mirabeau they do not justify his estimate of the latter's genius. The Gracchi, Agis, Cleomenes, and others of Plutarch's heroes do not in the record of facts equal their own fame. Sir Philip Sidney and Sir Walter Raleigh are men of great figure and of few deeds. We cannot find the smallest part of the personal weight of Washington in the narrative of his exploits. The authority of the name of Schiller is too great for his books. This inequality of the reputation to the works or the anecdotes is not accounted for by saying that the reverberation is longer than the thunder-clap; but something resided in these men which begot an expectation that outran all their performance. The largest part of their power was latent. This is that which we call character,—a reserved force which acts directly by presence, and without means. What others effect by talent or eloquence, the man of character accomplishes by some magnetism. "Half his strength he puts not forth." His victories are by demonstration of superiority, and not by crossing bayonets. He conquers, because his arrival alters the face of affairs. "O Iole! how didst thou know that Hercules was a god?" "Because," answered Iole, "I was content the moment my eyes fell on him. When I beheld Theseus, I desired that I might see him offer battle, or at least drive his horses in the chariot-race; but Hercules did not wait for a contest; he conquered whether he stood, or walked, or sat, or whatever else he did."

"Show me," said Omar the Caliph to Amru the warrior, "the sword with which you have fought so many battles and slain so many infidels." "Ah," replied Amru, "the sword without the arm of the master is no sharper nor heavier than the sword of Farezdak the poet." So one hundred and fifty pounds of flesh and blood without character is of no great value.

"No man throws away his vote," says Francis Willard, "when he places it in the ballot-box with his conviction behind it. The party which elected Lincoln in 1860 polled only seven thousand votes in 1840. Revolutions never go backward, and the fanaticisms of to-day are the victories of to-morrow."

"O sir, we are beaten," exclaimed the general in command of Sheridan's army, retreating before the victorious Early. "No, sir," replied the indignant Sheridan; "you are beaten, but this army is not beaten." Drawing his sword, he waved it above his head, and pointed it at the pursuing host, while his clarion voice rose above the horrid din in a command to charge once more. The lines paused, turned,—

"And with the ocean's mighty swing, When heaving to the tempest's wing, They hurled them on the foe;"

and the Confederate army was wildly routed.

When war with France seemed imminent, in 1798, President Adams wrote to George Washington, then a private citizen in retirement at Mount Vernon: "We must have your name, if you will permit us to use it; there will be more efficacy in it than in many an army." Character is power.

When Pope Paul IV. heard of the death of Calvin he exclaimed with a sigh, "Ah, the strength of that proud heretic lay in—riches? No! Honors? No! But nothing could move him from his course. Holy Virgin! With two such servants, our Church would soon be mistress of both worlds."

Eighteen hundred years ago, when night closed over the city of Pompeii, a lady sat in her house nursing her son of ten years of age. The child had been ill for some days; his form was wasted, his little limbs were shrunk; and we may imagine with what infinite anxiety she watched every motion of the helpless one, whose existence was so dear. What did take place we know with an exactness very remarkable. That distant mountain which reared its awful head on the shore of the bay, Vesuvius, was troubled that same night with an eruption, and threw into the air such clouds of pumice-stones that the streets and squares of Pompeii became filled, and gradually the stones grew higher and higher, until they reached the level of the windows. There was no chance of escape then by the doors; and those who attempted to get away stepped out of their first floor windows and rushed over the sulphurous stones—a short distance only, for they were quickly overpowered by the poisonous vapors and fell dead. After the stones there fell ashes, and after ashes hot water fell in showers, which changed the ashes into clay. Those who ran out of their houses during the fall of stones were utterly consumed, while those who waited until the ashes began to fall perished likewise, but their bodies were preserved by the ashes and water which fell upon them. The Pompeiian mother we have mentioned opened the window of her house when she thought the fall of stones was over, and with the child in her arms took a few hurried steps forward, when, overpowered by the sulphur, she fell forward, at which moment the shower of ashes began to fall, and quickly buried mother and child. The hot water afterward changed into a mould; the ashes and the sun baked the fatal clay to such a degree of hardness that it has endured to the present day. A short time ago the spot where mother and child lay was found, liquid plaster-of-Paris was poured into the mould formed by the bodies, and then the mould was broken up, leaving the plaster-cast whole. Thus one touching incident in the terrible tragedy of eighteen centuries ago has been preserved for the admiration and respect of posterity. *The arms and legs of the child showed a contraction and emaciation which could only result from illness.* Of the mother only the right arm was preserved; she fell upon the ashes, and the remaining portion of her body was consumed. *But the right hand still clasped the legs of the child*; on her arm were two gold bracelets, and on her fingers were two gold rings—one set with an emerald, the other with a cut amethyst. This touching illustration of *a mother's love* now rests in the museum of the celebrated city.

"I was sitting with Grant once," says General Fisk, "when a major-general entered, dressed in the uniform of his rank, who said: 'Boys, I have a good story to tell you. I believe there are no ladies present.' Grant said, 'No, but there are gentlemen present.'"

Mr. George W. Childs, in referring to this trait, said:

"Another great trait of his character was his purity in every way. I never heard him express or make an indelicate allusion in any way or shape. There is nothing I ever heard that man say that could not be repeated in the presence of women."

The writer has heard of several incidents illustrating his answer to impure stories. On one occasion, when Grant formed one of a dinner-party of American gentlemen in a foreign city, conversation drifted into references to questionable affairs, when he suddenly rose and said, "Gentlemen, please excuse me; I will retire."

When Attila, flushed with conquest, appeared with his barbarian horde before the gates of Rome in 452, Pope Leo alone of all the people dared go forth and try to turn his wrath aside. A single magistrate followed him. The Huns were awed by the fearless majesty of the unarmed old man, and led him before their chief, whose respect was so great that he agreed not to enter the city, provided a tribute should be paid to him.

Wellington said that Napoleon's presence in the French army was equivalent to forty thousand additional soldiers, and Richter said of the invincible Luther, "His words were half battles."

"I know no great men," says Voltaire, "except those who have rendered great services to the human race." Men are measured by what they do; not by what they seem or possess.

Francis Horner, of England, was a man of whom Sydney Smith said, that "the ten commandments were stamped upon his forehead." The valuable and peculiar light in which Horner's history is calculated to inspire every right-minded youth is this: he died at the age of thirty-eight, possessed of greater influence than any other private man, and admired, beloved, trusted, and deplored by all except the heartless and the base. No greater homage was ever paid in Parliament to any deceased member. How was this attained? By rank? He was the son of an Edinburgh merchant. By wealth? Neither he nor any of his relatives ever had a superfluous sixpence. By office? He held but one; and that for only a few years, of no influence, and with very little pay. By talents? His were not splendid, and he had no genius. Cautious and slow, his only ambition was to be right. By eloquence? He spoke in calm, good taste, without any of the oratory that either terrifies or seduces. By any fascination of manner? His was only correct and agreeable. By what was it, then? Merely by sense, industry, good principles and a good heart, qualities which no well constituted mind need ever despair of attaining. It was the force of his character that raised him; and this character was not impressed on him by nature, but formed, out of no peculiarly fine elements, by himself. There were many in the House of Commons of far greater ability and eloquence. But no one surpassed him in the combination of an adequate portion of these with moral worth. Horner was born to show what moderate powers, unaided by anything whatever except culture and goodness, may achieve, even when these powers are displayed amidst the competition and jealousies of public life.

A hundred years hence what difference will it make whether you were rich or poor, a peer or a peasant? But what difference may it not make whether you did what was right or what was wrong?

At a large dinner-party given by Lord Stratford after the Crimean War, it was proposed that every one should write on a slip of paper the name which appeared most likely to descend to posterity with renown. When the papers were opened everyone of them contained the name of Florence Nightingale.

Professor Blackie, of the University of Edinburgh, said to a class of young men: "Money is not needful; power is not needful; liberty is not needful; even health is not the one thing needful; but character alone is that which can truly save us, and if we are not saved in this sense, we certainly must be damned." It has been said that "when poverty is your inheritance, virtue must be your capital."

"Hence it was," said Franklin, speaking of the influence of his known integrity of character, "that I had so much weight with my fellow-citizens. I was but a bad speaker, never eloquent, subject to much hesitation in my choice of words, hardly correct in language, and yet I generally carried my point."

When a man's character is gone, all is gone. All peace of mind, all complacency in himself is fled forever. He despises himself. He is despised by his fellow-men. Within is shame and remorse; without neglect and reproach. He is of necessity a miserable and useless man; he is so even though he be clothed in purple and fine linen, and fare sumptuously every day. It is better to be poor; it is better to be reduced to beggary; it is better to be cast into prison, or condemned to perpetual slavery, than to be destitute of a good name or endure the pains and the evils of a conscious worthlessness of character.

The time is soon coming when, by the common consent of mankind, it will be esteemed more honorable to have been John Pounds, putting new and beautiful souls into the ragged children of the neighborhood while he mended his father's shoes, than to have sat upon the British throne. The time now is when, if Queen Victoria, in one of her magnificent progresses through her realms, were to meet that more than American queen, Miss Dix, in her "circumnavigation of charity" among the insane, the former should kneel and kiss the hand of the latter; and the ruler over more than a hundred millions of people should pay homage to the angel whom God has sent to the maniac.

"At your age," said to a youth an old man who had honorably held many positions of trust and responsibility, "both position and wealth appear enduring things; but at mine a man sees that nothing lasts but character."

Several eminent clergymen were discussing the qualities of self-made men. They each admitted that they belonged to that class, except a certain bishop, who remained silent, and was intensely absorbed in the repast. The host was determined to draw him out, and so, addressing him, said: "All at this table are self-made men, unless the bishop is an exception." The bishop promptly replied, "I am not made yet," and the reply contained a profound truth. So long as life lasts, with its discipline of joy or sorrow, its opportunities for good or evil, so long our characters are being shaped and fixed.

Milton said: "He who would write heroic poems, must make his whole life an heroic poem." We are responsible for our thoughts, and unless we could command them, mental and moral excellence would be impossible.

Charles Kingsley has well said: "Let any one set his heart to do what is right and nothing else, and it will not be long ere his brow is stamped with all that goes to make up the heroic expression, with noble indignation, noble self-restraint, great hopes, great sorrows, perhaps even with the print of the martyr's crown of thorns."

Said James Martineau: "God insists on having a concurrence between our practice and our thoughts. If we proceed to make a contradiction between them, He forthwith begins to abolish it, and if the will will not rise to the reason, the reason must be degraded to the will."

"When I say, in conducting your understanding," says Sidney Smith, "love knowledge with a great love, with a vehement love, with a love co-eval with life—what do I say but love innocence, love virtue, love purity of conduct, love that which, if you are rich and great, will vindicate the blind fortune which has made you so, and make them call it justice; love that which, if you are poor, will render your poverty respectable, and make the proudest feel that it is unjust to laugh at the meanness of your fortunes; love that which will comfort you, adorn you, and never quit you—which will open to you the kingdom of thought, and all the boundless regions of conception as an asylum against the cruelty, the injustice, and the pain that may be your lot in the world—that which will make your motives habitually great and honorable, and light up in an instant a thousand noble disdains at the very thought of meanness and of fraud?"

The Arabs express this by a parable that incarnates, as is their wont, the Word in the recital. King Nimrod, say they, one day summoned his three sons into his presence. He ordered to be set before them three urns under seal. One of the urns was of gold, another of amber, and the third of clay. The king bade the eldest of his sons choose among the urns that which appeared to him to contain the treasure of greatest price. The eldest chose the vase of gold, on which was written the word "Empire." He opened it and found it full of blood. The second chose the amber vase whereon was written the word "Glory." He opened it and found it contained the ashes of the great men who had made a sensation in the world. The third son took the only remaining vase, the one of clay; he found it quite empty, but on the bottom the potter had written the word "God." "Which of these vases weighs the most?" asked the king of the courtiers. The men of ambition replied it was the vase of gold; the poets and conquerors, the amber one; the sages that it was the empty vase, because a single letter of the name God weighs more than the entire globe. We are of the opinion of the sages. We believe the greatest things are great but in the proportion of divinity they contain.

"Although genius always commands admiration," says Smiles, "character most secures respect. The former is more the product of brain-power, the latter of heart-power; and in the long run it is the heart that rules in life. Men of genius stand to society in the relation of its intellect, as men of character of its conscience; and while the former are admired, the latter are followed.

"Commonplace though it may appear, this doing of one's duty embodies the highest ideal of life and character. There may be nothing heroic about it; but the common lot of men is not heroic. And though the abiding sense of duty upholds man in his highest attitudes, it also equally sustains him in the transaction of the ordinary affairs of every-day existence. The most influential of all the virtues are those which are the most in request for daily use. They wear the best and last the longest. We can always better understand and appreciate a man's real character by the manner in which he conducts himself toward those who are the most nearly related to him, and by his transaction of the seemingly commonplace details of daily duty, than by his public exhibition of himself as an author, an orator, or a statesman. Intellectual culture has no necessary relation to purity or excellence of character.

"On the contrary, a condition of comparative poverty is compatible with character in its highest form. A man may possess only his industry, his frugality, his integrity, and yet stand high in the rank of true manhood.

"Character is property. It is the noblest of possessions. It is an estate in the general good-will and respect of men; and they who invest in it—though they may not become rich in this world's goods—will find their reward in esteem and reputation fairly and honorably won. Without principles, a man is like a ship without rudder or compass, left to drift hither and thither with every wind that blows."

What a contrast is afforded by the lives of Bacon and More. Bacon sought office with as much desire as More avoided it; Bacon used as much solicitation to obtain it as More endured to accept it, and each, when in it, was equally true to his character. More was simple, as Bacon was ostentatious. More was as incorruptible as Bacon was venal. More spent his private fortune in office, and Bacon spent the wages of corruption there. Both left office poor in worldly goods; but while More was rich in honor and good deeds, Bacon was poor in everything; poor in the mammon for which he bartered his integrity; poor in the gawd for which he sacrificed his peace; poor in the presence of the worthless; covered with shame in the midst of the people; trusting his fame to posterity, of which posterity is only able to say, that the wisest of men was adviser to the silliest of kings, yet that such a king had a sort of majesty when morally compared with the official director of his conscience. Both More and Bacon served each a great purpose for the world. More illustrated the beauty of holiness; Bacon expounded the infinitude of science. Bacon became the prophet of intellect; More, the martyr of conscience. The one pours over our understandings the light of knowledge; but the other inflames our hearts with the love of virtue.

All have read of the proud Egyptian king who ordered a colossal staircase built in his new palace, and was chagrined to find that he required a ladder to climb from one step to the next. A king's legs are as short as those of a beggar. So, too, a prince's ability to enjoy the pleasures of life is no greater than that of a pauper.

"All that is valuable in this world is to be had for nothing. Genius, beauty, health, piety, love, are not bought and sold. The richest man on earth would vainly offer a fortune to be qualified to write a verse like Milton, or to compose a melody like Mozart. You may summon all the physicians, but they cannot procure for you the sweet, healthful sleep which the tired laborer gets without price. Let no man, then, call himself a proprietor. He owns but the breath as it traverses his lips and the idea as it flits across his mind; and of that breath he may be deprived by the sting of a bee, and that idea, perhaps, truly belongs to another."

"We live in deeds, not years; in thoughts, not breaths: In feelings, not in figures on a dial. We should count time by heart-throbs. He most lives Who thinks most, feels the noblest, acts the best; And he whose heart beats quickest lives the longest."

Moral Sunshine

I have gout, asthma, and seven other maladies, but am otherwise very well.—Sidney Smith

The inborn geniality of some people amounts to genius. —Whipple

This one sits shivering in fortune's smile,
Taking his joy with bated, doubtful breath;
This other, gnawed by hunger, all the while
Laughs in the teeth of death. —T. B. Aldrich

There is no real life but cheerful life. —Addison

Next to the virtue, the fun in this world is what we can least spare.—Agnes Strickland

Joy in one's work is the consummate tool. —Phillips Brooks

Joy is the mainspring in the whole
Of endless Natures calm rotation.
Joy moves the dazzling wheels that roll
In the great timepiece of Creation. —Schiller

"He is as stiff as a poker," said a friend of a man who could never be coaxed or tempted to smile. "Stiff as a poker," exclaimed another, "why he would set an example to a poker."

Even Christians are not celebrated for entering into the *joy* of their Lord.

We are told that "Pascal would not permit himself to be conscious of the relish of his food; he prohibited all seasonings and spices, however much he might wish for and need them; and he actually died because he forced his diseased stomach to receive at each meal a certain amount of aliment, neither more nor less, whatever might be his appetite at the time, or his utter want of appetite. He wore a girdle armed with iron spikes, which he was accustomed to drive in upon his body (his fleshless ribs) as often as he thought himself in need of such admonition. He was annoyed and offended if any in his hearing might chance to say that they had just seen a beautiful woman. He rebuked a mother who permitted her own children to give her their kisses. Toward a loving sister, who devoted herself to his comfort, he assumed an artificial harshness of manner for the *express purpose*, as he acknowledged, of revolting her sisterly affection."

And all this sprung from the simple principle that earthly enjoyment was inconsistent with religion.

We should fight against every influence which tends to depress the mind, as we would against a temptation to crime. A depressed mind prevents the free action of the diaphragm and the expansion of the chest. It stops the secretions of the body, interferes with the circulation of the blood in the brain, and deranges the entire functions of the body. Scrofula and consumption often follow protracted depressions of mind. That "fatal murmur" which is heard in the upper lobes of the lungs in the first stages of consumption, often follows depressed spirits after some great misfortune or sorrow. Victims of suicide are almost always in a depressed state from exhausted vitality, loss of nervous energy, dyspepsia, worry, anxiety, trouble, or grief.

"Mirth is God's medicine," says a wise writer; "everybody ought to bathe in it. Grim care, moroseness, anxiety—all the rust of life, ought to be scoured off by the oil of mirth." It is better than emery. Every man ought to rub himself with it. A man without mirth is like a wagon without springs, in which one is caused disagreeably to jolt by every pebble over which it runs. A man with mirth is like a chariot with springs, in which one can ride over the roughest roads and scarcely feel anything but a pleasant rocking motion.

"I have told you," said Southey, "of the Spaniard who always put on spectacles when about to eat cherries, in order that the fruit might look larger and more tempting. In like manner I make the most of my enjoyments; and though I do not cast my eyes away from my troubles, I pack them in as small a compass as I can for myself, and never let them annoy others." We all know the power of good cheer to magnify everything.

Travelers are told by the Icelanders, who live amid the cold and desolation of almost perpetual winter, that "Iceland is the best land the sun shines upon."

"You are on the shady side of seventy, I expect?" was asked of an old man. "No," was the reply, "I am on the sunny side; for I am on the side nearest to glory."

A cheerful man is pre-eminently a useful man. He does not cramp his mind, nor take half-views of men and things. He knows that there is much misery, but that misery need not be the rule of life. He sees that in every state people may be cheerful; the lambs skip, birds sing and fly joyously, puppies play, kittens are full of joyance, the whole air full of careering and rejoicing insects; that everywhere the good outbalances the bad, and that every evil has its compensating balm.

"Bishop Fénelon is a delicious man," said Lord Peterborough; "I had to run away from him to prevent his making me a Christian."

Hume, the historian, never said anything truer than—"To be happy, the person must be cheerful and gay, not gloomy and melancholy. A propensity to hope and joy is real riches; one to fear and sorrow, real poverty."

Dr. Johnson once remarked with his point and pith that the custom of looking on the bright side of every event was better than having a thousand pounds a year income. But Hume rated the value in dollars and cents of cheerfulness still higher. He said he would rather have a cheerful disposition always inclined to look on the bright side of things than to be master of an estate with 10,000 pounds a year.

"We have not fulfilled every duty, unless we have fulfilled that of being pleasant."

"If a word or two will render a man happy," said a Frenchman, "he must be a wretch indeed, who will not give it. It is like lighting another man's candle with your own, which loses none of its brilliancy by what the other gains."

The sensible young man, in theory at least, chooses for his wife one who will be able to keep his house, to be the mother of sturdy children, one who will of all things meet life's experiences with a sweet temper. It is impossible to imagine a pleasant home with a cross wife, mother or sister, as its presiding genius. And it is a rule, with exceptions, that good appetite and sound sleep induce amiability. If, with these advantages, a girl or woman, boy or man, is still snappish or surly, why it must be due to her or his total depravity.

Some things she should not do; she shouldn't dose herself, or study up her case, or plunge suddenly into vigorous exercise. Moderation is a safe rule to begin with, and, indeed, to keep on with—moderation in study, in work, in exercise, in everything except fresh air, good, simple food, and sleep. Few people have too much of these. The average girl at home can find no more sanitary gymnastics than in doing part of the lighter housework. This sort of exercise has object, and interest, and use, which raises it above mere drill. Add to this a merry romp with younger brothers and sisters, a brisk daily walk, the use for a few moments twice a day of dumb bells in a cool, airy room, and it is safe to predict a steady advance toward that ideal state of being in which we forget our bodies and just enjoy ourselves.

"It is not work that kills men," says Beecher; "it is worry. Work is healthy; you can hardly put more on a man than he can bear. But worry is rust upon the blade. It is not movement that destroys the machinery, but friction."

Helen Hunt says there is one sin which seems to be everywhere, and by everybody is underestimated and quite too much overlooked in valuations of character. It is the sin of fretting. It is as common as air, as speech; so common that unless it rises above its usual monotone we do not even observe it. Watch any ordinary coming together of people, and we see how many minutes it will be before somebody frets—that is, makes more or less complaint of something or other, which probably every one in the room, or car, or on the street corner knew before, and which most probably nobody can help. Why say anything about it? It is cold, it is hot, it is wet, it is dry, somebody has broken an appointment, ill-cooked a meal; stupidity or bad faith somewhere has resulted in discomfort. There are plenty of things to fret about. It is simply astonishing, how much annoyance and discomfort may be found in the course of every-day living, even of the simplest, if one only keeps a sharp eye out on that side of things. Some people seem to be always hunting for deformities, discords and shadows, instead of beauty, harmony and light. We are born to trouble, as sparks fly upward. But even to the sparks flying upward, in the blackest of smoke, there is a blue sky above, and the less time they waste on the road, the sooner they will reach it. Fretting is all time wasted on the road.

About two things we should never fret, that which we cannot help, and that which we can help. Better find one of your own faults than ten of your neighbor's.

It is not the troubles of to-day, but those of to-morrow and next week and next year, that whiten our heads and wrinkle our faces.

"Every man we meet looks as if he'd gone out to borrow trouble, with plenty of it on hand," said a French lady driving in New York.

The pendulum of a certain clock began to calculate how often it would have to swing backward and forward in the week and in the month to come; then looking further into the future, it made a calculation for a year, etc. The pendulum got frightened and stopped. Do one day's work at a time. Do not worry about the trouble of to-morrow. Most of the trouble in life is borrowed trouble, which never actually comes.

"As all healthy action, physical, intellectual and moral, depends primarily on cheerfulness," says E. P. Whipple, "and as every duty, whether it be to follow a plow or to die at the stake, should be done in a cheerful spirit, the exploration of the sources and conditions of this most vigorous, exhilarating and creative of the virtues may be as useful as the exposition of any topic of science or system of prudential art."

Christ, the great teacher, did not shut Himself up with monks, away from temptation of the great world outside. He taught no long-faced, gloomy theology. He taught the gospel of gladness and good cheer. His doctrines are touched with the sunlight, and flavored with the flowers of the fields. The birds of the air, the beasts of the field, and happy, romping children are in them. True piety is cheerful as the day.

Cranmer cheers his brother martyrs, and Latimer walks with a face shining with cheerfulness to the stake, upholds his fellow's spirits, and seasons all his sermons with pleasant anecdotes.

"Nothing will supply the want of sunshine to peaches," said Emerson, "and to make knowledge valuable, you must have the cheerfulness of wisdom."

In answer to the question, "How shall we overcome temptation," a noted writer said, "Cheerfulness is the first thing, cheerfulness is the second, and cheerfulness is the third." A habit of cheerfulness, enabling one to transmute apparent misfortunes into real blessings, is a fortune to a young man or young woman just crossing the threshold of active life. He who has formed a habit of looking at the bright, happy side of things, who sees the glory in the grass, the sunshine in the flowers, sermons in stones, and good in everything, has a great advantage over the chronic dyspeptic, who sees no good in anything. His habitual thought sculptures his face into beauty and touches his manner with grace.

We often forget that the priceless charm which will secure to us all these desirable gifts is within our reach. It is the charm of a sunny temper, a talisman more potent than station, more precious than gold, more to be desired than fine rubies. It is an aroma, whose fragrance fills the air with the odors of Paradise.

"It is from these enthusiastic fellows," says an admirer, "that you hear—what they fully believe, bless them!—that all countries are beautiful, all dinners grand, all pictures superb, all mountains high, all women beautiful. When such a one has come back from his country trip, after a hard year's work, he has always found the cosiest of nooks, the cheapest houses, the best of landladies, the finest views, and the best dinners. But with the other the case is indeed altered. He has always been robbed; he has positively seen nothing; his landlady was a harpy, his bedroom was unhealthy, and the mutton was so tough that he could not get his teeth through it."

"He goes on to talk of the sun in his glory," says Izaak Walton, "the fields, the meadows, the streams which they have seen, the birds which they have heard; he asks what would the blind and deaf give to see and hear what they have seen."

Of Lord Holland's sunshiny face, Rogers said: "He always comes to breakfast like a man upon whom some sudden good fortune has fallen."

But oh, for the glorious spectacles worn by the good-natured man!—oh, for those wondrous glasses, finer than the Claude Lorraine glass, which throw a sunlit view over everything, and make the heart glad with little things, and thankful for small mercies! Such glasses had honest Izaak Walton, who, coming in from a fishing expedition on the river Lea, burst out into such grateful little talks as this: "Let us, as we walk home under the cool shade of this honeysuckle hedge, mention some of the thoughts and joys that have possessed my soul since we two met. And that our present happiness may appear the greater, and we more thankful for it, I beg you to consider with me, how many do at this very time lie under the torment of the gout or the toothache, and this we have been free from; and let me tell you, that every misery I miss is a new blessing."

The hypochondriac who nurses his spleen never looks forward cheerfully, but lounges in his invalid chair, and croaks like a raven, foreboding woe. "Ah," says he, "you will never succeed; these things always fail."

The Thug of India, whose prayer is a homicide, and whose offering is the body of a victim, is melancholy.

The Fijiian, waiting to smash the skull of a victim, and to prepare a bakola for his gods, is gloomy as fear and death.

The melancholy of the Eastern Jews after their black fast, and the ill-temper of monks and nuns after their Fridays and Wednesdays, is very observable; it is the recompense which a proud nature takes out of the world for its selfish sacrifice. Melancholia is the black bile which the Greeks presumed overran and pervaded the bodies of such persons; and fasting does undoubtedly produce this.

"I once talked with a Rosicrucian about the Great Secret," said Addison. "He talked of it as a spirit that lived in an emerald, and converted everything that was near it to the highest perfection. 'It gives lustre to the sun,' said he, 'and water to the diamond. It irradiates every metal, and enriches lead with the property of gold. It brightens smoke into flame, flame into light, and light into glory. A single ray dissipates pain and care from the person on whom it falls.' Then I found his great secret was Content."

My crown is in my heart, not on my head:
Not decked with diamonds and Indian stones,
Nor to be seen: my crown is called content:
A crown it is, that seldom kings enjoy. —Shakespeare
Yet, with a heart that's ever kind,
A gentle spirit gay,
You've spring perennial in your mind,
And round you make a May. —Thackeray

Hold up Your Head

Thoroughly to believe in one's own self, so one's self were thorough, were to do great things. —Tennyson

If there be a faith that can remove mountains, it is faith in one's own power. —Marie Ebner-Eschenbach

Let no one discourage self-reliance; it is, of all the rest, the greatest quality of true manliness. —Kossuth

It needs a divine man to exhibit anything divine. Trust thyself; every breast vibrates to that iron string. Accept the place that divine Providence has found for you, the society of your contemporaries, the connection of events. Great men have always done so. Nothing is at last sacred but the integrity of our own mind. —Emerson

This above all,—to thine own self be true;
And it must follow, as the night the day,
Thou canst not then be false to any man. —Shakespeare

"Yes," said a half-drunken man in a cellar to a parish visitor, a young girl, "I am a tough and a drunkard, and am just out of jail, and my wife is starving; but that doesn't give you the right to come into my house without knocking to ask questions."

Another zealous girl declared in a reform club in New York City that she always went to visit the poor in her carriage, with the crest on the door and liveried servants. "It gives me authority," she said. "They listen to my words with more respect."

The Fräulein Barbara, who founded the home for degraded and drunken sailors in London, used other means to gain influence over them. "I too," she would say, taking the poor applicant by the hand when he came to her door, "I, too, as well as you, am one of those for whom Christ died. We are brother and sister, and will help each other."

An English artist, engaged in painting a scene in the London slums, applied to the Board of Guardians of the poor in Chelsea for leave to sketch into it, as types of want and wretchedness, certain picturesque paupers then in the almshouse. The board refused permission on the ground that "a man does not cease to have self-respect and rights because he is a pauper, and that his misfortunes should not be paraded before the world."

The incident helps to throw light on the vexed problem of the intercourse of the rich with the poor. Kind but thoughtless people, who take up the work of "slumming," intent upon elevating and reforming the needy classes, are apt to forget that these unfortunates have self-respect and rights and sensitive feelings.

"But I am not derided," said Diogenes, when some one told him he was derided. "Only those are ridiculed who feel the ridicule and are discomposed by it."

Dr. Franklin used to say that if a man makes a sheep of himself the wolves will eat him. Not less true is it that if a man is supposed to be a sheep, wolves will very likely try to eat him.

"O God, assist our side," prayed the Prince of Anhalt-Dessau, a general in the Prussian service, before going into battle. "At least, avoid assisting the enemy, and leave the result to me."

"If a man possesses the consciousness of what he is," said Schelling, "he will soon also learn what he ought to be; let him have a theoretical respect for himself, and a practical will soon follow." A person under the firm persuasion that he can command resources virtually has them. "Humility is the part of wisdom, and is most becoming in men," said Kossuth; "but let no one discourage self-reliance; it is, of all the rest, the greatest quality of true manliness." Froude wrote: "A tree must be rooted in the soil before it can bear flowers or fruit. A man must learn to stand upright upon his own feet, to respect himself, to be independent of charity or accident. It is on this basis only that any superstructure of intellectual cultivation worth having can possibly be built."

"I think he is a most extraordinary man," said John J. Ingalls, speaking of Grover Cleveland. "While the Senate was in session to induct Hendricks into office, I had an opportunity to study Cleveland, as he sat there like a sphinx. He occupied a seat immediately in front of the vice-president's stand, and from where I sat, I had an unobstructed view of him.

"I wanted to fathom, if possible, what manner of a man it was who had defeated us and taken the patronage of the government over to the democracy. We had a new master, so to speak, and a democrat at that, and I looked him over with a good deal of curiosity.

"There sat a man, the president of the United States, beginning his rule over the destinies of sixty millions of people, who less than three years before was an obscure lawyer, scarcely known outside of Erie County, shut up in a dingy office over a livery stable. He had been mayor of the city of Buffalo at a time when a crisis in its affairs demanded a courageous head and a firm hand and he supplied them. The little prestige thus gained made him the democratic nominee for governor, and at a time (his luck still following him) when the Republican party of the State was rent with dissensions. He was elected, and (still more luck) by the unprecedented and unheard of majority of nearly 200,000 votes. Two years later his party nominated him for president and he was elected.

"There sat this man before me, wholly undisturbed by the pageantry of the occasion, calmly waiting to perform his part in the drama, just as an actor awaits his cue to appear on a stage. It was his first visit to Washington. He had never before seen the Capitol and knew absolutely nothing of the machinery of government. All was a mystery to him, but a stranger not understanding the circumstances would have imagined that the proceedings going on before him were a part of his daily life.

"The man positively did not move a limb, shut an eye or twitch a muscle during the entire hour he sat in the Senate chamber. Nor did he betray the faintest evidence of self-consciousness or emotion, and as I thought of the dingy office over the livery stable but three years before he struck me as a remarkable illustration of the possibilities of American citizenship.

"But the most marvelous exhibition of the man's nerve and of the absolute confidence he has in himself was yet to come. After the proceedings in the Senate chamber Cleveland was conducted to the east end of the Capitol to take the oath of office and deliver his inaugural address. He wore a close buttoned Prince Albert coat, and between the buttons he thrust his right hand, while his left he carried behind him. In this position he stood until the applause which greeted him had subsided, when he began his address.

"I looked for him to produce a manuscript, but he did not, and as he progressed in clear and distinct tones, without hesitation, I was amazed. With sixty millions of people, yes, with the entire civilized world looking on, this man had the courage to deliver an inaugural address making him President of the United States as coolly and as unconcernedly as if he were addressing a ward meeting. It was the most remarkable spectacle this or any other country has ever beheld."

Believe in yourself; you may succeed when others do not believe in you, but never when you do not believe in yourself.

"Ah! John Hunter, still hard at work!" exclaimed a physician on finding the old anatomist at the dissecting table. "Yes, doctor, and you'll find it difficult to meet with another John Hunter when I am gone."

"Heaven takes a hundred years to form a great genius for the regeneration of an empire and afterward rests a hundred years," said Kaunitz, who had administered the affairs of his country with great success for half a century. "This makes me tremble for the Austrian monarchy after my death."

"Isn't it beautiful that I can sing so?" asked Jenny Lind, naïvely, of a friend.

"My Lord," said William Pitt in 1757 to the Duke of Devonshire, "I am sure that I can save this country and that nobody else can." He did save it.

What seems to us disagreeable egotism in others is often but a strong expression of confidence in their ability to attain. Great men have usually had great confidence in themselves. Wordsworth felt sure of his place in history and never hesitated to say so. Dante predicted his own fame. Kepler said it did not matter whether his contemporaries read his books or not. "I may well wait a century for a reader since God has waited six thousand years for an observer like myself." "Fear not," said Julius Cæsar to his pilot frightened in a storm, "thou bearest Cæsar and his good fortunes."

When the Directory at Paris found that Napoleon had become in one month the most famous man in Europe they determined to check his career, and appointed Kellerman his associate in command. Napoleon promptly, but respectfully, tendered his resignation, saying, "One bad general is better than two good ones; war, like government, is mainly decided by tact." This decision immediately brought the Directory to terms.

Emperor Francis was extremely anxious to prove the illustrious descent of his prospective son-in-law. Napoleon refused to have the account published, remarking, "I had rather be the descendant of an honest man than of any petty tyrant of Italy. I wish my nobility to commence with myself and derive all my titles from the French people. I am the Rudolph of Hapsburg of my family. My patent of nobility dates from the battle of Montenotte."

When Napoleon was informed that the British Government had decreed that he should be recognized only as general, he said, "They cannot prevent me from being myself."

An Englishman asked Napoleon at Elba who was the greatest general of the age, adding, "I think Wellington." To which the Emperor replied, "He has not yet measured himself against me."

"Well matured and well disciplined talent is always sure of a market," said Washington Irving; "but it must not cower at home and expect to be sought for. There is a good deal of cant, too, about the success of forward and impudent men, while men of retiring worth are passed over with neglect. But it usually happens that those forward men have that valuable quality of promptness and activity, without which worth is a mere inoperative property. A barking dog is often more useful than a sleeping lion."

"Self-respect is the early form in which greatness appears."

"You may deceive all the people some of the time," said Lincoln, "some of the people all the time, but not all the people all the time." We cannot deceive ourselves any of the time, and the only way to enjoy our own respect is to deserve it. What would you think of a man who would neglect himself and treat his shadow with the greatest respect?

"Self-reliance is a grand element of character," says Michael Reynolds. "It has won Olympic crowns and Isthmian laurels; it confers kinship with men who have vindicated their divine right to be held in the world's memory."

Books and Success

Ignorance is the curse of God,
Knowledge the wing wherewith we fly to heaven. —Shakespeare

Prefer knowledge to wealth; for the one is transitory, the other perpetual.—Socrates

If a man empties his purse into his head, no man can take it away from him. An investment in knowledge always pays the best interest. —Franklin

My early and invincible love of reading, I would not exchange for the treasures of India. —Gibbon

If the crowns of all the kingdoms of the empire were laid down at my feet in exchange for my books and my love of reading, I would spurn them all.—Fénelon

Who of us can tell
What he had been, had Cadmus never taught
The art that fixes into form the thought,—
Had Plato never spoken from his cell,
Or his high harp blind Homer never strung? —Bulwer

When friends grow cold and the converse of intimates languishes into vapid civility and common-place, these only continue the unaltered countenance of happier days, and cheer us with that true friendship which never deceived hope, nor deserted sorrow. —Washington Irving

"Do you want to know," asks Robert Collyer, "how I manage to talk to you in this simple Saxon? I read Bunyan, Crusoe, and Goldsmith when I was a boy, morning, noon, and night. All the rest was task work; these were my delight, with the stories in the Bible, and with Shakespeare, when at last the mighty master came within our doors. The rest were as senna to me. These were like a well of pure water, and this is the first step I seem to have taken of my own free will toward the pulpit. * * * I took to these as I took to milk, and, without the least idea what I was doing, got the taste for simple words into the very fibre of my nature. There was day-school for me until I was eight years old, and then I had to turn in and work thirteen hours a day. From the days when we used to spell out Crusoe and old Bunyan there had grown up in me a devouring hunger to read books. It made small matter what they were, so they were books. Half a volume of an old encyclopædia came along—the first I had ever seen. How many times I went through that I cannot even guess. I remember that I read some old reports of the Missionary Society with the greatest delight.

"There were chapters in them about China and Labrador. Yet I think it is in reading, as it is in eating, when the first hunger is over you begin to be a little critical, and will by no means take to garbage if you are of a wholesome nature. And I remember this because it touches this beautiful valley of the Hudson. I could not go home for the Christmas of 1839, and was feeling very sad about it all, for I was only a boy; and sitting by the fire, an old farmer came in and said: 'I notice thou's fond of reading, so I brought thee summat to read.' It was Irving's 'Sketch Book.' I had never heard of the work. I went at it, and was 'as them that dream.' No such delight had touched me since the old days of Crusoe. I saw the Hudson and the Catskills, took poor Rip at once into my heart, as everybody has, pitied Ichabod while I laughed at him, thought the old Dutch feast a most admirable thing, and long before I was through, all regret at my lost Christmas had gone down with the wind, and I had found out there are books and books. That vast hunger to read never left me. If there was no candle, I poked my head down to the fire; read while I was eating, blowing the bellows, or walking from one place to another. I could read and walk four miles an hour. The world centred in books. There was no thought in my mind of any good to come out of it; the good lay in the reading. I had no more idea of being a minister than you elder men who were boys then, in this town, had that I should be here to-night to tell this story. Now, give a boy a passion like this for anything, books or business, painting or farming, mechanism or music, and you give him thereby a lever to lift his world, and a patent of nobility, if the thing he does is noble. There were two or three of my mind about books. We became companions, and gave the roughs a wide berth. The books did their work, too, about that drink, and fought the devil with a finer fire."

"In education," says Herbert Spencer, "the process of self-development should be encouraged to the fullest extent. Children should be led to make their own investigations, and to draw their own inferences. They should be *told* as little as possible, and induced to *discover* as much as possible. Humanity has progressed solely by self-instruction; and that to achieve the best results each mind must progress somewhat after the same fashion, is continually proved by the marked success of self-made men."

"My books," said Thomas Hood, "kept me from the ring, the dog-pit, the tavern, and the saloon. The associate of Pope and Addison, the mind accustomed to the noble though silent discourse of Shakespeare and Milton, will hardly seek or put up with low or evil company or slaves."

"When I get a little money," said Erasmus, "I buy books, and if any is left, I buy food and clothes."

"Hundreds of books read once," says Robertson, "have passed as completely from us as if we had never read them; whereas the discipline of mind got by writing down, not copying, an abstract of a book which is worth the trouble fixes it on the mind for years, and, besides, enables one to read other books with more attention and more profit."

"This habit of reading, I make bold to tell you," says Trollope, "is your pass to the greatest, the purest, and the most perfect pleasures that God has prepared for His creatures. Other pleasures may be more ecstatic; but the habit of reading is the only enjoyment I know, in which there is no alloy."

The Bible was begun in the desert in Arabia ages before Homer sang and flourished in Asia Minor. Millions of books have since gone into oblivion.

Empires have risen and fallen. Revolutions have swept over and changed the earth. It has always been subject to criticism and obloquy. Mighty men have sought its overthrow. Works of Greek poets who catered to men's depraved tastes have, in spite of everything, perished. The Bible is a book of religion; and can be tried by no other standard.

"Read Plutarch," said Emerson, "and the world is a proud place peopled with men of positive quality, with heroes and demi-gods standing around us who will not let us sleep."

"There is no business, no avocation whatever," says Wyttenbach, "which will not permit a man, who has an inclination, to give a little time, every day, to the studies of his youth."

"All the sport in the park," said Lady Jane Grey, "is but a shadow of that pleasure I find in Plato."

"In the lap of Eternity," said Heinsius, "among so many divine souls, I take my seat with so lofty a spirit and such sweet content, that I pity all the great ones and rich men, that have not this happiness."

"Death itself divides not the wise," says Bulwer. "Thou meetest Plato when thine eyes moisten over the Phædo. May Homer live with all men forever!"

"When a man reads," says President Porter, "he should put himself into the most intimate intercourse with his author, so that all his energies of apprehension, judgment and feeling may be occupied with, and aroused by, what his author furnishes, whatever it may be. If repetition or review will aid him in this, as it often will, let him not disdain or neglect frequent reviews. If the use of the pen, in brief or full notes, in catchwords or other symbols, will aid him, let him not shrink from the drudgery of the pen and the commonplace book."

"Reading is to the mind," says Addison, "what exercise is to the body. As by the one health is preserved, strengthened and invigorated, by the other, virtue (which is the health of the mind) is kept alive, cherished and confirmed."

"There is a world of science necessary in choosing books," said Bulwer. "I have known some people in great sorrow fly to a novel, or the last light book in fashion. One might as well take a rose draught for the plague! Light reading does not do when the heart is really heavy. I am told that Goethe, when he lost his son, took to study a science that was new to him. Ah! Goethe was a physician who knew what he was about."

"When I served when a young man in India," said a distinguished English soldier and diplomatist; "when it was the turning point in my life; when it was a mere chance whether I should become a mere card-playing, hooka-smoking lounger, I was fortunately quartered for two years in the neighborhood of an excellent library, which was made accessible to me."

"Books," says E. P. Whipple, "are lighthouses erected in the great sea of time."

"As a rule," said Benjamin Disraeli, "the most successful man in life is the man who has the best information."

"You get into society, in the widest sense," says Geikie, "in a great library, with the huge advantage of needing no introductions, and not dreading repulses. From that great crowd you can choose what companions you please, for in the silent levees of the immortals there is no pride, but the highest is at the service of the lowest, with a grand humility. You may speak freely with any, without a thought of your inferiority; for books are perfectly well-bred, and hurt no one's feelings by any discriminations." Sir William Waller observed, "In my study, I am sure to converse with none but wise men, but abroad it is impossible for me to avoid the society of fools." "It is the glorious prerogative of the empire of knowledge," says Webster, "that what it gains it never loses. On the contrary, it increases by the multiple of its own power; all its ends become means, all its attainments help to new conquests."

"At this hour, five hundred years since their creation," says De Quincey, "the tales of Chaucer, never equaled on this earth for their tenderness and for life of picturesqueness, are read familiarly by many in the charming language of their natal day, and by others in the modernization of Dryden, of Pope, and Wordsworth. At this hour, one thousand eight hundred years since their creation, the pagan tales of Ovid, never equaled on this earth for the gayety of their movement and the capricious graces of their narrative, are read by all Christendom."

"There is no Past so long as Books shall live," says Lytton.

"No wonder Cicero said that he would part with all he was worth so he might live and die among his books," says Geikie. "No wonder Petrarch was among them to the last, and was found dead in their company. It seems natural that Bede should have died dictating, and that Leibnitz should have died with a book in his hand, and Lord Clarendon at his desk. Buckle's last words, 'My poor book!' tell a passion that forgot death; and it seemed only a fitting farewell when the tear stole down the manly cheeks of Scott as they wheeled him into his library, when he had come back to Abbotsford to die. Southey, white-haired, a living shadow, sitting stroking and kissing the books he could no longer open or read, is altogether pathetic."

"No entertainment is so cheap as reading," says Mary Wortley Montagu; "nor any pleasure so lasting." Good books elevate the character, purify the taste, *take the attractiveness out of low pleasures*, and lift us upon a higher plane of thinking and living. It is not easy to be mean directly after reading a noble and inspiring book. The conversation of a man who reads for improvement or pleasure will be flavored by his reading; but it will not be about his reading.

Perhaps no other thing has such power to lift the poor out of his poverty, the wretched out of his misery, to make the burden-bearer forget his burden, the sick his sufferings, the sorrower his grief, the downtrodden his degradation, as books. They are friends to the lonely, companions to the deserted, joy to the joyless, hope to the hopeless, good cheer to the disheartened, a helper to the helpless. They bring light into darkness, and sunshine into shadow.

"Twenty-five years ago, when I was a boy," said Rev. J. A. James, "a school-fellow gave me an infamous book, which he lent me for only fifteen minutes. At the end of that time it was returned to him, but that book has haunted me like a spectre ever since. I have asked God on my knees to obliterate that book from my mind, but I believe that I shall carry down with me to the grave the spiritual damage I received during those fifteen minutes."

Did Homer and Plato and Socrates and Virgil ever dream that their words would echo through the ages, and aid in shaping men's lives in the nineteenth century? They were mere infants when on earth in comparison with the mighty influence and power they now yield. Every life on the American continent has in some degree been influenced by them. Christ, when on earth, never exerted one millionth part of the influence He wields to-day. While He reigns supreme in few human hearts, He touches all more or less, the atheist as well as the saint. On the other hand who shall say how many crimes were committed the past year by wicked men buried long ago? Their books, their pictures, their terrible examples, live in all they reach, and incite to evil deeds. How important, then, is the selection of books which are to become a part of your being.

Knowledge cannot be stolen from us. It cannot be bought or sold. We may be poor, and the sheriff may come and sell our furniture, or drive away our cow, or take our pet lamb, and leave us homeless and penniless; but he cannot lay the law's hand upon the jewelry of our minds.

"Good books and the wild woods are two things with which man can never become too familiar," says George W. Cable. "The friendship of trees is a sort of self-love and is very wholesome. All inanimate nature is but a mirror, and it is greater far to have the sense of beauty than it is to be only its insensible depository.

"The books that inspire imagination, whether in truth or fiction; that elevate the thoughts, are the right kind to read. Our emotions are simply the vibrations of our soul.

"The moment fiction becomes mendacious it is bad, for it induces us to believe a lie. Fiction purely as fiction must be innocent and beautiful, and its beauty must be more than skin deep. Every field of art is a playground and we are extra pleased when the artist makes that field a gymnasium also."

Cotton Mather's "Essay to do Good" read by the boy Franklin influenced the latter's whole life. He advised everybody to read with a pen in hand and to make notes of all they read.

James T. Fields visited Jesse Pomeroy, the boy murderer, in jail. Pomeroy told him he had been a great reader of "blood and thunder" stories; that he had read sixty dime novels about scalping and other bloody performances; and he thought there was no doubt that these books had put the horrible thoughts into his mind which led to his murderous acts.

Many a boy has gone to sea and become a rover for life under the influence of Marryat's novels. Abbott's "Life of Napoleon," read at the age of seven years, sent one boy whom I knew to the army before he was fourteen. Many a man has committed crime from the leavening, multiplying influence of a bad book read when a boy. The chaplain of Newgate prison in London, in one of his annual reports to the Lord Mayor, referring to many fine-looking lads of respectable parentage in the city prison, said that he discovered that "all these boys, without exception, had been in the habit of reading those cheap periodicals" which were published for the alleged amusement of youth of both sexes. There is not a police court or a prison in this country where similar cases could not be found. One can hardly measure the moral ruin that has been caused in this generation by the influence of bad books.

In the parlor window of the old mossy vicarage where Coleridge spent his dreamy childhood lay a well-thumbed copy of that volume of Oriental fancy, the "Arabian Nights," and he has told us with what mingled desire and apprehension he was wont to look at the precious book, until the morning sunshine had touched and illuminated it, when, seizing it hastily, he would carry it off in triumph to some leafy nook in the vicarage garden, and plunge delightedly into its maze of marvels and enchantments.

Beecher said that Ruskin's works taught him the secret of seeing, and that no man could ever again be quite the same man or look at the world in the same way after reading him. Samuel Drew said, "Locke's 'Essay on the Understanding' awakened me from stupor, and induced me to form a resolution to abandon the groveling views I had been accustomed to maintain." An English tanner, whose leather gained a great reputation, said he should not have made it so good if he had not read Carlyle. The lives of Washington and Henry Clay, which Lincoln borrowed from neighbors in the wilderness, and devoured by the light of the cabin fire, inspired his life. In his early manhood he read Paine's "Age of Reason," and Volney's "Ruins," which so influenced his mind that he wrote an essay to prove the unreliability of the Bible. These two books nearly unbalanced his moral character. But, fortunately, the books which fell into his hands in after years corrected this evil influence. The trend of many a life for good or ill, for success or failure, has been determined by a single book. The books which we read early in life are those which influence us most. When Garfield was working for a neighbor he read "Sinbad the Sailor" and the "Pirate's Own Book." These books revealed a new world to him, and his mother with difficulty kept him from going to sea. He was fascinated with the sea life which these books pictured to his young imagination. The "Voyages of Captain Cook" led William Carey to go on a mission to the heathen. "The Imitation of Christ" and Taylor's "Holy Living and Dying" determined the character of John Wesley. "Shakespeare and the Bible," said John Sharp, "made me Archbishop of York." The "Vicar of Wakefield" awakened the poetical genius in Goethe.

"I have been the bosom friend of Leander and Romeo," said Lowell. "I seem to go behind Shakespeare, and to get my intelligence at first hand. Sometimes, in my sorrow, a line from Spenser steals in upon my memory as if by some vitality and external volition of its own, like a blast from the distant trump of a knight pricking toward the court of Faerie, and I am straightway lifted out of that sadness and shadow into the sunshine of a previous and long-agone experience."

"Who gets more enjoyment out of eating," asks Amos R. Wells, "the pampered millionaire, whose tongue is the wearied host of myriads of sugary, creamy, spicy guests, or the little daughter of the laborer, trotting about all the morning with helpful steps, who has come a long two miles with her father's dinner to eat it with him from a tin pail? And who gets the more pleasure out of reading, the satiated fiction-glutton, her brain crammed with disordered fragments of countless scenes of adventure, love and tragedy, impatient of the same old situations, the familiar characters, the stale plots—she or the girl who is fired with a love for history, say, who wants to know all about the grand old, queer old Socrates, and then about his friends, and then about the times in which he lived, and then about the way in which they all lived, then about the Socratic legacy to the ages? Why, will that girl ever be done with the feast? Can you not see, looking down on her joy with a blessing, the very Lord of the banquet, who has ordered all history and ordained that the truth He fashions shall be stranger always than the fiction man contrives? Take the word of a man who has made full trial of both. Solid reading is as much more interesting and attractive than frivolous reading as solid living is more recreative than frivolous living."

"I solemnly declare," said Sidney Smith, "that but for the love of knowledge, I should consider the life of the meanest hedger and ditcher as preferable to that of the greatest and richest man in existence; for the fire of our minds is like the fires which the Persians burn in the mountains, it flames night and day, and is immortal, and not to be quenched! Upon something it must act and feed—upon the pure spirit of knowledge, or upon the foul dregs of polluting passions. Therefore, when I say, in conducting your understanding, love knowledge with a great love, with a vehement love, with a love co-eval with life—what do I say but love innocence, love virtue, love purity of conduct, love that which, if you are rich and great, will vindicate the blind fortune which has made you so, and make men call it justice; love that which, if you are poor, will render your poverty respectable, and make the proudest feel it unjust to laugh at the meanness of your fortunes; love that which will comfort you, adorn you, and never quit you—which will open to you the kingdom of thought, and all the boundless regions of conception, as an asylum against the cruelty, the injustice, and the pain that may be your lot in the world—that which will make your motives habitually great and honorable, *and light up in an instant a thousand noble disdains at the very thought of meanness and of fraud?"*

Do I feel like hearing an eloquent sermon? Spurgeon and Beecher, Whitefield, Hall, Collyer, Phillips Brooks, Canon Farrar, Dr. Parker, Talmage, are all standing on my bookcase, waiting to give me their greatest efforts at a moment's notice. Do I feel indisposed, and need a little recreation? This afternoon I will take a trip across the Atlantic, flying against the wind and over breakers without fear of seasickness on the ocean greyhounds. I will inspect the world renowned Liverpool docks; take a run up to Hawarden, call on Mr. Gladstone; fly over to London, take a run through the British Museum and see the wonderful collection from all nations; go through the National Art Gallery, through the Houses of Parliament, visit Windsor Castle and Buckingham Palace, call upon Queen Victoria, the Prince of Wales; take a run through the lake region and call upon the great writers, visit Oxford and Cambridge; cross the English Channel, stop at Rouen, where Joan of Arc was burned to death by the English, take a flying trip to Paris, visit the tomb of Napoleon, the Louvre Gallery; take a peep at one of the greatest pieces of sculpture in existence, the Venus de Milo (which a rich and ignorant person offered to buy if they would give him a fresh one), take a glance at some of the greatest paintings in existence along the miles of galleries; take a peep into the Grand Opera House, the grandest in the world (to make room for which 427 buildings were demolished), promenade through the Champs de Elysée, pass under the triumphal arch of Napoleon, take a run out to Versailles and inspect the famous palace of Louis XIV., upon which he spent perhaps $100,000,000.

Do I desire to hear eloquent speeches? Through my books I can enter the Parliament and listen to the thrilling oratory of Disraeli, of Gladstone, of Bright, of O'Connor; they will admit me to the floor of the Senate, where I can hear the matchless oratory of a Webster, of a Clay, of a Calhoun, of a Sumner, of Everett, of Wilson. They will pass me into the Roman Forum, where I can hear Cicero, or to the rostrums of Greece, where I may listen spell-bound to the magic oratory of a Demosthenes.

"No matter how poor I am," says Channing; "no matter though the prosperous of my own time will not enter my obscure dwelling; if the sacred writers will enter and take up their abode under my roof; if Milton will cross my threshold to sing to me of paradise, and Shakespeare to open to me the worlds of imagination and the workings of the human heart, and Franklin to enrich me with his practical wisdom,—I shall not pine for the want of intellectual companionship, and I may become a cultivated man, though excluded from what is called the best society in the place where I live."

"With the dead there is no rivalry," says Macaulay. "In the dead there is no change. Plato is never sullen; Cervantes is never petulant; Demosthenes never comes unseasonably; Dante never stays too long; no difference of political opinion can alienate Cicero; no heresy can excite the horror of Bossuet."

"Heed not the idle assertion that literary pursuits will disqualify you for the active business of life," says Alexander H. Everett. "Reject it as a mere imagination, inconsistent with principle, unsupported by experience."

The habit of reading may become morbid. There is a novel-reading disease. There are people who are almost as much tied to their novels as an intemperate man is tied to his bottle. The more of these novels they read, the weaker their minds become. They remember nothing; they read for the stimulus; their reasoning powers become weaker and weaker, their memory more treacherous. The mind is ruined for healthy intellectual food. They have no taste for history or biography, or anything but cheap, trashy, sensational novels.

The passive reception of other men's thoughts is not education. Beware of intellectual dram drinking and intellectual dissipation. It is emasculating. Beware of the book which does not make you determined to go and do something and be something in the world.

The great difference between the American graduate and the graduates from the English universities is that the latter have not read many books superficially, but a few books well. The American graduate has a smattering of many books, but has not become master of any. The same is largely true of readers in general; they want to know a little of everything. They want to read all the latest publications, good, bad and indifferent, if it is only new. As a rule our people want light reading, "something to read" that will take up the attention, kill time on the railroad or at home. As a rule English people read more substantial books, older books, books which have established their right to exist. They are not so eager for "recent publications."

Joseph Cook advises youth to always make notes of their reading. Mr. Cook uses the margins of his books for his notes, and marks all of his own books very freely, so that every volume in his library becomes a notebook. He advises all young men and young women to keep commonplace books. We cannot too heartily recommend this habit of taking notes. It is a great aid to memory, and it helps wonderfully to locate or to find for future use what we have read. It helps to assimilate and make our own whatever we read. The habit of taking notes of lectures and sermons is an excellent one. One of the greatest aids to education is the habit of writing out an analysis or a skeleton of a book or article after we have read it; also of a sermon or a lecture. This habit has made many a strong, vigorous thinker and writer. In this connection we cannot too strongly recommend the habit of saving clippings from our readings wherever possible of everything which would be likely to assist us in the future. These scrap-books, indexed, often become of untold advantage, especially if in the line of our work. Much of what we call genius in great men comes from these note-books and scrap-books.

How many poor boys and girls who thought they had "no chance" in life have been started upon noble careers by the grand books of Smiles, Todd, Mathews, Munger, Whipple, Geikie, Thayer, and others.

You should bring your mind to the reading of a book, or to the study of any subject, as you take an axe to the grindstone; not for what you get from the stone, but for the sharpening of the axe. While it is true that the facts learned from books are worth more than the dust from the stone, even in much greater ratio is the mind more valuable than the axe. Bacon says: "Some books are to be tasted, others to be swallowed, and some few to be chewed and digested; that is, some books are to be read only in parts; others to be read, but not curiously; and some few to be read wholly, and with diligence and attention. Reading maketh a full man, conference a ready man, and writing an exact man; and, therefore, if a man write little, he had need have a great memory; if he confer little, he had need have a present wit; and if he read little, he had need have much cunning, to seem to know that he doth not. Histories make men wise; poets witty; the mathematics subtle; natural philosophy deep; morals grave; logic and rhetoric able to contend."

Riches Without Wings

Walk worthy of the vocation wherewith ye are called. —Eph IV. I

Abundance consists not alone in material possession, but in an uncovetous spirit. —Selden

Less coin, less care; to know how to dispense with wealth is to possess it.—Reynolds

Rich, from the very want of wealth,
In heaven's best treasures, peace and health. —Gray

Money never made a man happy yet; there is nothing in its nature to produce happiness. The more a man has, the more he wants. Instead of filling a vacuum, it makes one. —Franklin

There are treasures laid up in the heart, treasures of charity, piety, temperance, and soberness. These treasures a man takes with him beyond death, when he leaves this world. —Buddhist Scriptures

"It is better to get wisdom than gold; for wisdom is better than rubies, and all things that may be desired are not to be compared to it."
"Better a cheap coffin and a plain funeral after a useful, unselfish life, than a grand mausoleum after a loveless, selfish life."
I ought not to allow any man, because he has broad lands, to feel that he is rich in my presence. I ought to make him feel that I can do without his riches, that I cannot be bought—neither by comfort, neither by pride,—and although I be utterly penniless, and receiving bread from him, that he is the poor man beside me. —Emerson

"I don't want such things," said Epictetus to the rich Roman orator who was making light of his contempt for money-wealth; "and besides," said the stoic, "you are poorer than I am, after all. You have silver vessels, but earthenware reasons, principles, appetites. My mind to me a kingdom is, and it furnishes me with abundant and happy occupation in lieu of your restless idleness. All your possessions seem small to you; mine seem great to me. Your desire is insatiate, mine is satisfied."
"Lord, how many things are in the world of which Diogenes hath no need!" exclaimed the stoic, as he wandered among the miscellaneous articles at a country fair.
"One would think," said Boswell, "that the proprietor of all this (Keddlestone, the seat of Lord Scarsfield) must be happy." "Nay, sir," said Johnson, "all this excludes but one evil, poverty."

"What property has he left behind him?" people ask when a man dies; but the angel who receives him asks, "What good deeds hast thou sent before thee?"

"What is the best thing to possess?" asked an ancient philosopher of his pupils. One answered, "Nothing is better than a good eye,"—a figurative expression for a liberal and contented disposition. Another said, "A good companion is the best thing in the world;" a third chose a good neighbor; and a fourth, a wise friend. But Eleazar said: "A good heart is better than them all." "True," said the master; "thou hast comprehended in two words all that the rest have said, for he that hath a good heart will be contented, a good companion, a good neighbor, and will easily see what is fit to be done by him."

"My kingdom for a horse," said Richard III. of England amid the press of Bosworth Field. "My kingdom for a moment," said Queen Elizabeth on her death-bed. And millions of others, when they have felt earth, its riches and power slipping from their grasp, have shown plainly that deep down in their hearts they value such things at naught when really compared with the blessed light of life, the stars and flowers, the companionship of friends, and far above all else, the opportunity of growth and development here and of preparation for future life.

Queen Caroline Matilda of Denmark wrote on the window of her prison, with her diamond ring: "Oh, keep me innocent; make others great."

"These are my jewels," said Cornelia to the Campanian lady who asked to see her gems; and she pointed with pride to her boys returning from school. The reply was worthy the daughter of Scipio Africanus and wife of Tiberius Gracchus. The most valuable production of any country is its crop of men.

"I will take away thy treasures," said a tyrant to a philosopher. "Nay, that thou canst not," was the retort; "for, in the first place, I have none that thou knowest of. My treasure is in heaven, and my heart is there."

Some people are born happy. No matter what their circumstances are they are joyous, content and satisfied with everything. They carry a perpetual holiday in their eye and see joy and beauty everywhere. When we meet them they impress us as just having met with some good luck, or that they have some good news to tell you. Like the bees that extract honey from every flower, they have a happy alchemy which transmutes even gloom into sunshine. In the sick room they are better than the physician and more potent than drugs. All doors open to these people. They are welcome everywhere.

We make our own worlds and people them, while memory, the scribe, faithfully registers the account of each as we pass the milestones dotting the way. Are we not, then, responsible for the inhabitants of our little worlds? We should fill them with the true, the beautiful and the good, since we are endowed with the faculty of creating.

"Genius," says Whipple, "may almost be defined as the faculty of acquiring poverty." It is the men of talent who make money out of the work of the men of genius. Somebody has truly said, that the greatest works have brought the least benefit to their authors. They were beyond the reach of appreciation before appreciation came.

There is an Eastern legend of a powerful genius, who promised a beautiful maiden a gift of rare value if she would pass through a field of corn and, without pausing, going backward, or wandering hither and thither, select the largest and ripest ear,—the value of the gift to be in proportion to the size and perfection of the ear she should choose. She passed through the field, seeing a great many well worth gathering, but always hoping to find a larger and more perfect one, she passed them all by, when, coming to a part of the field where the stalks grew more stunted, she disdained to take one from these, and so came through to the other side without having selected any.

A man may make millions and be a failure still. Money-making is not the highest success. The life of a well-known millionaire was not truly successful. He had but one ambition. He coined his very soul into dollars. The almighty dollar was his sun, and was mirrored in his heart. He strangled all other emotions and hushed and stifled all nobler aspirations. He grasped his riches tightly, till stricken by the scythe of death; when, in the twinkling of an eye, he was transformed from one of the richest men who ever lived in this world to one of the poorest souls that ever went out of it.

Lincoln always yearned for a rounded wholeness of character; and his fellow lawyers called him "perversely honest." Nothing could induce him to take the wrong side of a case, or to continue on that side after learning that it was unjust or hopeless. After giving considerable time to a case in which he had received from a lady a retainer of two hundred dollars, he returned the money, saying: "Madam, you have not a peg to hang your case on." "But you have earned that money," said the lady. "No, no," replied Lincoln, "that would not be right. I can't take pay for doing my duty."

Agassiz would not lecture at five hundred dollars a night, because he had no time to make money. Charles Sumner, when a senator, declined to lecture at any price, saying that his time belonged to Massachusetts and the nation. Spurgeon would not speak for fifty nights in America at one thousand dollars a night, because he said he could do better: he could stay in London and try to save fifty souls. All honor to the comparative few in every walk of life who, amid the strong materialistic tendencies of our age, still speak and act earnestly, inspired by the hope of rewards other than gold or popular favor. These are our truly great men and women. They labor in their ordinary vocations with no less zeal because they give time and thought to higher things.

King Midas, in the ancient myth, asked that everything he touched might be turned to gold, for then, he thought, he would be perfectly happy. His request was granted, but when his clothes, his food, his drink, the flowers he plucked, and even his little daughter, whom he kissed, were all changed into yellow metal, he begged that the Golden Touch might be taken from him. He had learned that many other things are intrinsically far more valuable than all the gold that was ever dug from the earth.

The "beggarly Homer, who strolled, God knows when, in the infancy and barbarism of the world," was richer far than Croesus and added more wealth to the world than the Rothschilds, the Vanderbilts and Goulds.

An Arab who fortunately escaped death after losing his way in the desert, without provisions, tells of his feelings when he found a bag full of pearls, just as he was about to abandon all hope. "I shall never forget," said he, "the relish and delight that I felt on supposing it to be dried wheat, nor the bitterness and despair I suffered on discovering that the bag contained pearls."

It is an interesting fact in this money-getting era that a poor author, or a seedy artist, or a college president with frayed coat-sleeves, has more standing in society and has more paragraphs written about him in the papers than many a millionaire. This is due, perhaps, to the malign influence of money-getting and to the benign effect of purely intellectual pursuits. As a rule every great success in the money world means the failure and misery of hundreds of antagonists. Every success in the world of intellect and character is an aid and profit to society. Character is a mark cut upon something, and this indelible mark determines the only true value of all people and all their work. Dr. Hunter said: "No man was ever a great man who wanted to be one." Artists cannot help putting themselves and their own characters into their works. The vulgar artist cannot paint a virtuous picture. The gross, the bizarre, the sensitive, the delicate, all come out on the canvas and tell the story of his life.

Who would not choose to be a millionaire of deeds with a Lincoln, a Grant, a Florence Nightingale, a Childs; a millionaire of ideas with Emerson, with Lowell, with Shakespeare, with Wordsworth; a millionaire of statesmanship with a Gladstone, a Bright, a Sumner, a Washington?

Some men are rich in health, in constant cheerfulness, in a mercurial temperament which floats them over troubles and trials enough to sink a shipload of ordinary men. Others are rich in disposition, family, and friends. There are some men so amiable that everybody loves them; some so cheerful that they carry an atmosphere of jollity about them. Some are rich in integrity and character.

"Who is the richest of men?" asked Socrates. "He who is content with the least, for contentment is nature's riches."

"Do you know, sir," said a devotee of Mammon to John Bright, "that I am worth a million sterling?" "Yes," said the irritated but calm-spirited respondent, "I do; and I know that it is all you are worth."

A bankrupt merchant, returning home one night, said to his noble wife, "My dear, I am ruined; everything we have is in the hands of the sheriff." After a few moments of silence the wife looked into his face and asked, "Will the sheriff sell you?" "Oh, no." "Will the sheriff sell me?" "Oh, no." "Then do not say we have lost everything. All that is most valuable remains to us—manhood, womanhood, childhood. We have lost but the results of our skill and industry. We can make another fortune if our hearts and hands are left us."

"We say a man is 'made'," said Beecher. "What do we mean? That he has got the control of his lower instincts, so that they are only fuel to his higher feelings, giving force to his nature? That his affections are like vines, sending out on all sides blossoms and clustering fruits? That his tastes are so cultivated that all beautiful things speak to him, and bring him their delights? That his understanding is opened, so that he walks through every hall of knowledge, and gathers its treasures? That his moral feelings are so developed and quickened that he holds sweet commerce with Heaven? O, no—none of these things. He is cold and dead in heart, and mind, and soul. Only his passions are alive; but—he is worth five hundred thousand dollars!

"And we say a man is 'ruined.' Are his wife and children dead? O, no. Have they had a quarrel, and are they separated from him? O, no. Has he lost his reputation through crime? No. Is his reason gone? O, no; it is as sound as ever. Is he struck through with disease? No. He has lost his property, and he is ruined. The *man* ruined! When shall we learn that 'a man's life consisteth not in the abundance of the things which he possesseth?'"

"How is it possible," asks an ancient philosopher, "that a man who has nothing, who is naked, houseless, without a hearth, squalid, without a slave, without a city, can pass a life that flows easily? See, God has sent you a man to show you that it is possible. Look at me who am without a city, without a house, without possessions, without a slave; I sleep on the ground; I have no wife, no children, no prætorium, but only the earth and heavens, and one poor cloak. And what do I want? Am I not without sorrow? Am I not without fear? Am I not free? When did any of you see me failing in the object of my desire? or even falling into that which I would avoid? Did I ever blame God or man? Did I ever accuse any man? Did any of you ever see me with a sorrowful countenance?"

"You are a plebeian," said a patrician to Cicero. "I am a plebeian," replied the great Roman orator; "the nobility of my family begins with me, that of yours will end with you." No man deserves to be crowned with honor whose life is a failure, and he who lives only to eat and drink and accumulate money is surely not successful. The world is no better for his living in it. He never wiped a tear from a sad face, never kindled a fire upon a frozen hearth. There is no flesh in his heart; he worships no god but gold.

Why should I scramble and struggle to get possession of a little portion of this earth? This is my world now; why should I envy others its mere legal possession? It belongs to him who can see it, enjoy it. I need not envy the so-called owners of estates in Boston and New York. They are merely taking care of my property and keeping it in excellent condition for me. For a few pennies for railroad fare whenever I wish I can see and possess the best of it all. It has cost me no effort, it gives me no care; yet the green grass, the shrubbery, and the statues on the lawns, the finer sculptures and paintings within, are always ready for me whenever I feel a desire to look upon them. I do not wish to carry them home with me, for I could not give them half the care they now receive; besides, it would take too much of my valuable time, and I should be worrying continually lest they be spoiled or stolen. I have much of the wealth of the world now. It is all prepared for me without any pains on my part. All around me are working hard to get things that will please me, and competing to see who can give them the cheapest. The little I pay for the use of libraries, railroads, galleries, parks, is less than it would cost to care for the least of all I use. Life and landscape are mine, the stars and flowers, the sea and air, the birds and trees. What more do I want? All the ages have been working for me; all mankind are my servants. I am only required to feed and clothe myself, an easy task in this land of opportunity.

There is scarcely an idea more infectious or potent than the love of money. It is a yellow fever, decimating its votaries and ruining more families in the land, than all the plagues or diseases put together. Instances of its malevolent power occur to every reader. Almost every square foot of land of our continent during the early buccaneer period (some call it the march of civilization), has been ensanguined through the madness for treasure. Read the pages of our historian Prescott, and you will see that the whole anti-Puritan history of America resolves itself into an awful slaughter for gold. Discoveries were only side issues.

Speak, history, who are life's victors? Unroll thy long scroll and say, have they won who first reached the goal, heedless of a brother's rights? And has he lost in life's great race who stopped "to raise a fallen child, and place him on his feet again," or to give a fainting comrade care; or to guide or assist a feeble woman? Has he lost who halts before the throne when duty calls, or sorrow, or distress? Is there no one to sing the pæan of the conquered who fell in the battle of life? of the wounded, the beaten, who died overwhelmed in the strife? of the low and humble, the weary and broken-hearted, who strove and who failed, in the eyes of men, but who did their duty as God gave them to see it?

"We have yet no man who has leaned *entirely* on his character, and eaten angel's food," said Emerson; "who, trusting to his sentiments, found life made of miracles; who, working for *universal aims*, found himself fed, he knew not how; clothed, sheltered, and weaponed, he knew not how, and yet it was done by his own hands."

At a time when it was considered dangerous to society in Europe for the common people to read books and listen to lectures on any but religious subjects, Charles Knight determined to enlighten the masses by cheap literature. He believed that a paper might be instructive and not be dull, cheap without being wicked. He started the "Penny Magazine," which acquired a circulation of two hundred thousand the first year. Knight projected the "Penny Cyclopedia," the "Library of Entertaining Knowledge," "Half-Hours with the Best Authors," and other useful works at a low price. His whole adult life was spent in the work of elevating the common people by cheap, yet wholesome publications. He died in poverty, but grateful people have erected a noble monument over his ashes.

How many rich dwellings there are, crowded with every appointment of luxury, that are only glittering caverns of selfishness and discontent! "Better a dinner of herbs where love is, than a stalled ox and hatred therewith."

"No man can tell whether he is rich or poor by turning to his ledger," says Beecher. "It is the heart that makes a man rich. He is rich or poor according to what he *is*, not according to what he *has*."

If our thoughts are great and noble, no mean surroundings can make us miserable. It is the mind that makes the body rich.

Howe'er it be, it seems to me,
'Tis only noble to be good.
Kind hearts are more than coronets,
And simple faith than Norman blood. —Tennyson

Be noble! and the nobleness that lies
In other men, sleeping, but never dead,
Will rise in majesty to meet thine own. —Lowell

An Iron Will

Table of Contents:

Training the Will

"The education of the will is the object of our existence," says Emerson.

Nor is this putting it too strongly, if we take into account the human will in its relations to the divine. This accords with the saying of J. Stuart Mill, that "a character is a completely fashioned will."

In respect to mere mundane relations, the development and discipline of one's will-power is of supreme moment in relation to success in life. No man can ever estimate the power of will. It is a part of the divine nature, all of a piece with the power of creation. We speak of God's fiat "*Fiat lux*, Let light be." Man has his fiat. The achievements of history have been the choices, the determinations, the creations, of the human will. It was the will, quiet or pugnacious, gentle or grim, of men like Wilberforce and Garrison, Goodyear and Cyrus Field, Bismarck and Grant, that made them indomitable. They simply would do what they planned. Such men can no more be stopped than the sun can be, or the tide. Most men fail, not through lack of education or agreeable personal qualities, but from lack of dogged determination, from lack of dauntless will.

"It is impossible," says Sharman, "to look into the conditions under which the battle of life is being fought, without perceiving how much really depends upon the extent to which the will-power is cultivated, strengthened, and made operative in right directions." Young people need to go into training for it. We live in an age of athletic meets. Those who are determined to have athletic will-power must take for it the kind of exercise they need.

This is well illustrated by a report I have seen of the long race from Marathon in the recent Olympian games, which was won by the young Greek peasant, Sotirios Louès.

A Struggle in the Race of Life

There had been no great parade about the training of this champion runner. From his work at the plough he quietly betook himself to the task of making Greece victorious before the assembled strangers from every land. He was known to be a good runner, and without fuss or bustle he entered himself as a competitor. But it was not his speed alone, out-distancing every rival, that made the young Greek stand out from among his fellows that day. When he left his cottage home at Amarusi, his father said to him, "Sotiri, you must only return a victor!" The light of a firm resolve shone in the young man's eye. The old father was sure that his boy would win, and so he made his way to the station, there to wait till Sotiri should come in ahead of all the rest. No one knew the old man and his three daughters as they elbowed their way through the crowd. When at last the excitement of the assembled multitude told that the critical moment had arrived, that the racers were nearing the goal, the old father looked up through eyes that were a little dim as he realized that truly Sotiri was leading the way. He *was* "returning a victor." How the crowd surged about the young peasant when the race was fairly won! Wild with excitement, they knew not how to shower upon him sufficient praise. Ladies overwhelmed him with flowers and rings; some even gave him their watches, and one American lady bestowed upon him her jewelled smelling-bottle. The princes embraced him, and the king himself saluted him in military fashion. But the young Sotirios was seeking for other praise than theirs. Past the ranks of royalty and fair maidenhood, past the outstretched hands of his own countrymen, past the applauding crowd of foreigners, his gaze wandered till it fell upon an old man trembling with eagerness, who resolutely pushed his way through the excited, satisfied throng. Then the young face lighted, and as old Louès advanced to the innermost circle with arms outstretched to embrace his boy, the young victor said, simply: "You see, father, I have obeyed."

Mental Discipline

The athlete trains for his race; and the mind must be put into training if one will win life's race.

"It is," says Professor Mathews, "only by continued, strenuous efforts, repeated again and again, day after day, week after week, and month after month, that the ability can be acquired to fasten the mind to one subject, however abstract or knotty, to the exclusion of everything else. The process of obtaining this self-mastery—this complete command of one's mental powers—is a gradual one, its length varying with the mental constitution of each person; but its acquisition is worth infinitely more than the utmost labor it ever costs."

"Perhaps the most valuable result of all education," it was said by Professor Huxley, "is the ability to make yourself do the thing you have to do when it ought to be done, whether you like it or not; it is the first lesson which ought to be learned, and, however early a man's training begins, it is probably the last lesson which he learns thoroughly."

Doing Things Once

When Henry Ward Beecher was asked how it was that he could accomplish so much more than other men, he replied:

"I don't do more, but less, than other people. They do all their work three times over: once in anticipation, once in actuality, once in rumination. I do mine in actuality alone, doing it once instead of three times."

This was by the intelligent exercise of Mr. Beecher's will-power in concentrating his mind upon what he was doing at a given moment, and then turning to something else. Any one who has observed business men closely, has noticed this characteristic. One of the secrets of a successful life is to be able to hold all of our energies upon one point, to focus all of the scattered rays of the mind upon one place or thing.

Centralizing Force

The mental reservoir of most people is like a leaky dam which we sometimes see in the country, where the greater part of the water flows out without going over the wheel and doing the work of the mill. The habit of mind-wandering, of worrying about this and that,

"Genius, that power which dazzles mortal eyes, Is oft but Perseverance in disguise."

Many a man would have been a success had he connected his fragmentary efforts. Spasmodic, disconnected attempts, without concentration, uncontrolled by any fixed idea, will never bring success. It is continuity of purpose alone that achieves results.

Learning to Swim

The way to learn to run is to run, the way to learn to swim is to swim. The way to learn to develop will-power is by the actual exercise of will-power in the business of life. "The man that exercises his will," says an English essayist, "makes it a stronger and more effective force in proportion to the extent to which such exercise is intelligently and perseveringly maintained." The forth-putting of will-power is a means of strengthening will-power. The will becomes strong by exercise. To stick to a thing till you are master, is a test of intellectual discipline and power.

Dr. Cuyler

"It is astonishing," says Dr. Theodore Cuyler, "how many men lack this power of 'holding on' until they reach the goal. They can make a sudden dash, but they lack grit. They are easily discouraged. They get on as long as everything goes smoothly, but when there is friction they lose heart. They depend on stronger personalities for their spirit and strength. They lack independence or originality. They only dare to do what others do. They do not step boldly from the crowd and act fearlessly."

The Big Trees

What is needed by him who would succeed in the highest degree possible is careful planning. He is to accumulate reserved power, that he may be equal to all emergencies. Thomas Starr King said that the great trees of California gave him his first impression of the power of reserve. "It was the thought of the reserve energies that had been compacted into them," he said, "that stirred me. The mountains had given them their iron and rich stimulants, the hills had given them their soil, the clouds had given their rain and snow, and a thousand summers and winters had poured forth their treasures about their vast roots."

No young man can hope to do anything above the commonplace who has not made his life a reservoir of power on which he can constantly draw, which will never fail him in any emergency. Be sure that you have stored away, in your power-house, the energy, the knowledge that will be equal to the great occasion when it comes. "If I were twenty, and had but ten years to live," said a great scholar and writer, "I would spend the first nine years accumulating knowledge and getting ready for the tenth."

"I Will"

"There are no two words in the English language which stand out in bolder relief, like kings upon a checker-board, to so great an extent as the words 'I will.' There is strength, depth and solidity, decision, confidence and power, determination, vigor and individuality, in the round, ringing tone which characterizes its delivery. It talks to you of triumph over difficulties, of victory in the face of discouragement, of will to promise and strength to perform, of lofty and daring enterprise, of unfettered aspirations, and of the thousand and one solid impulses by which man masters impediments in the way of progression."

As one has well said: "He who is silent is forgotten; he who does not advance falls back; he who stops is overwhelmed, distanced, crushed; he who ceases to become greater, becomes smaller; he who leaves off gives up; the stationary is the beginning of the end—it precedes death; to live is to achieve, to will without ceasing."

Be thou a hero; let thy might Tramp on eternal snows its way, And through the ebon walls of night, Hew down a passage unto day. —Park Benjamin.

The Rulers of Destiny

There is no chance, no destiny, no fate,
Can circumvent, or hinder, or control
The firm resolve of a determined soul.
Gifts count for nothing; will alone is great;
All things give way before it soon or late.
What obstacle can stay the mighty force
Of the sea-seeking river in its course,
Or cause the ascending orb of day to wait?
Each well-born soul must win what it deserves.
Let the fool prate of luck. The fortunate
Is he whose earnest purpose never swerves,
Whose slightest action or inaction serves
The one great aim. —Ella Wheeler Wilcox

There is always room for a man of force.—Emerson

The king is the man who can.—Carlyle

A strong, defiant purpose is many-handed, and lays hold of whatever is near that can serve it; it has a magnetic power that draws to itself whatever is kindred.—T.T. Munger

What is will-power, looked at in a large way, but energy of character? Energy of will, self-originating force, is the soul of every great character. Where it is, there is life; where it is not, there is faintness, helplessness, and despondency. "Let it be your first study to teach the world that you are not wood and straw; that there is some iron in you." Men who have left their mark upon the world have been men of great and prompt decision. The achievements of will-power are almost beyond computation. Scarcely anything seems impossible to the man who can will strongly enough and long enough. One talent with a will behind it will accomplish more than ten without it, as a thimbleful of powder in a rifle, the bore of whose barrel will give it direction, will do greater execution than a carload burned in the open air.

"The Wills, the Won'ts, and the Can'ts"
"There are three kinds of people in the world," says a recent writer, "the wills, the won'ts, and the can'ts. The first accomplish everything; the second oppose everything; the third fail in everything."

The shores of fortune, as Foster says, are covered with the stranded wrecks of men of brilliant ability, but who have wanted courage, faith, and decision, and have therefore perished in sight of more resolute but less capable adventurers, who succeeded in making port.

Were I called upon to express in a word the secret of so many failures among those who started out with high hopes, I should say they lacked will-power. They could not half will: and what is a man without a will? He is like an engine without steam. Genius unexecuted is no more genius than a bushel of acorns is a forest of oaks.

Will has been called the spinal column of personality. "The will in its relation to life," says an English writer, "may be compared at once to the rudder and to the steam engine of a vessel, on the confined and related action of which it depends entirely for the direction of its course and the vigor of its movement."

Strength of will is the test of a young man's possibilities. Can he will strong enough, and hold whatever he undertakes with an iron grip? It is the iron grip that takes and holds. What chance is there in this crowding, pushing, selfish, greedy world, where everything is pusher or pushed, for a young man with no will, no grip on life? The man who would forge to the front in this competitive age must be a man of prompt and determined decision.

A Tailor's Needle

It is in one of Ben Jonson's old plays: "When I once take the humor of a thing, I am like your tailor's needle—I go through with it."

This is not different from Richelieu, who said: "When I have once taken a resolution, I go straight to my aim; I overthrow all, I cut down all."

And in business affairs the counsel of Rothschild is to the same effect: "Do without fail that which you determine to do."

Gladstone's children were taught to accomplish *to the end* whatever they might begin, no matter how insignificant the undertaking might be.

What Is Worse than Rashness

It is irresolution that is worse than rashness. "He that shoots," says Feltham, "may sometimes hit the mark; but he that shoots not at all can never hit it. Irresolution is like an ague; it shakes not this nor that limb, but all the body is at once in a fit."

The man who is forever twisting and turning, backing and filling, hesitating and dawdling, shuffling and parleying, weighing and balancing, splitting hairs over non-essentials, listening to every new motive which presents itself, will never accomplish anything. But the positive man, the decided man, is a power in the world, and stands for something; you can measure him, and estimate the work that his energy will accomplish.

Opportunity is coy, is swift, is gone, before the slow, the unobservant, the indolent, or the careless can seize her. "Vigilance in watching opportunity," said Phelps, "tact and daring in seizing upon opportunity; force and persistence in crowding opportunity to its utmost of possible achievement—these are the martial virtues which must command success." "The best men," remarked Chapin, "are not those who have waited for chances, but who have taken them; besieged the chance; conquered the chance; and made chance the servitor."

Is it not possible to classify successes and failures by their various degrees of will-power? A man who can resolve vigorously upon a course of action, and turns neither to the right nor to the left, though a paradise tempt him, who keeps his eyes upon the goal, whatever distracts him, is sure of success.

"Not every vessel that sails from Tarshish will bring back the gold of Ophir. But shall it therefore rot in the harbor? No! Give its sails to the wind!"

Conscious Power

"Conscious power," says Mellès, "exists within the mind of every one. Sometimes its existence is unrealized, but it is there. It is there to be developed and brought forth, like the culture of that obstinate but beautiful flower, the orchid. To allow it to remain dormant is to place one's self in obscurity, to trample on one's ambition, to smother one's faculties. To develop it is to individualize all that is best within you, and give it to the world. It is by an absolute knowledge of yourself, the proper estimate of your own value."

"There is hardly a reader," says an experienced educator, "who will not be able to recall the early life of at least one young man whose childhood was spent in poverty, and who, in boyhood, expressed a firm desire to secure a higher education. If, a little later, that desire became a declared resolve, soon the avenues opened to that end. That desire and resolve created an atmosphere which attracted the forces necessary to the attainment of the purpose. Many of these young men will tell us that, as long as they were hoping and striving and longing, mountains of difficulty rose before them; but that when they fashioned their hopes into fixed purposes aid came unsought to help them on the way."

Do You Believe in Yourself?

The man without self-reliance and an iron will is the plaything of chance, the puppet of his environment, the slave of circumstances. Are not doubts the greatest of enemies? If you would succeed up to the limit of your possibilities, must you not constantly hold to the belief that you are success-organized, and that you will be successful, no matter what opposes? You are never to allow a shadow of doubt to enter your mind that the Creator intended you to win in life's battle. Regard every suggestion that your life may be a failure, that you are not made like those who succeed, and that success is not for you, as a traitor, and expel it from your mind as you would a thief from your house.

There is something sublime in the youth who possesses the spirit of boldness and fearlessness, who has proper confidence in his ability to do and dare.

The world takes us at our own valuation. It believes in the man who believes in himself, but it has little use for the timid man, the one who is never certain of himself; who cannot rely on his own judgment, who craves advice from others, and is afraid to go ahead on his own account.

It is the man with a positive nature, the man who believes that he is equal to the emergency, who believes he can do the thing he attempts, who wins the confidence of his fellow-man. He is beloved because he is brave and self-sufficient.

Those who have accomplished great things in the world have been, as a rule, bold, aggressive, and self-confident. They dared to step out from the crowd, and act in an original way. They were not afraid to be generals.

There is little room in this crowding, competing age for the timid, vacillating youth. He who would succeed to-day must not only be brave, but must also dare to take chances. He who waits for certainty never wins.

"The law of the soul is eternal endeavor, That bears the man onward and upward forever."

"A man can be too confiding in others, but never too confident in himself."

Never admit defeat or poverty. Stoutly assert your divine right to hold your head up and look the world in the face; step bravely to the front whatever opposes, and the world will make way for you. No one will insist upon your rights while you yourself doubt that you have any. Believe you were made for the place you fill. Put forth your whole energies. Be awake, electrify yourself; go forth to the task. A young man once said to his employer, "Don't give me an easy job. I want to handle heavy boxes, shoulder great loads. I would like to lift a big mountain and throw it into the sea,"—and he stretched out two brawny arms, while his honest eyes danced and his whole being glowed with conscious strength.

The world in its heart admires the stern, determined doer. "The world turns aside to let any man pass who knows whither he is going." "It is wonderful how even the apparent casualties of life seem to bow to a spirit that will not bow to them, and yield to assist a design, after having in vain attempted to frustrate it."

"The man who succeeds," says Prentice Mulford, "must always in mind or imagination live, move, think, and act as if he gained that success, or he never will gain it."

"We go forth," said Emerson, "austere, dedicated, believing in the iron links of Destiny, and will not turn on our heels to save our lives. A book, a bust, or only the sound of a name shoots a spark through the nerves, and we suddenly believe in will. We cannot hear of personal vigor of any kind, great power of performance, without fresh resolution."

Force of Will in Camp and Field

Oh, what miracles have been wrought by the self-confidence, the self-determination of an iron will! What impossible deeds have been performed by it! It was this that took Napoleon over the Alps in midwinter; it took Farragut and Dewey past the cannons, torpedoes, and mines of the enemy; it led Nelson and Grant to victory; it has been the great tonic in the world of discovery, invention, and art; it has helped to win the thousand triumphs in war and science which were deemed impossible.

The secret of Jeanne d'Arc's success was not alone in rare decision of character, but in the seeing of visions which inspired her to self-confidence—confidence in her divine mission.

It was an iron will that gave Nelson command of the British fleet, a title, and a statue at Trafalgar Square It was the keynote of his character when he said, "When I don't know whether to fight or not, I always fight."

It was an iron will that was brought into play when Horatius with two companions held ninety thousand Tuscans at bay until the bridge across the Tiber had been destroyed—when Leonidas at Thermopylæ checked the mighty march of Xerxes—when Themistocles off the coast of Greece shattered the Persian's Armada—when Cæsar finding his army hard pressed seized spear and buckler and snatched victory from defeat—when Winkelried gathered to his breast a sheaf of Austrian spears and opened a path for his comrades—when Wellington fought in many climes without ever being conquered—when Ney on a hundred fields changed apparent disaster into brilliant triumph—when Sheridan arrived from Winchester as the Union retreat was becoming a route and turned the tide—when Sherman signaled his men to hold the fort knowing that their leader was coming.

History furnishes thousands of examples of men who have seized occasions to accomplish results deemed impossible by those less resolute. Prompt decision and whole-souled action sweep the world before them. Who was the organizer of the modern German empire? Was he not the man of iron?

Napoleon and Grant

"What would you do if you were besieged in a place entirely destitute of provisions?" asked the examiner, when Napoleon was a cadet.

"If there were anything to eat in the enemy's camp, I should not be concerned."

When Paris was in the hands of a mob, and the authorities were panic-stricken, in came a man who said, "I know a young officer who can quell this mob."

"Send for him."

Napoleon was sent for; he came, he subjugated the mob, he subjugated the authorities, he ruled France, then conquered Europe.

May 10, 1796, Napoleon carried the bridge at Lodi, in the face of the Austrian batteries, trained upon the French end of the structure. Behind them were six thousand troops. Napoleon massed four thousand grenadiers at the head of the bridge, with a battalion of three hundred carbineers in front. At the tap of the drum the foremost assailants wheeled from the cover of the street wall under a terrible hail of grape and canister, and attempted to pass the gateway to the bridge. The front ranks went down like stalks of grain before a reaper; the column staggered and reeled backward, and the valiant grenadiers were appalled by the task before them. Without a word or a look of reproach, Napoleon placed himself at their head, and his aids and generals rushed to his side. Forward again over heaps of dead that choked the passage, and a quick run counted by seconds only carried the column across two hundred yards of clear space, scarcely a shot from the Austrians taking effect beyond the point where the platoons wheeled for the first leap. *The guns of the enemy were not aimed at the advance. The advance was too quick for the Austrian gunners.* So sudden and so miraculous was it all, that the Austrian artillerists abandoned their guns instantly, and their supports fled in a panic instead of rushing to the front and meeting the French onslaught. This Napoleon had counted on in making the bold attack.

What was Napoleon but the thunderbolt of war? He once journeyed from Spain to Paris at seventeen miles an hour in the saddle.

"Is it *possible* to cross the path?" asked Napoleon of the engineers who had been sent to explore the dreaded pass of St. Bernard.

"Perhaps," was the hesitating reply, "it is within the limits of *possibility*."

"*Forward, then.*"

Yet Ulysses S. Grant, a young man unknown to fame, with neither money nor influence, with no patrons or friends, in six years fought more battles, gained more victories, captured more prisoners, took more spoils, commanded more men, than Napoleon did in twenty years. "The great thing about him," said Lincoln, "is cool persistence."

"Don't Swear—fight"

When the Spanish fire on San Juan Hill became almost unbearable, some of the Rough Riders began to swear. Colonel Wood, with the wisdom of a good leader, called out, amid the whistle of the Mauser bullets: "Don't swear—fight!"

In a skirmish at Salamanca, while the enemy's guns were pouring shot into his regiment, Sir William Napier's men became disobedient. He at once ordered a halt, and flogged four of the ringleaders under fire. The men yielded at once, and then marched three miles under a heavy cannonade as coolly as if it were a review.

When Pellisier, the Crimean chief of Zouaves, struck an officer with a whip, the man drew a pistol that missed fire. The chief replied: "Fellow, I order you a three days' arrest for not having your arms in better order."

The man of iron will is cool in the hour of danger.

"I Had to Run like a Cyclone"

This was what Roosevelt said about his pushing on up San Juan Hill ahead of his regiment: "I had to run like a cyclone to stay in front and keep from being run over."

The personal heroism of Hobson, or of Cushing, who blew up the "Albemarle" forty years ago, was but the expression of a magnificent will power. It was this which was the basis of General Wheeler's unparalleled military advancement: a second lieutenant at twenty-three, a colonel at twenty-four, a brigadier-general at twenty-five, a major-general at twenty-six, a corps commander at twenty-seven, and a lieutenant-general at twenty-eight.

General Wheeler had sixteen horses killed under him, and a great number wounded. His saddle equipments and clothes were frequently struck by the missiles of the enemy. He was three times wounded, once painfully. He had thirty-two staff officers, or acting staff officers, killed or wounded. In almost every case they were immediately by his side. No officer was ever more exposed to the missiles of death than Joseph Wheeler.

What is this imperial characteristic of manhood, an iron will, but that which underlies all magnificent achievement, whether by heroes of the "Light Brigade" or the heroic fire-fighters of our great cities?

Will Power in its Relation to Health and Disease

There is no doubt that, as a rule, great decision of character is usually accompanied by great constitutional firmness. Men who have been noted for great firmness of character have usually been strong and robust. As a rule it is the strong physical man who carries weight and conviction. Take, as an example, William the Conqueror, as he is pictured by Green in his history:

"The very spirit of the sea-robbers from whom he sprang seemed embodied in his gigantic form, his enormous strength, his savage countenance, his desperate bravery. No other knight under heaven, his enemies confessed, was William's peer. No other man could bend William's bow. His mace crashed through a ring of English warriors to the foot of the standard. He rose to his greatest heights in moments when other men despaired. No other man who ever sat upon the throne of England was this man's match."

Or, take Webster. Sydney Smith said: "Webster is a living lie; because no man on earth can be as great as he looks." Carlyle said of him: "One would incline at sight to back him against the world." His very physique was eloquent. Men yielded their wills to his at sight.

The great prizes of life ever fall to the robust, the stalwart, the strong,—not to a huge muscle or powerful frame necessarily, but to a strong vitality, a great nervous energy. It is the Lord Broughams, working almost continuously one hundred and forty-four hours; it is the Napoleons, twenty hours in the saddle; it is the Franklins, camping out in the open air at seventy; it is the Gladstones, firmly grasping the helm of the ship of state at eighty-four, tramping miles every day, and chopping down huge trees at eighty-five,—who accomplish the great things of life.

To prosper you must improve your brain power; and nothing helps the brain more than a healthy body. The race of to-day is only to be won by those who will study to keep their bodies in such good condition that their minds are able and ready to sustain that high pressure on memory and mind, which our present fierce competition engenders. It is health rather than strength that is now wanted. Health is essentially the requirement of our time to enable us to succeed in life. In all modern occupations—from the nursery to the school, from the school to the shop or world beyond—the brain and nerve strain go on, continuous, augmenting, and intensifying.

As a rule physical vigor is the condition of a great career. Stonewall Jackson, early in life, determined to conquer every weakness he had, physical, mental, and moral. He held all of his powers with a firm hand. To his great self-discipline and self-mastery he owed his success. So determined was he to harden himself to the weather that he could not be induced to wear an overcoat in winter. "I will not give in to the cold," he said. For a year, on account of dyspepsia, he lived on buttermilk and stale bread, and wore a wet shirt next his body because his doctor advised it, although everybody else ridiculed the idea. This was while he was professor at the Virginia Military Institute. His doctor advised him to retire at nine o'clock; and, no matter where he was, or who was present, he always sought his bed on the minute.

He adhered rigidly through life to this stern system of discipline. Such self-training, such self-conquest, gives one great power over others. It is equal to genius itself.

"I can do nothing," said Grant, "without nine hours' sleep."

What else is so grand as to stand on life's threshold, fresh, young, hopeful, with a consciousness of power equal to any emergency,—a master of the situation? The glory of a young man is his strength.

Our great need of the world to-day is for men and women who are good animals. To endure the strain of our concentrated civilization, the coming man and woman must have an excess of animal spirits. They must have a robustness of health. Mere absence of disease is not health. It is the overflowing fountain, not the one half full, that gives life and beauty to the valley below. Only he is healthy who exults in mere animal existence; whose very life is a luxury; who feels a bounding pulse throughout his body; who feels life in every limb, as dogs do when scouring over the field, or as boys do when gliding over fields of ice.

Yet in spite of all this, in defiance of it, we know that an iron will is often triumphant in the contest with physical infirmity.

"Brave spirits are a balsam to themselves: There is a nobleness of mind that heals Wounds beyond salves."

"One day," said a noted rope-walker, "I signed an agreement to wheel a barrow along a rope on a given day. A day or two before I was seized with lumbago. I called in my medical man, and told him I must be cured by a certain day; not only because I should lose what I hoped to earn, but also forfeit a large sum. I got no better, and the doctor forbade my getting up. I told him, 'What do I want with your advice? If you cannot cure me, of what good is your advice?' When I got to the place, there was the doctor protesting I was unfit for the exploit. I went on, though I felt like a frog with my back. I got ready my pole and my barrow, took hold of the handles and wheeled it along the rope as well as I ever did. When I got to the end I wheeled it back again, and when this was done I was a frog again. What made me that I could wheel the barrow? It was my reserve will."

"What does he know," asks the sage, "who has not suffered?" Did not Schiller produce his greatest tragedies in the midst of physical suffering almost amounting to torture? Handel was never greater than when, warned by palsy of the approach of death, and struggling with distress and suffering, he sat down to compose the great works which have made his name immortal in music. Beethoven was almost totally deaf and burdened with sorrow when he produced his greatest works. Milton writing "Who best can suffer, best can do," wrote at his best when in feeble health, and when poor and blind.

"... Yet I argue not
Against Heaven's hand or will, nor bate a jot
Of heart or hope; but still bear up and steer
Right onward."

The Rev. William H. Milburn, who lost his sight when a child, studied for the ministry, and was ordained before he attained his majority. He has written half a dozen books, among them a very careful history of the Mississippi Valley. He has long been chaplain of the lower house of Congress.

Blind Fanny Crosby, of New York, was a teacher of the blind for many years. She has written nearly three thousand hymns, among which are: "Pass Me not, O Gentle Saviour," "Rescue the Perishing," "Saviour More than Life to Me," and "Jesus keep Me near the Cross."

"The truest help we can render one who is afflicted," said Bishop Brooks, "is not to take his burden from him, but to call out his best energy, that he may be able to bear."

What a mighty will Darwin had! He was in continual ill health. He was in constant suffering. His patience was marvellous. No one but his wife knew what he endured. "For forty years," says his son, "he never knew one day of health;" yet during those forty years he unremittingly forced himself to do the work from which the mightiest minds and the strongest constitutions would have shrunk. He had a wonderful power of sticking to a subject. He used almost to apologize for his patience, saying that he could not bear to be beaten, as if it were a sign of weakness.

Bulwer advises us to refuse to be ill, never to tell people we are ill, never to own it ourselves. Illness is one of those things which a man should resist on principle. Do not dwell upon your ailments nor study your symptoms. Never allow yourself to be convinced that you are not complete master of yourself. Stoutly affirm your own superiority over bodily ills. We should keep a high ideal of health and harmony constantly before the mind.

Is not the mind the natural protector of the body? We cannot believe that the Creator has left the whole human race entirely at the mercy of only about half a dozen specific drugs which always act with certainty. There is a divine remedy placed within us for many of the ills we suffer. If we only knew how to use this power of will and mind to protect ourselves, many of us would be able to carry youth and cheerfulness with us into the teens of our second century. The mind has undoubted power to preserve and sustain physical youth and beauty, to keep the body strong and healthy, to renew life, and to preserve it from decay, many years longer than it does now. The longest-lived men and women have, as a rule, been those who have attained great mental and moral development. They have lived in the upper region of a higher life, beyond the reach of much of the jar, the friction, and the discords which weaken and shatter most lives.

Every physician knows that courageous people, with indomitable will, are not half as likely to contract contagious diseases as the timid, the vacillating, the irresolute. A thoughtful physician once assured a friend that if an express agent were to visit New Orleans in the yellow-fever season, having forty thousand dollars in his care, he would be in little danger of the fever so long as he kept possession of the money. Let him once deliver that into other hands, and the sooner he left the city the better.

Napoleon used to visit the plague hospitals even when the physicians dreaded to go, and actually put his hands upon the plague-stricken patients. He said the man who was not afraid could vanish the plague. A will power like this is a strong tonic to the body. Such a will has taken many men from apparent death-beds, and enabled them to perform wonderful deeds of valor. When told by his physicians that he must die, Douglas Jerrold said: "And leave a family of helpless children? I won't die." He kept his word, and lived for years.

The Romance of Achievement Under Difficulties

What doth the poor man's son inherit?
Stout muscles, and a sinewy heart,
A hardy frame, a hardier spirit!
King of two hands he does his part
In every useful toil and art:
A heritage it seems to me,
A king might wish to hold in fee. —Lowell

Has not God given every man a capital to start with? Are we not born rich? He is rich who has good health, a sound body, good muscles; he is rich who has a good head, a good disposition, a good heart; he is rich who has two good hands, with five chances on each. Equipped? Every man is equipped as only God could equip him. What a fortune he possesses in the marvellous mechanism of his body and mind. It is individual effort that has achieved everything worth achieving.

The Fun of the Little Game

A big Australian, six feet four, James Tyson, died not long since, with a property of $25,000,000, who began life as a farm hand. Tyson cared little for money. He used to say of it:

"I shall just leave it behind me when I go. I shall have done with it then, and it will not concern me afterwards. But," he would add, with a characteristic semi-exultant snap of the fingers, "the money is nothing. It was the little game that was the fun."

Being asked, "What was the little game?" he replied with an energy of concentration peculiar to him: *Fighting the desert. That has been my work. I have been fighting the desert all my life, and I have won. I have put water where was no water, and beef where was no beef. I have put fences where there were no fences, and roads where there were no roads. Nothing can undo what I have done, and millions will be happier for it after I am long dead and forgotten.*

Has not self-help accomplished about all the great things of the world? How many young men falter, faint, and dally with their purpose because they have no capital to start with, and wait and wait for some good luck to give them a lift. But success is the child of drudgery and perseverance. It cannot be coaxed or bribed; pay the price, and it is yours. A constant struggle, a ceaseless battle to bring success from inhospitable surroundings, is the price of all great achievements.

Conquerors of Fortune

Benjamin Franklin had this tenacity of purpose in a wonderful degree. When he started in the printing business in Philadelphia, he carried his material through the streets on a wheelbarrow. He hired one room for his office, work-room, and sleeping-room. He found a formidable rival in the city and invited him to his room. Pointing to a piece of bread from which he had just eaten his dinner, he said:

"Unless you can live cheaper than I can, you cannot starve me out."

It was so that he proved the wisdom of Edmund Burke's saying, that "He that wrestles with us strengthens our nerves, and sharpens our skill: our antagonist is our helper."

The poor and friendless lad, George Peabody, weary, footsore, and hungry, called at a tavern in Concord, N.H., and asked to be allowed to saw wood for lodging and breakfast. Yet he put in work for everything he ever received, and out-matched the poverty of early days.

Gideon Lee could not even get shoes to wear in winter, when a boy, but he went to work barefoot in the snow. He made a bargain with himself to work sixteen hours a day. He fulfilled it to the letter, and when from interruption he lost time, he robbed himself of sleep to make it up. He became a wealthy merchant of New York, mayor of the city, and a member of Congress.

Commercial Courage

The business affairs of a gentleman named Rouss were once in a complicated condition, owing to his conflicting interests in various states, and he was thrown into prison. While confined he wrote on the walls of his cell:

"I am forty years of age this day. When I am fifty, I shall be worth half a million; and by the time I am sixty, I shall be worth a million dollars."

He lived to accumulate more than three million dollars.

"The ruin which overtakes so many merchants," says Whipple, "is due not so much to their lack of business talent as to their lack of business nerve."

Cyrus W. Field had retired from business with a large fortune when he became possessed with the idea that by means of a cable laid upon the bottom of the Atlantic Ocean, telegraphic communication could be established between Europe and America. He plunged into the undertaking with all the force of his being. It was an incredibly hard contest: the forests of Newfoundland, the lobby in Congress, the unskilled handling of brakes on his Agamemnon cable, a second and a third breaking of the cable at sea, the cessation of the current in a well-laid cable, the snapping of a superior cable on the Great Eastern—all these availed not to foil the iron will of Field, whose final triumph was that of mental energy in the application of science.

Four New York Journalists

To Horace Greeley, the founder of the "Tribune," I need not allude; his story is or ought to be in every school-book.

James Brooks, once the editor and proprietor of the "Daily Express," and later an eminent congressman, began life as a clerk in a store in Maine, and when twenty-one received for his pay a hogshead of New England rum. He was so eager to go to college that he started for Waterville with his trunk on his back, and when he was graduated he was so poor and plucky that he carried his trunk on his back to the station as he went home.

When James Gordon Bennett was forty years old he collected all his property, three hundred dollars, and in a cellar with a board upon two barrels for a desk, himself his own typesetter, office boy, publisher, newsboy, clerk, editor, proofreader, and printer's devil, he started the "New York Herald." He did this, after many attempts and defeats in trying to follow the routine, instead of doing his own way. Never was any man's early career a better illustration of Wendell Phillips' dictum: "What is defeat? Nothing but education; nothing but the first steps to something better."

Thurlow Weed, who was a journalist for fifty-seven years, strong, sensible, genial, tactful, and of magnificent physique, who did so much to shape public policy in the Empire State, tells a most romantic story of his boyhood:—

"I cannot ascertain how much schooling I got at Catskill, probably less than a year, certainly not a year and a half, and this was when I was not more than five or six years old. I felt a necessity, at an early age, of trying to do something for my own support.

"My first employment was in sugar-making, an occupation to which I became much attached. I now look with great pleasure upon the days and nights passed in the sap-bush. The want of shoes (which, as the snow was deep, was no small privation) was the only drawback upon my happiness. I used, however, to tie pieces of an old rag carpet around my feet, and got along pretty well, chopping wood and gathering up sap. But when the spring advanced, and bare ground appeared in spots, I threw off the old carpet encumbrance and did my work barefoot.

"There is much leisure time for boys who are making maple sugar. I devoted this time to reading, when I could obtain books; but the farmers of that period had few or no books, save their Bibles. I borrowed books whenever and wherever I could.

"I heard that a neighbor, three miles off, had borrowed from a still more distant neighbor a book of great interest. I started off, barefoot, in the snow, to obtain the treasure. There were spots of bare ground, upon which I would stop to warm my feet. And there were also, along the road, occasional lengths of log-fence from which the snow had melted, and upon which it was a luxury to walk. The book was at home, and the good people consented, upon my promise that it should be neither torn nor soiled, to lend it to me. In returning with the prize, I was too happy to think of the snow or my naked feet.

"Candles were then among the luxuries, not the necessaries, of life. If boys, instead of going to bed after dark, wanted to read, they supplied themselves with pine knots, by the light of which, in a horizontal position, they pursued their studies. In this manner, with my body in the sugar-house, and my head out of doors, where the fat pine was blazing, I read with intense interest the book I had borrowed, a 'History of the French Revolution.'"

Weed's next earning was in an iron foundry at Onondaga:

"My business was, after a casting, to temper and prepare the molding 'dogs,' myself. This was night and day work. We ate salt pork and rye and Indian bread, three times a day, and slept on straw in bunks. I liked the excitement of a furnace life."

When he went to the "Albany Argus" to learn the printing business he worked from five in the morning till nine at night.

From Humblest Beginnings

The more difficulties one has to encounter, within and without, the more significant and the higher in inspiration his life will be.—Horace Bushnell

The story of Weed and of Greeley is not an uncommon one in America. Some of the most eminent men on the globe have struggled with poverty in early life and triumphed over it.

The astronomer Kepler, whose name can never die, was kept in constant anxieties; and he told fortunes by astrology for a livelihood, saying that astrology, as the daughter of astronomy, ought to keep her mother. All sorts of service he had to accept; he made almanacs and worked for any one who would pay him.

Linnæus was so poor when getting his education that he had to mend his shoes with folded paper, and often had to beg his meals of his friends.

During the ten years in which he made his greatest discoveries, Isaac Newton could hardly pay two shillings a week to the Royal Society of which he was a member. Some of his friends wanted to get him excused from this payment, but he would not allow them to act.

Humphry Davy had but a slender chance to acquire great scientific knowledge, yet he had true mettle in him, and he made even old pans, kettles, and bottles contribute to his success, as he experimented and studied in the attic of the apothecary store where he worked.

George Stephenson was one of eight children whose parents were so poor that all lived in a single room. George had to watch cows for a neighbor, but he managed to get time to make engines of clay, with hemlock sticks for pipes. At seventeen he had charge of an engine, with his father for fireman. He could neither read nor write, but the engine was his teacher, and he a faithful student. While the other hands were playing games or loafing in liquor shops during the holidays, George was taking his machine to pieces, cleaning it, studying it, and making experiments in engines. When he had become famous as a great inventor of improvements in engines, those who had loafed and played called him lucky.

It was by steadfastly keeping at it, by indomitable will power, that these men won their positions in life.

"We rise by the things that are under our feet; By what we have mastered of good or gain."

Talent in Tatters

Among the companions of Sir Joshua Reynolds, while he was studying his art at Rome, was a fellow-pupil of the name of Astley. They made an excursion, with some others, on a sultry day, and all except Astley took off their coats. After several taunts he was persuaded to do the same, and displayed on the back of his waistcoat a foaming waterfall. Distress had compelled him to patch his clothes with one of his own landscapes.

James Sharpies, the celebrated blacksmith artist of England, was very poor, but he often rose at three o'clock to copy books he could not buy. He would walk eighteen miles to Manchester and back after a hard day's work, to buy a shilling's worth of artist's materials. He would ask for the heaviest work in the blacksmith shop, because it took a longer time to heat at the forge, and he could thus have many spare minutes to study the precious book, which he propped up against the chimney. He was a great miser of spare moments, and used every one as though he might never see another. He devoted his leisure hours for five years to that wonderful production, "The Forge," copies of which are to be seen in many a home. It was by one unwavering aim, carried out by an iron will, that he wrought out his life triumph.

"That boy will beat me one day," said an old painter as he watched a little fellow named Michael Angelo making drawings of pot and brushes, easel and stool, and other articles in the studio. The barefoot boy did persevere until he had overcome every difficulty and become the greatest master of art the world has known. Although Michael Angelo made himself immortal in three different occupations,—and his fame might well rest upon his dome of St. Peter as an architect, upon his "Moses" as a sculptor, or upon his "Last Judgment" as a painter,—yet we find by his correspondence, now in the British Museum, that when he was at work on his colossal bronze statue of Pope Julius II., he was so poor that he could not have his younger brother come to visit him at Bologna, because he had but one bed in which he and three of his assistants slept together. Yet

"The star of an unconquered will
Arose in his breast,
Serene, and resolute and still,
And calm and self-possessed."

Concentrated Energy

The struggles and triumphs of those who are bound to win is a never-ending tale. Nor will the procession of enthusiastic workers cease so long as the globe is turning on its axle.

Say what we will of genius, specialized in a hundred callings, yet the fact remains that no amount of genius has ever availed upon the earth unless enforced by will power to overcome the obstacles that hedge about every one who would rise above the circumstances in which he was born, or become greater than his calling. Was not Virgil the son of a porter, Horace of a shopkeeper, Demosthenes of a cutler, Milton of a money scrivener, Shakespeare of a wool stapler, and Cromwell of a brewer?

Ben Jonson, when following his trade of a mason, worked on Lincoln's Inn in London with trowel in hand and a book in his pocket. Joseph Hunter was a carpenter in youth, Robert Burns a plowman, Keats a druggist, Thomas Carlyle and Hugh Miller masons. Dante and Descartes were soldiers. Cardinal Wolsey, Defoe, and Kirke White were butchers' sons. Faraday was the son of a hostler, and his teacher, Humphry Davy, was an apprentice to an apothecary. Kepler was a waiter boy in a German hotel, Bunyan a tinker, Copernicus the son of a Polish baker. They rose by being greater than their callings, as Arkwright rose above mere barbering, Bunyan above tinkering, Wilson above shoemaking, Lincoln above rail-splitting, and Grant above tanning. By being first-class barbers, tinkers, shoemakers, rail-splitters, tanners, they acquired the power which enabled them to become great inventors, authors, statesmen, generals. John Kay, the inventor of the fly-shuttle, James Hargreaves, who introduced the spinning-jenny, and Samuel Compton, who originated mule-spinning, were all artisans, uneducated and poor, but were endowed with natural faculties which enabled them to make a more enduring impression upon the world than anything that could have been done by the mere power of scholarship or wealth.

It cannot be said of any of these great names that their individual courses in life would have been what they were, had there been lacking a superb will power resistless as the tide to bear them upward and onward.

> Let Fortune empty her whole quiver on me,
> I have a soul that, like an ample shield,
> Can take in all, and verge enough for more;
> Fate was not mine, nor am I Fate's:
> Souls know no conquerors. —Dryden

Staying Power

"Never give up, there are chances and changes,
Helping the hopeful, a hundred to one;
And, through the chaos, High Wisdom arranges
Ever success, if you'll only hold on.
Never give up; for the wisest is boldest,
Knowing that Providence mingles the cup,
And of all maxims, the best, as the oldest,
Is the stern watchword of 'Never give up!'"
Be firm; one constant element of luck
Is genuine, solid, old Teutonic pluck. —Holmes

Success in most things depends on knowing how long it takes to succeed.—Montesquieu

The power to hold on is characteristic of all men who have accomplished anything great; they may lack in some other particular, have many weaknesses or eccentricities, but the quality of persistence is never absent from a successful man. No matter what opposition he meets or what discouragement overtakes him, drudgery cannot disgust him, obstacles cannot discourage him, labor cannot weary him; misfortune, sorrow, and reverses cannot harm him. It is not so much brilliancy of intellect, or fertility of resource, as persistency of effort, constancy of purpose, that makes a great man. Those who succeed in life are the men and women who keep everlastingly at it, who do not believe themselves geniuses, but who know that if they ever accomplish anything they must do it by determined and persistent industry.

Audubon after years of forest life had two hundred of his priceless drawings destroyed by mice.

"A poignant flame," he relates, "pierced my brain like an arrow of fire, and for several weeks I was prostrated with fever. At length physical and moral strength awoke within me. Again I took my gun, my game-bag, my portfolio, and my pencils, and plunged once more into the depths of the forests."

All are familiar with the misfortune of Carlyle while writing his "History of the French Revolution." After the first volume was ready for the press, he loaned the manuscript to a neighbor, who left it lying on the floor, and the servant girl took it to kindle the fire. It was a bitter disappointment, but Carlyle was not the man to give up. After many months of poring over hundreds of volumes of authorities and scores of manuscripts, he reproduced that which had burned in a few minutes.

Proceed, and Light Will Dawn
The slightest acquaintance with literary history would bring to light a multitude of heroes of poverty or misfortune, of men and women perplexed

and disheartened, who have yet aroused themselves to new effort at every new obstacle.

It is related by Arago that he found under the cover of a text book he was binding a short note from D'Alembert to a student:

"Go on, sir, go on. The difficulties you meet with will resolve themselves as you advance. Proceed; and light will dawn, and shine with increasing clearness on your path."

"That maxim," said Arago, "was my greatest master in mathematics."

Had Balzac been easily discouraged he would have hesitated at the words of warning given by his father:

"Do you know that in literature a man must be either a king or a beggar?"

"Very well," was the reply, "*I will be a king.*"

His parents left him to his fate in a garret. For ten years he fought terrible battles with hardship and poverty, but won a great victory at last. He won it after producing forty novels that did not win.

Zola's early manhood witnessed a bitter struggle against poverty and deprivation. Until twenty he was a spoiled child; but, on his father's death, he and his mother began the battle of life in Paris. Of his dark time, Zola himself says:

"Often I went hungry for so long, that it seemed as if I must die. I scarcely tasted meat from one month's end to another, and for two days I lived on three apples. Fire, even on the coldest nights, was an undreamed-of luxury; and I was the happiest man in Paris when I could get a candle, by the light of which I might study at night."

Samuel Johnson's bare feet at Oxford showed through the holes in his shoes, yet he threw out at his window the new pair that some one left at his door. He lived for a time in London on nine cents a day. For thirteen years he had a hard struggle with want. John Locke once lived on bread and water in a Dutch garret, and Heyne slept many a night on a barn floor with only a book for his pillow. It was to poverty as a thorn urging the breast of Harriet Martineau that we owe her writings.

There are no more interesting pages in biography than those which record how Emerson, as a child, was unable to read the second volume of a certain book, because his widowed mother could not afford the amount (five cents) necessary to obtain it from the circulating library.

"Poor fellow!" said Emerson, as he looked at his delicately-reared little son, "how much he loses by not having to go through the hard experiences I had in my youth."

It was through the necessity laid upon him to earn that Emerson made his first great success in life as a teacher. "I know," he said, "no such unquestionable badge and ensign of a sovereign mind as that tenacity of purpose, which, through all change of companions or parties or fortunes, changes never, bates no jot of heart or hope, but wearies out opposition and arrives at its port.

"She Can Never Succeed"

Louisa Alcott earned two hundred thousand dollars by her pen. Yet, when she was first dreaming of her power, her father handed her a manuscript one day that had been rejected by Mr. Fields, editor of the "Atlantic," with the message:

"Tell Louisa to stick to her teaching; she can never succeed as a writer."

"Tell him I *will* succeed as a writer, and some day I shall write for the 'Atlantic.'"

Not long after she wrote for the "Atlantic" a poem that Longfellow attributed to Emerson. And there came a time when she wrote in her diary:

"Twenty years ago I resolved to make the family independent if I could. At forty, that is done. Debts all paid, even the outlawed ones, and we have enough to be comfortable. It has cost me my health, perhaps."

"I Trample on Impossibilities":

So it was said by Lord Chatham. "Why," asked Mirabeau, "should we call ourselves men, unless it be to succeed in everything everywhere?"

"It is all very well," said Charles J. Fox, "to tell me that a young man has distinguished himself by a brilliant first speech. He may go on satisfied with his first triumph; but show me a young man who has not succeeded at first, and has then gone on, and I will back that man to do better than those who succeeded at the first trial." Cobden broke down completely the first time he appeared on a platform in Manchester, and the chairman apologized for him; but he did not give up speaking until every poor man in England had a larger, better, and cheaper loaf. Young Disraeli sprung from a hated and persecuted race, pushed his way up through the middle classes and upper classes, until he stood self-poised upon the topmost round of political and social power. At first he was scoffed at, ridiculed, rebuffed, hissed from the House of Commons; he simply said, "The time will come when you will hear me." The time did come, and he swayed the sceptre of England for a quarter of a century.

How massive was the incalculable reserve power of Lincoln as a youth; or of President Garfield, wood-chopper, bell-ringer, and sweeper-general in college!

Persistent Purpose

We hear a great deal of talk about genius, talent, luck, chance, cleverness, and fine manners playing a large part in one's success. Leaving out luck and chance, all these elements are important factors. Yet the possession of any or all of them, unaccompanied by a definite aim, a determined purpose, will not insure success. Men drift into business. They drift into society. They drift into politics. They drift into what they fondly and but vainly imagine is religion. If winds and tides are favorable, all is well; if not, all is wrong. Stalker says: "Most men merely drift through life, and the work they do is determined by a hundred different circumstances; they might as well be doing anything else, or they would prefer to be doing nothing at all." Yet whatever else may have been lacking in the giants of the race, the men who have been conspicuously successful have all had one characteristic in common—doggedness and persistence of purpose.

It does not matter how clever a youth may be, whether he leads his class in college or outshines all the other boys in his community, he will never succeed if he lacks this essential of determined persistence. Many men who might have made brilliant musicians, artists, teachers, lawyers, able physicians or surgeons, in spite of predictions to the contrary, have fallen short of success because deficient in this quality.

Persistency of purpose is a power. It creates confidence in others. Everybody believes in the determined man. When he undertakes anything his battle is half won, because not only he himself, but every one who knows him, believes that he will accomplish whatever he sets out to do. People know that it is useless to oppose a man who uses his stumbling-blocks as stepping-stones; who is not afraid of defeat; who never, in spite of calumny or criticism, shrinks from his task; who never shirks responsibility; who always keeps his compass pointed to the north star of his purpose, no matter what storms may rage about him.

The persistent man never stops to consider whether he is succeeding or not. The only question with him is how to push ahead, to get a little farther along, a little nearer his goal. Whether it lead over mountains, rivers, or morasses, he must reach it. Every other consideration is sacrificed to this one dominant purpose.

The success of a dull or average youth and the failure of a brilliant one is a constant surprise in American history. But if the different cases are closely analyzed we shall find that the explanation lies in the staying power of the seemingly dull boy, the ability to stand firm as a rock under all circumstances, to allow nothing to divert him from his purpose.

Three Necessary Things

"Three things are necessary," said Charles Sumner, "first, backbone; second, backbone; third, backbone."

A good chance alone is nothing. Education is nothing without strong and vigorous resolution and stamina to make one accomplish something in the world. An encouraging start is nothing without backbone. A man who cannot stand erect, who wabbles first one way and then the other, who has no opinion of his own, or courage to think his own thought, is of very little use in this world. It is grit, it is perseverance, it is moral stamina and courage that govern the world.

At the trial of the seven bishops of the Church of England for refusing to aid the king to overthrow the Protestant faith, it was necessary to watch the officers at the doors, lest they send food to some juryman, and aid him to starve the others into an agreement. Nothing was allowed to be sent in but water for the jurymen to wash in, and they were so thirsty they drank it up. At first nine were for acquitting, and three for convicting. Two of the minority soon gave way; the third, Arnold, was obstinate. He declined to argue. Austin said to him, "Look at me. I am the largest and the strongest of the twelve; and before I will find such a petition as this libel, here will I stay till I am no bigger than a tobacco pipe." Arnold yielded at six in the morning.

Success Against Odds

Yes, to this thought I hold with firm persistence;
The last result of wisdom stamps it true:
He only earns his freedom and existence
Who daily conquers them anew. —Goethe

"It is interesting to notice how some minds seem almost to create themselves," says Irving, "springing up under every disadvantage, and working their solitary but irresistible way through a thousand obstacles." Opposing circumstances create strength. Opposition gives us greater power of resistance. To overcome one barrier gives us greater ability to overcome the next. History is full of examples of men and women who have redeemed themselves from disgrace, poverty, and misfortune, by the firm resolution of an iron will.

Success is not measured by what a man accomplishes, but by the opposition he has encountered, and the courage with which he has maintained the struggle against overwhelming odds. Not the distance we have run, but the obstacles we have overcome, the disadvantages under which we have made the race, will decide the prizes.

"It is defeat," says Henry Ward Beecher, "that turns bone to flint, and gristle to muscle, and makes men invincible, and formed those heroic natures that are now in ascendency in the world. Do not, then, be afraid of defeat. You are never so near to victory as when defeated in a good cause."

Governor Seymour of New York, a man of great force and character, said, in reviewing his life: "If I were to wipe out twenty acts, what should they be? Should it be my business mistakes, my foolish acts (for I suppose all do foolish acts occasionally), my grievances? No; for, after all, these are the very things by which I have profited. So I finally concluded I should expunge, instead of my mistakes, my triumphs. I could not afford to dismiss the tonic of mortification, the refinement of sorrow; I needed them every one."

"Every condition, be it what it may," says Channing, "has hardships, hazards, pains. We try to escape them; we pine for a sheltered lot, for a smooth path, for cheering friends, and unbroken success. But Providence ordains storms, disasters, hostilities, sufferings; and the great question whether we shall live to any purpose or not, whether we shall grow strong in mind and heart, or be weak and pitiable, depends on nothing so much as on our use of the adverse circumstances. Outward evils are designed to school our passions, and to rouse our faculties and virtues into intenser action. Sometimes they seem to create new powers. Difficulty is the element, and resistance the true work of man. Self-culture never goes on so fast as when embarrassed circumstances, the opposition of men or the elements, unexpected changes of the times, or other forms of suffering, instead of disheartening, throw us on our inward resources, turn us for strength to God, clear up to us the great purpose of life, and inspire calm resolution. No greatness or goodness is worth much, unless tried in these fires."

> Better to stem with heart and hand
> The roaring tide of life, than lie,
> Unmindful, on its flowery strand,
> Of God's occasions drifting by!
> Better with naked nerve to bear
> The needles of this goading air,
> Than in the lap of sensual ease forego
> The godlike power to do, the godlike aim to know. —Whittier

The Degree of "O.O."

When Moody first visited Ireland he was introduced by a friend to an Irish merchant who asked at once:

"Is he an O.O.?"

"Out and Out"—that was what "O.O." stood for.

"Out and Out" for God—that was what this merchant meant. He indeed is but a wooden man, and a poor stick at that, who is decided in everything else, but who never knows "where he is at" in all moral relations, being religiously nowhere.

The early books of the Hebrews have much to say about "The Valley of Decision" and the development of "Out and Out" moral character.

Wofully lacking in a well-balanced will power is the man who stands side by side with moral evil personified, in hands with it, to serve it willingly as a tool and servant.

Morally made in God's image, what is more sane, more wholesome, more fitting, for a man than his rising up promptly, decidedly, to make the Divine Will his own will in all moral action, to take it as the supreme guide to go by? It is the glory of the human will to coincide with the Divine Will. Doing this, a man's Iron Will, instead of being a malignant selfish power, will be useful in uplifting mankind.

God has spoken, or he has not spoken. If he has spoken, the wise will hear.

We search the world for truth; we cull
The good, the pure, the beautiful,
From graven stone and written scroll,
From all the flower-fields of the soul:
And, weary seekers of the best,
We come back laden from our quest,
To find that all the sages said
Is in the *Book* our mother read. —Whittier
O earth that blooms and birds that sing,
O stars that shine when all is dark!
In type and symbol thou dost bring
The Life Divine, and bid us hark,
That we may catch the chant sublime,
And, rising, pass the bounds of time;
So shall we win the goal divine,
Our immortality. —Carrol Norton

Cheerfulness as a Life Power

Table of Contents.

Foreword

The soul-consuming and friction-wearing tendency of this hurrying, grasping, competing age is the excuse for this booklet. Is it not an absolute necessity to get rid of all irritants, of everything which worries and frets, and which brings discord into so many lives? Cheerfulness has a wonderful lubricating power. It lengthens the life of human machinery, as lubricants lengthen the life of inert machinery. Life's delicate bearings should not be carelessly ground away for mere lack of oil. What is needed is a habit of cheerfulness, to enjoy every day as we go along; not to fret and stew all the week, and then expect to make up for it Sunday or on some holiday. It is not a question of mirth so much as of cheerfulness; not alone that which accompanies laughter, but serenity,—a calm, sweet soul-contentment and inward peace. Are there not multitudes of people who have the "blues," who yet wish well to their neighbors? They would say kind words and make the world happier—but they "haven't the time." To lead them to look on the sunny side of things, and to take a little time every day to speak pleasant words, is the message of the hour.

The Author

In the preparation of these pages, amid the daily demands of journalistic work, the author has been assisted by Mr. E. P. Tenney, of Cambridge.

What Vanderbilt Paid for Twelve Laughs

William K. Vanderbilt, when he last visited Constantinople, one day invited Coquelin the elder, so celebrated for his powers as a mimic, who happened to be in the city at the time, to give a private recital on board his yacht, lying in the Bosphorus. Coquelin spoke three of his monologues. A few days afterwards Coquelin received the following memorandum from the millionaire:—

"You have brought tears to our eyes and laughter to our hearts. Since all philosophers are agreed that laughing is preferable to weeping, your account with me stands thus:—

"For tears, six times . . . $600 "For laughter, twelve times . . 2,400 ———— $3,000

"Kindly acknowledge receipt of enclosed check."

"I find nonsense singularly refreshing," said Talleyrand. There is good philosophy in the saying, "Laugh and grow fat." If everybody knew the power of laughter as a health tonic and life prolonger the tinge of sadness which now clouds the American face would largely disappear, and many physicians would find their occupation gone.

The power of laughter was given us to serve a wise purpose in our economy. It is Nature's device for exercising the internal organs and giving us pleasure at the same time.

Laughter begins in the lungs and diaphragm, setting the liver, stomach, and other internal organs into a quick, jelly-like vibration, which gives a pleasant sensation and exercise, almost equal to that of horseback riding. During digestion, the movements of the stomach are similar to churning. Every time you take a full breath, or when you cachinnate well, the diaphragm descends and gives the stomach an extra squeeze and shakes it. Frequent laughing sets the stomach to dancing, hurrying up the digestive process. The heart beats faster, and sends the blood bounding through the body. "There is not," says Dr. Green, "one remotest corner or little inlet of the minute blood-vessels of the human body that does not feel some wavelet from the convulsions occasioned by a good hearty laugh." In medical terms, it stimulates the vasomotor centers, and the spasmodic contraction of the blood-vessels causes the blood to flow quickly. Laughter accelerates the respiration, and gives warmth and glow to the whole system. It brightens the eye, increases the perspiration, expands the chest, forces the poisoned air from the least-used lung cells, and tends to restore that exquisite poise or balance which we call health, which results from the harmonious action of all the functions of the body. This delicate poise, which may be destroyed by a sleepless night, a piece of bad news, by grief or anxiety, is often wholly restored by a good hearty laugh.

There is, therefore, sound sense in the caption,—"Cheerfulness as a Life Power,"—relating as it does to the physical life, as well as the mental and moral; and what we may call

The Laugh Cure

is based upon principles recognized as sound by the medical profession—so literally true is the Hebrew proverb that "a merry heart doeth good like a medicine."

"Mirth is God's medicine," said Dr. Oliver Wendell Holmes; "everybody ought to bathe in it. Grim care, moroseness, anxiety,—all the rust of life,—ought to be scoured off by the oil of mirth." Elsewhere he says: "If you are making choice of a physician be sure you get one with a cheerful and serene countenance."

Is not a jolly physician of greater service than his pills? Dr. Marshall Hall frequently prescribed "cheerfulness" for his patients, saying that it is better than anything to be obtained at the apothecary's.

In Western New York, Dr. Burdick was known as the "Laughing Doctor." He always presented the happiest kind of a face; and his good humor was contagious. He dealt sparingly in drugs, yet was very successful.

The London "Lancet," the most eminent medical journal in the world, gives the following scientific testimony to the value of joviality:—

"This power of 'good spirits' is a matter of high moment to the sick and weakly. To the former, it may mean the ability to survive; to the latter, the possibility of outliving, or living in spite of, a disease. It is, therefore, of the greatest importance to cultivate the highest and most buoyant frame of mind which the conditions will admit. The same energy which takes the form of mental activity is vital to the work of the organism. Mental influences affect the system; and a joyous spirit not only relieves pain, but increases the momentum of life in the body."

Dr. Ray, superintendent of Butler Hospital for the Insane, says in one of his reports, "A hearty laugh is more desirable for mental health than any exercise of the reasoning faculties."

Grief, anxiety, and fear are great enemies of human life. A depressed, sour, melancholy soul, a life which has ceased to believe in its own sacredness, its own power, its own mission, a life which sinks into querulous egotism or vegetating aimlessness, has become crippled and useless. We should fight against every influence which tends to depress the mind, as we would against a temptation to crime. It is undoubtedly true that, as a rule, the mind has power to lengthen the period of youthful and mature strength and beauty, preserving and renewing physical life by a stalwart mental health.

I read the other day of a man in a neighboring city who was given up to die; his relatives were sent for, and they watched at his bedside. But an old acquaintance, who called to see him, assured him smilingly that he was all right and would soon be well. He talked in such a strain that the sick man was forced to laugh; and the effort so roused his system that he rallied, and he was soon well again.

Was it not Shakespere who said that a light heart lives long?

The San Francisco "Argonaut" says that a woman in Milpites, a victim of almost crushing sorrow, despondency, indigestion, insomnia, and kindred ills, determined to throw off the gloom which was making life so heavy a burden to her, and established a rule that she would laugh at least three times a day, whether occasion was presented or not; so she trained herself to laugh heartily at the least provocation, and would retire to her room and make merry by herself. She was soon in excellent health and buoyant spirits; her home became a sunny, cheerful abode.

It was said, by one who knew this woman well, and who wrote an account of the case for a popular magazine, that at first her husband and children were amused at her, and while they respected her determination because of the griefs she bore, they did not enter into the spirit of the plan. "But after awhile," said this woman to me, with a smile, only yesterday, "the funny part of the idea struck my husband, and he began to laugh every time we spoke of it. And when he came home, he would ask me if I had had my 'regular laughs;' and he would laugh when he asked the question, and again when I answered it. My children, then very young, thought 'mamma's notion very queer,' but they laughed at it just the same. Gradually, my children told other children, and they told their parents. My husband spoke of it to our friends, and I rarely met one of them but he or she would laugh and ask me, 'How many of your laughs have you had to-day?' Naturally, they laughed when they asked, and of course that set me laughing. When I formed this apparently strange habit I was weighed down with sorrow, and my rule simply lifted me out of it. I had suffered the most acute indigestion; for years I have not known what it is. Headaches were a daily dread; for over six years I have not had a single pain in the head. My home seems different to me, and I feel a thousand times more interest in its work. My husband is a changed man. My children are called 'the girls who are always laughing,' and, altogether, my rule has proved an inspiration which has worked wonders."

The queen of fashion, however, says that we must never laugh out loud; but since the same tyrannical mistress kills people by corsets, indulges in cosmetics, and is out all night at dancing parties, and in China pinches up the women's feet, I place much less confidence in her views upon the laugh cure for human woes. Yet in all civilized countries it is a fundamental principle of refined manners not to be ill-timed and unreasonably noisy and boisterous in mirth. One who is wise will never violate the proprieties of well-bred people.

"Yet," says a wholesome writer upon health, "we should do something more than to simply cultivate a cheerful, hopeful spirit,—we should cultivate a spirit of mirthfulness that is not only easily pleased and smiling, but that indulges in hearty, hilarious laughter; and if this faculty is not well marked in our organization we should cultivate it, being well assured that hearty, body-shaking laughter will do us good."

Ordinary good looks depend on one's sense of humor,—"a merry heart maketh a cheerful countenance." Joyfulness keeps the heart and face young. A good laugh makes us better friends with ourselves and everybody around us, and puts us into closer touch with what is best and brightest in our lot in life.

Physiology tells the story. The great sympathetic nerves are closely allied; and when one set carries bad news to the head, the nerves reaching the stomach are affected, indigestion comes on, and one's countenance becomes doleful. Laugh when you can; it is

A Cheap Medicine

Merriment is a philosophy not well understood. The eminent surgeon Chavasse says that we ought to begin with the babies and train children to habits of mirth:—

"Encourage your child to be merry and laugh aloud; a good hearty laugh expands the chest and makes the blood bound merrily along. Commend me to a good laugh,—not to a little snickering laugh, but to one that will sound right through the house. It will not only do your child good, but will be a benefit to all who hear, and be an important means of driving the blues away from a dwelling. Merriment is very catching, and spreads in a remarkable manner, few being able to resist its contagion. A hearty laugh is delightful harmony; indeed, it is the best of all music." "Children without hilarity," says an eminent author, "will never amount to much. Trees without blossoms will never bear fruit."

Hufeland, physician to the King of Prussia, commends the ancient custom of jesters at the king's table, whose quips and cranks would keep the company in a roar.

Did not Lycurgus set up the god of laughter in the Spartan eating-halls? There is no table sauce like laughter at meals. It is the great enemy of dyspepsia.

How wise are the words of the acute Chamfort, that the most completely lost of all days is the one in which we have not laughed!

"A crown, for making the king laugh," was one of the items of expense which the historian Hume found in a manuscript of King Edward II.

"It is a good thing to laugh, at any rate," said Dryden, the poet, "and if a straw can tickle a man, it is an instrument of happiness."

"I live," said Laurence Sterne, one of the greatest of English humorists, "in a constant endeavor to fence against the infirmities of ill health and other evils by mirth; I am persuaded that, every time a man smiles,—but much more so when he laughs,—it adds something to his fragment of life."

"Give me an honest laugher," said Sir Walter Scott, and he was himself one of the happiest men in the world, with a kind word and pleasant smile for every one, and everybody loved him.

"How much lies in laughter!" exclaimed the critic Carlyle. "It is the cipher-key wherewith we decipher the whole man. Some men wear an everlasting barren simper; in the smile of others lies the cold glitter, as of ice; the fewest are able to laugh what can be called laughing, but only sniff and titter and snicker from the throat outward, or at least produce some whiffing, husky cachinnation, as if they were laughing through wool. Of none such comes good."

"The power to laugh, to cease work and begin to frolic and make merry in forgetfulness of all the conflict of life," says Campbell Morgan, "is a divine bestowment upon man."

Happy, then, is the man, who may well laugh to himself over his good luck, who can answer the old question, "How old are you?" by Sambo's reply:—

"If you reckon by the years, sah, I'se twenty-five; but if you goes by the fun I's 'ad, I guess I's a hundred."

Why Don't You Laugh?
From the "Independent"

"Why don't you laugh, young man, when troubles come, Instead of sitting 'round so sour and glum? You cannot have all play, And sunshine every day; When troubles come, I say, why don't you laugh?

"Why don't you laugh? 'T will ever help to soothe The aches and pains. No road in life is smooth; There's many an unseen bump, And many a hidden stump O'er which you'll have to jump. Why don't you laugh?

"Why don't you laugh? Don't let your spirits wilt; Don't sit and cry because the milk you've spilt; If you would mend it now, Pray let me tell you how: Just milk another cow! Why don't you laugh?

"Why don't you laugh, and make us all laugh, too, And keep us mortals all from getting blue? A laugh will always win; If you can't laugh, just grin,— Come on, let's all join in! Why don't you laugh?"

The Cure for Americanitis

Prince Wolkonsky, during a visit to this country, declared that "Business is the alpha and omega of American life. There is no pleasure, no joy, no satisfaction. There is no standard except that of profit. There is no other country where they speak of a man as worth so many dollars. In other countries they live to enjoy life; here they exist for business." A Boston merchant corroborated this statement by saying he was anxious all day about making money, and worried all night for fear he should lose what he had made.

"In the United States," a distinguished traveler once said, "there is everywhere comfort, but no joy. The ambition of getting more and fretting over what is lost absorb life."

"Every man we meet looks as if he'd gone out to borrow trouble, with plenty of it on hand," said a French lady, upon arriving in New York.

"The Americans are the best-fed, the best-clad, and the best-housed people in the world," says another witness, "but they are the most anxious; they hug possible calamity to their breasts."

"I question if care and doubt ever wrote their names so legibly on the faces of any other population," says Emerson; "old age begins in the nursery."

How quickly we Americans exhaust life! With what panting haste we pursue everything! Every man you meet seems to be late for an appointment. Hurry is stamped in the wrinkles of the national face. We are men of action; we go faster and faster as the years go by, speeding our machinery to the utmost. Bent forms, prematurely gray hair, restlessness and discontent, are characteristic of our age and people. We earn our bread, but cannot digest it; and our over-stimulated nerves soon become irritated, and touchiness follows,—so fatal to a business man, and so annoying in society.

"It is not work that kills men," says Beecher; "it is worry. Work is healthy; you can hardly put more on a man than he can bear. But worry is rust upon the blade. It is not movement that destroys the machinery, but friction."

It is not so much the great sorrows, the great burdens, the great hardships, the great calamities, that cloud over the sunshine of life, as the little petty vexations, insignificant anxieties and fear, the little daily dyings, which render our lives unhappy, and destroy our mental elasticity, without advancing our life-work one inch. "Anxiety never yet bridged any chasm."

"What," asks Dr. George W. Jacoby, in an "Evening Post" interview, "is the ultimate physical effect of worry? Why, the same as that of a fatal bullet-wound or sword-thrust. Worry kills as surely, though not so quickly, as ever gun or dagger did, and more people have died in the last century from sheer worry than have been killed in battle."

Dr. Jacoby is one of the foremost of American brain doctors. "The investigations of the neurologists," he says, "have laid bare no secret of Nature in recent years more startling and interesting than the discovery that worry kills." This is the final, up-to-date word. "Not only is it known," resumes the great neurologist, counting off his words, as it were, on his finger-tips, "that worry kills, but the most minute details of its murderous methods are familiar to modern scientists. It is a common belief of those who have made a special study of the science of brain diseases that hundreds of deaths attributed to other causes each year are due simply to worry. In plain, untechnical language, worry works its irreparable injury through certain cells of the brain life. The insidious inroads upon the system can be best likened to the constant falling of drops of water in one spot. In the brain it is the insistent, never-lost idea, the single, constant thought, centered upon one subject, which in the course of time destroys the brain cells. The healthy brain can cope with occasional worry; it is the iteration and reiteration of disquieting thoughts which the cells of the brain cannot successfully combat.

"The mechanical effect of worry is much the same as if the skull were laid bare and the brain exposed to the action of a little hammer beating continually upon it day after day, until the membranes are disintegrated and the normal functions disabled. The maddening thought that will not be downed, the haunting, ever-present idea that is not or cannot be banished by a supreme effort of the will, is the theoretical hammer which diminishes the vitality of the sensitive nerve organisms, the minuteness of which makes them visible to the eye only under a powerful microscope. The 'worry,' the thought, the single idea grows upon one as time goes on, until the worry victim cannot throw it off. Through this, one set or area of cells is affected. The cells are intimately connected, joined together by little fibres, and they in turn are in close relationship with the cells of the other parts of the brain.

"Worry is itself a species of monomania. No mental attitude is more disastrous to personal achievement, personal happiness, and personal usefulness in the world, than worry and its twin brother, despondency. The remedy for the evil lies in training the will to cast off cares and seek a change of occupation, when the first warning is sounded by Nature in intellectual lassitude. Relaxation is the certain foe of worry, and 'don't fret' one of the healthiest of maxims."

In a life of constant worrying, we are as much behind the times as if we were to go back to use the first steam engines that wasted ninety per cent. of the energy of the coal, instead of having an electric dynamo that utilizes ninety per cent. of the power. Some people waste a large percentage of their energy in fretting and stewing, in useless anxiety, in scolding, in complaining about the weather and the perversity of inanimate things. Others convert nearly all of their energy into power and moral sunshine. He who has learned the true art of living will not waste his energies in friction, which accomplishes nothing, but merely grinds out the machinery of life.

It must be relegated to the debating societies to determine which is the worse—A Nervous Man or

A Worrying Woman

"I'm awfully worried this morning," said one woman. "What is it?" "Why, I thought of something to worry about last night, and now I can't remember it."

A famous actress once said: "Worry is the foe of all beauty." She might have added: "It is the foe to all health."

"It seems so heartless in me, if I do not worry about my children," said one mother.

Women nurse their troubles, as they do their babies. "Troubles grow larger," said Lady Holland, "by nursing."

The White Knight who carried about a mousetrap, lest he be troubled with mice upon his journeys, was not unlike those who anticipate their burdens.

"He grieves," says Seneca, "more than is necessary, who grieves before it is necessary."

"My children," said a dying man, "during my long life I have had a great many troubles, most of which never happened." A prominent business man in Philadelphia said that his father worried for twenty-five years over an anticipated misfortune which never arrived.

We try to grasp too much of life at once; since we think of it as a whole, instead of living one day at a time. Life is a mosaic, and each tiny piece must be cut and set with skill, first one piece, then another.

A clock would be of no use as a time-keeper if it should become discouraged and come to a standstill by calculating its work a year ahead, as the clock did in Jane Taylor's fable. It is not the troubles of to-day, but those of to-morrow and next week and next year, that whiten our heads, wrinkle our faces, and bring us to a standstill.

"There is such a thing," said Uncle Eben, "as too much foresight. People get to figuring what might happen year after next, and let the fire go out and catch their death of cold, right where they are."

Nervous prostration is seldom the result of present trouble or work, but of work and trouble anticipated. Mental exhaustion comes to those who look ahead, and climb mountains before reaching them. Resolutely build a wall about to-day, and live within the inclosure. The past may have been hard, sad, or wrong,—but it is over.

Why not take a turn about? Instead of worrying over unforeseen misfortune, set out with all your soul to rejoice in the unforeseen blessings of all your coming days. "I find the gayest castles in the air that were ever piled," says Emerson, "far better for comfort and for use than the dungeons in the air that are daily dug and caverned out by grumbling, discontented people."

What is this world but as you take it? Thackeray calls the world a looking-glass that gives back the reflection of one's own face. "Frown at it, and it will look sourly upon you; laugh at it, and it is a jolly companion."

"There is no use in talking," said a woman. "Every time I move, I vow I'll never move again. Such neighbors as I get in with! Seems as though they grow worse and worse." "Indeed?" replied her caller; "perhaps you take the worst neighbor with you when you move."

"In the sudden thunder-storm of Independence Day," says a news correspondent, "we were struck by the contrast between two women, each of whom had had some trying experience with the weather. One came through the rain and hail to take refuge at the railway station, under the swaying and uncertain shelter of an escorting man's umbrella. Her skirts were soaked to the knees, her pink ribbons were limp, the purple of the flowers on her hat ran in streaks down the white silk. And yet, though she was a poor girl and her holiday finery must have been relatively costly, she made the best of it with a smile and cheerful words. The other was well sheltered; but she took the disappointment of her hopes and the possibility of a little spattering from a leaky window with frowns and fault-finding."

"Cries little Miss Fret, In a very great pet: 'I hate this warm weather; it's horrid to tan! It scorches my nose, And it blisters my toes, And wherever I go I must carry a fan.'

"Chirps little Miss Laugh: 'Why, I couldn't tell half The fun I am having this bright summer day! I sing through the hours, I cull pretty flowers, And ride like a queen on the sweet-smelling hay.'"

Happily a new era has of late opened for our worried housekeepers, who spend their time in "the half-frantic dusting of corners, spasmodic sweeping, impatient snatching or pushing aside obstacles in the room, hurrying and skurrying upstairs and down cellar." "It is not," says Prentice Mulford, "the work that exhausts them,—it is the mental condition they are in that makes so many old and haggard at forty." All that is needful now to ease up their burdens is to go to

Our Hawaiian Paradise

A newspaper correspondent, Annie Laurie, has told us all about the new kind of American girls just added to our country:—

"They are as straight as an arrow, and walk as queens walk in fairy stories; they have great braids of sleek, black hair, soft brown eyes, and gleaming white teeth; they can swim and ride and sing; and they are brown with a skin that shines like bronze ... There isn't a worried woman in Hawaii. The women there can't worry. They don't know how. They eat and sing and laugh, and see the sun and the moon set, and possess their souls in smiling peace.

"If a Hawaii woman has a good dinner, she laughs and invites her friends to eat it with her; if she hasn't a good dinner, she laughs and goes to sleep,—and forgets to be hungry. She doesn't have to worry about what the people in the downstairs flat will think if they don't see the butcher's boy arrive on time. If she can earn the money, she buys a nice, new, glorified Mother Hubbard; and, if she can't get it, she throws the old one into the surf and washes it out, puts a new wreath of fresh flowers in her hair, and starts out to enjoy the morning and the breezes thereof.

"They are not earnest workers; they haven't the slightest idea that they were put upon earth to reform the universe,—they're just happy. They run across great stretches of clear, white sand, washed with resplendent purple waves, and, when the little brown babies roll in the surf, their brown mothers run after them, laughing and splashing like a lot of children. Or, perhaps we see them in gay cavalcades mounted upon garlanded ponies, adorned by white jasmine wreaths with roses and pinks. And here in this paradise of laughter and light hearts and gentle music, there's absolutely nothing to do but to care for the children and old people and to swim or ride. You couldn't start a 'reform circle' to save your life; there isn't a jail in the place, nor a tenement quarter, and there are no outdoor poor. There isn't a woman's club in Honolulu,—not a club. There was a culture circle once for a few days; a Boston woman who went there for her health organized it, but it interfered with afternoon nap-time, so nobody came."

When, hereafter, we talk about worrying women, we must take into account our Hawaiian sisters, if we will average up the amount of worry *per capita*, in our nation.

A Weather Breeder

It is probably quite within bounds to say that one out of three of our American farming population, women and men, never enjoy a beautiful day without first reminding you that "It is one of those infernal weather breeders."

Habitual fretters see more trouble than others. They are never so well as their neighbors. The weather never suits them. The climate is trying. The winds are too high or too low; it is too hot or too cold, too damp or too dry. The roads are either muddy or dusty.

"I met Mr. N. one wet morning," says Dr. John Todd; "and, bound as I was to make the best of it, I ventured:

"'Good morning. This rain will be fine for your grass crop.'

"'Yes, perhaps,' he replied, 'but it is very bad for corn; I don't think we'll have half a crop.'

"A few days later, I met him again. 'This is a fine sun for corn, Mr. N.'

"'Yes,' said he, 'but it's awful for rye; rye wants cold weather.'

"One cool morning soon after, I said: 'This is a capital day for rye.'

"'Yes,' he said, 'but it is the worst kind of weather for corn and grass; they want heat to bring them forward.'"

There are a vast number of fidgety, nervous, and eccentric people who live only to expect new disappointments or to recount their old ones.

"Impatient people," said Spurgeon, "water their miseries, and hoe up their comforts."

"Let's see," said a neighbor to a farmer, whose wagon was loaded down with potatoes, "weren't we talking together last August?" "I believe so." "At that time, you said corn was all burnt up." "Yes." "And potatoes were baking in the ground." "Yes." "And that your district could not possibly expect more than half a crop." "I remember." "Well, here you are with your wagon loaded down. Things didn't turn out so badly, after all,—eh?" "Well, no-o," said the farmer, as he raked his fingers through his hair, "but I tell you my geese suffered awfully for want of a mud-hole to paddle in."

What is a pessimist but "a man who looks on the sun only as a thing that casts a shadow"?

In Pepys's "Diary" we learn the difference between "eyes shut and ears open," and "ears shut and eyes open." In going from John o' Groat's House to Land's End, a blind man would hear that the country was going to destruction, but a deaf man with eyes open could see great prosperity.

"I dare no more fret than curse or swear," said John Wesley.

"A discontented mortal is no more a man than discord is music."

"Why should a man whose blood is warm within Sit like his grandsire cut in alabaster? Sleep when he wakes? and creep into the jaundice By being peevish?"

Who are the "lemon squeezers of society"? They are people who predict evil, extinguish hope, and see only the worst side,—"people whose very look curdles the milk and sets your teeth on edge." They are often worthy people who think that pleasure is wrong; people, said an old divine, who lead us heavenward and stick pins into us all the way. They say depressing things and do disheartening things; they chill prayer-meetings, discourage charitable institutions, injure commerce, and kill churches; they are blowing out lights when they ought to be kindling them.

A man without mirth is like a wagon without springs, in which one jolts over every pebble; with mirth, he is like a chariot with springs, riding over the roughest roads and scarcely feeling anything but a pleasant rocking motion.

"Difficulties melt away before the man who carries about a cheerful spirit and persistently refuses to be discouraged, while they accumulate before the one who is always groaning over his hard luck and scanning the horizon for clouds not yet in sight."

"To one man," says Schopenhauer, "the world is barren, dull, and superficial; to another, rich, interesting, and full of meaning." If one loves beauty and looks for it, he will see it wherever he goes. If there is music in his soul, he will hear it everywhere; every object in nature will sing to him. Two men who live in the same house and do the same work may not live in the same world. Although they are under the same roof, one may see only deformity and ugliness; to him the world is out of joint, everything is cross-grained and out of sorts: the other is surrounded with beauty and harmony; everybody is kind to him; nobody wishes him harm. These men see the same objects, but they do not look through the same glasses; one looks through a smoked glass which drapes the whole world in mourning, the other looks through rose-colored lenses which tint everything with loveliness and touch it with beauty.

Take two persons just home from a vacation. "One has positively seen nothing, and has always been robbed; the landlady was a harpy, the bedroom was unhealthy, and the mutton was tough. The other has always found the coziest nooks, the cheapest houses, the best landladies, the finest views, and the best dinners."

"What Is an Optimist?"
This is the question a farmer's boy asked of his father.

"Well, John," replied his father, "you know I can't give ye the dictionary meanin' of that word any more 'n I can of a great many others. But I've got a kind of an idee what it means. Probably you don't remember your Uncle Henry; but I guess if there ever was an optimist, he was one. Things was always comin' out right with Henry, and especially anything hard that he had to do; it wa' n't a-goin' to be hard,—'t was jest kind of solid-pleasant.

"Take hoein' corn, now. If anything ever tuckered me out, 'twas hoein' corn in the hot sun. But in the field, 'long about the time I begun to lag back a little, Henry he'd look up an' say:—

"'Good, Jim! When we get these two rows hoed, an' eighteen more, the piece'll be half done.' An' he'd say it in such a kind of a cheerful way that I couldn't 'a' ben any more tickled if the piece had been all done,—an' the rest would go light enough.

"But the worst thing we had to do—hoein corn was a picnic to it—was pickin' stones. There was no end to that on our old farm, if we wanted to raise anything. When we wa'n't hurried and pressed with somethin' else, there was always pickin' stones to do; and there wa'n't a plowin' but what brought up a fresh crop, an' seems as if the pickin' had all to be done over again.

"Well, you'd' a' thought, to hear Henry, that there wa'n't any fun in the world like pickin' stones. He looked at it in a different way from anybody I ever see. Once, when the corn was all hoed, and the grass wa'n't fit to cut yet, an' I'd got all laid out to go fishin', and father he up and set us to pickin' stones up on the west piece, an' I was about ready to cry, Henry he says:—

"'Come on, Jim. I know where there's lots of nuggets.'

"An' what do you s'pose, now? That boy had a kind of a game that that there field was what he called a plasser mining field; and he got me into it, and I could 'a' sworn I was in Californy all day,—I had such a good time.

"'Only,' says Henry, after we'd got through the day's work, 'the way you get rich with these nuggets is to get rid of 'em, instead of to get 'em.'

"That somehow didn't strike my fancy, but we'd had play instead of work, anyway, an' a great lot of stones had been rooted out of that field.

"An', as I said before, I can't give ye any dictionary definition of optimism; but if your Uncle Henry wa'n't an optimist, I don't know what one is."

At life's outset, says one, a cheerful optimistic temperament is worth everything. A cheerful man, who always "feels first-rate," who always looks on the bright side, who is ever ready to snatch victory from defeat, is the successful man.

Everybody avoids the company of those who are always grumbling, who are full of "ifs" and "buts," and "I told you so's." We like the man who always looks toward the sun, whether it shines or not. It is the cheerful, hopeful man we go to for sympathy and assistance; not the carping, gloomy critic,—who always thinks it is going to rain, and that we are going to have a terribly hot summer, or a fearful thunder-storm, or who is forever complaining of hard times and his hard lot. It is the bright, cheerful, hopeful, contented man who makes his way, who is respected and admired.

Gloom and depression not only take much out of life, but detract greatly from the chances of winning success. It is the bright and cheerful spirit that wins the final triumph.

Living up Thanksgiving Avenue

"I see our brother, who has just sat down, lives on Grumbling street," said a keen-witted Yorkshireman. "I lived there myself for some time, and never enjoyed good health. The air was bad, the house bad, the water bad; the birds never came and sang in the street; and I was gloomy and sad enough. But I 'flitted.' I got into Thanksgiving avenue; and ever since then I have had good health, and so have all my family. The air is pure, the house good; the sun shines on it all day; the birds are always singing; and I am happy as I can live. Now, I recommend our brother to 'flit.' There are plenty of houses to let on Thanksgiving avenue; and he will find himself a new man if he will only come; and I shall be right glad to have him for a neighbor."

This world was not intended for a "vale of tears," but as a sweet Vale of Content. Travelers are told by the Icelanders, who live amid the cold and desolation of almost perpetual winter, that "Iceland is the best land the sun shines upon." "In the long Arctic night, the Eskimo is blithe, and carolsome, far from the approach of the white man; while amid the glorious scenery and Eden-like climate of Central America, the native languages have a dozen words for pain and misery and sorrow, for one with any cheerful signification."

When a Persian king was directed by his wise men to wear the shirt of a contented man, the only contented man in the kingdom had no shirt. The most contented man in Boston does not live on Commonwealth avenue or do business on State street: he is poor and blind, and he peddles needles and thread, buttons and sewing-room supplies, about the streets of Boston from house to house. Dr. Minot J. Savage used to pity this man very much, and once in venturing to talk with him about his condition, he was utterly amazed to find that the man was perfectly happy. He said that he had a faithful wife, and a business by which he earned sufficient for his wants; and, if he were to complain of his lot, he should feel mean and contemptible. Surely, if there are any "solid men" in Boston, he is one.

Content is the magic lamp, which, according to the beautiful picture painted for us by Goethe, transforms the rude fisherman's hut into a palace of silver; the logs, the floors, the roof, the furniture, everything being changed and gleaming with new light.

"My crown is in my heart, not on my head;
Not decked with diamonds and Indian stones,
Nor to be seen; my crown is called content;
A crown it is that seldom kings enjoy."

Oiling Your Business Machinery

Business is king. We often say that cotton is king, or corn is king, but with greater propriety we may say that the king is that great machine which is kept in motion by the Law of Supply and Demand: the destinies of all mankind are ruled by it.

"Were the question asked," says Stearns, "what is at this moment the strongest power in operation for controlling, regulating, and inciting the actions of men, what has most at its disposal the condition and destinies of the world, we must answer at once, it is business, in its various ranks and departments; of which commerce, foreign and domestic, is the most appropriate representation. In all prosperous and advancing communities,—advancing in arts, knowledge, literature, and social refinement,—business is king. Other influences in society may be equally indispensable, and some may think far more dignified, but *Business is King*. The statesman and the scholar, the nobleman and the prince, equally with the manufacturer, the mechanic, and the laborer, pursue their several objects only by leave granted and means furnished by this potentate."

Oil is better than sand for keeping this vast machinery in good running condition. Do not shovel grit or gravel stones upon the bearings. A tiny copper shaving in a wheel box, or a scratch on a journal, may set a railway train on fire. The running of the business world is damaged by whatever creates friction.

Anxiety mars one's work. Nobody can do his best when, fevered by worry. One may rush, and always be in great haste, and may talk about being busy, fuming and sweating as if he were doing ten men's duties; and yet some quiet person alongside, who is moving leisurely and without anxious haste, is probably accomplishing twice as much, and doing it better. Fluster unfits one for good work.

Have you not sometimes seen a business manager whose stiffness would serve as "a good example to a poker?" He acts toward his employees as the father of Frederick the Great did toward his subjects, caning them on the streets, and shouting, "I wish to be loved and not feared." "Growl, Spitfire and Brothers," says Talmage, "wonder why they fail, while Messrs. Merriman and Warmheart succeed."

There is no investment a business man can make that will pay him a greater per cent, than patience and amiability. Good humor will sell the most goods.

John Wanamaker's clerks have been heard to say: "We can work better for a week after a pleasant 'Good morning' from Mr. Wanamaker."

This kindly disposition and cheerful manner, and a desire to create a pleasant feeling and diffuse good cheer among those who work for him, have had a great deal to do with the great merchant's remarkable success. On the other hand, a man who easily finds fault, and is never generous-spirited, who never commends the work of subordinates when he can do so justly, who is unwilling to brighten their hours, fails to secure the best of service. "Why not try love's way?" It will pay better, and be better.

A habit of cheerfulness, enabling one to transmute apparent misfortunes into real blessings, is a fortune to a young man or young woman just crossing the threshold of active life. There is nothing but ill fortune in a habit of grumbling, which "requires no talent, no self-denial, no brains, no character." Grumbling only makes an employee more uncomfortable, and may cause his dismissal. No one would or should wish to make him do grudgingly what so many others would be glad to do in a cheerful spirit.

If you dislike your position, complain to no one, least of all to your employer. Fill the place as it was never filled before. Crowd it to overflowing. Make yourself more competent for it. Show that you are abundantly worthy of better things. Express yourself in this manner as freely as you please, for it is the only way that will count.

No one ever found the world quite as he would like it. You will be sure to have burdens laid upon you that belong to other people, unless you are a shirk yourself; but don't grumble. If the work needs doing and you can do it, never mind about the other one who ought to have done it and didn't; do it yourself. Those workers who fill up the gaps, and smooth away the rough spots, and finish up the jobs that others leave undone,—they are the true peacemakers, and worth a regiment of grumblers.

"Oh, what a sunny, winsome face she has!" said a Christian Endeavorer, in reporting of a clerk whom he saw in a Bay City store. "The customers flocked about her like bees about a honey-bush in full bloom."

Singing at Your Work

"Give us, therefore,"—let us cry with Carlyle,—"oh, give us the man who sings at his work! He will do more in the same time, he will do it better, he will persevere longer. One is scarcely sensible of fatigue whilst he marches to music. The very stars are said to make harmony as they revolve in their spheres. Wondrous is the strength of cheerfulness, altogether past calculation its powers of endurance. Efforts, to be permanently useful, must be uniformly joyous, a spirit all sunshine, graceful from very gladness, beautiful because bright."

"It is a good sign," says another writer, "when girlish voices carol over the steaming dish-pan or the mending-basket, when the broom moves rhythmically, and the duster flourishes in time to some brisk melody. We are sure that the dishes shine more brightly, and that the sweeping and dusting and mending are more satisfactory because of this running accompaniment of song. Father smiles when he hears his girl singing about her work, and mother's tired face brightens at the sound. Brothers and sisters, without realizing it, perhaps, catch the spirit of the cheerful worker."

There are singing milkers in Switzerland; a milkmaid or man gets better wages if gifted with a good voice, for a cow will yield one-fifth more milk when soothed by a pleasing melody.

It was said by Buffon that even sheep fatten better to the sound of music. And when field-hands are singing, as you sometimes hear them in the old country, you may be sure the labor is lightened.

It is Mrs. Howitt who has told us of the musical bells of the farm teams in a rural district in England:—"It was no regular tune, but a delicious melody in that soft, sunshiny air, which was filled at the same time with the song of birds. Angela had heard all kinds of music in London, but this was unlike anything she had heard before, so soft, and sweet, and gladsome. On it came, ringing, ringing as softly as flowing water. The boys and grandfather knew what it meant. Then it came in sight,—the farm team going to the mill with sacks of corn to be ground, each horse with a little string of bells to its harness. On they came, the handsome, well-cared-for creatures, nodding their heads as they stepped along; and at every step the cheerful and cheering melody rang out.

"'Do all horses down here have bells?' asked Angela.

"'By no means,' replied her grandfather. 'They cost something; but if we can make labor easier to a horse by giving him a little music, which he loves, he is less worn by his work, and that is a saving worth thinking of. A horse is a generous, noble-spirited animal, and not without intellect, either; and he is capable of much enjoyment from music.'"

A spirit of song, if not the singing itself, is a constant delight to us. "It is like passing sweet meadows alive with bobolinks."

"Some men," says Beecher, "move through life as a band of music moves down the street, flinging out pleasures on every side, through the air, to every one far and near who can listen; others fill the air with harsh clang and clangor. Many men go through life carrying their tongue, their temper, their whole disposition so that wherever they go, others dread them. Some men fill the air with their presence and sweetness, as orchards in October days fill the air with the perfume of ripe fruit."

Good Humor

"Health and good humor," said Massillon, "are to the human body like sunshine to vegetation."

The late Charles A. Dana fairly bubbled over with the enjoyment of his work, and was, up to his last illness, at his office every day. A Cabinet officer once said to him: "Well, Mr. Dana, I don't see how you stand this infernal grind."

"Grind?" said Mr. Dana. "You never were more mistaken. I have nothing but fun."

"Bully" was a favorite word with him; a slang word used to express uncommon pleasure, such as had been afforded by a trip abroad, or by a run to Cuba or Mexico, or by the perusal of something especially pleasing in the "Sun's" columns.

"One of my neighbors is a very ill-tempered man," said Nathan Rothschild. "He tries to vex me, and has built a great place for swine close to my walk. So, when I go out, I hear first, 'Grunt, grunt,' then 'Squeak, squeak.' But this does me no harm. I am always in good humor."

Offended by a pungent article, a gentleman called at the "Tribune" office and inquired for the editor. He was shown into a little seven-by-nine sanctum, where Greeley sat, with his head close down to his paper, scribbling away at a two-forty rate. The angry man began by asking if this was Mr. Greeley. "Yes, sir; what do you want?" said the editor quickly, without once looking up from his paper. The irate visitor then began using his tongue, with no reference to the rules of propriety, good breeding, or reason. Meantime Mr. Greeley continued to write. Page after page was dashed off in the most impetuous style, with no change of features, and without paying the slightest attention to the visitor. Finally, after about twenty minutes of the most impassioned scolding ever poured out in an editor's office, the angry man became disgusted, and abruptly turned to walk out of the room. Then, for the first time, Mr. Greeley quickly looked up, rose from his chair, and, slapping the gentleman familiarly on his shoulder, in a pleasant tone of voice said: "Don't go, friend; sit down, sit down, and free your mind; it will do you good,—you will feel better for it. Besides, it helps me to think what I am to write about. Don't go."

"One good hearty laugh," says Talmage, "is like a bomb-shell exploding in the right place, and spleen and discontent like a gun that kicks over the man shooting it off."

"Every one," says Lubbock, "likes a man who can enjoy a laugh at his own expense,—and justly so, for it shows good humor and good sense. If you laugh at yourself, other people will not laugh at you."

People differ very much in their sense of humor. As some are deaf to certain sounds and blind to certain colors, so there are those who seem deaf and blind to certain pleasures. What makes me laugh until I almost go into convulsions moves them not at all.

Is it not worth while to make an effort to see the funny side of our petty annoyances? How could the two boys but laugh, after they had contended long over the possession of a box found by the wayside, when they agreed to divide its contents, and found nothing in it?

The ability to get on with scolding, irritating people is a great art in doing business. To preserve serenity amid petty trials is a happy gift.

A sunny temper is also conducive to health. A medical authority of highest repute affirms that "excessive labor, exposure to wet and cold, deprivation of sufficient quantities of necessary and wholesome food, habitual bad lodging, sloth, and intemperance are all deadly enemies to human life, but they are none of them so bad as violent and ungoverned passions;" that men and women have frequently lived to an advanced age in spite of these; but that instances are very rare in which people of irascible tempers live to extreme old age.

Poultney Bigelow, in "Harper's Magazine," in relating the story of Jameson's raid upon the Boers of South Africa, says that the triumphant Boers fell on their knees, thanking God for their victory; and that they prayed for their enemies, and treated their prisoners with the utmost kindness. Our foreign missionary books relate similar anecdotes, it being a characteristic feature of their childlike piety for new converts to take literally the words of our Lord,—"Love your enemies."

It is not true that the devil has his tail in everything. A stalwart confidence in God, and faith in the happy outcome of life, will do more to lubricate the creaking machinery of our daily affairs than anything else.

"Le Diable Est Mort"

"*Courage, ami, le diable est mort!*" "Courage, friend, the devil is dead!" was Denys's constant countersign, which he would give to everybody. "They don't understand it," he would say, "but it wakes them up. I carry the good news from city to city, to uplift men's hearts." Once he came across a child who had broken a pitcher. "*Courage, amie, le diable est mort!*" said he, which was such cheering news that she ceased crying, and ran home to tell it to her grandma.

Give me the man who, like Emerson, sees longevity in his cause, and who believes there is a remedy for every wrong, a satisfaction for every longing soul; the man who believes the best of everybody, and who sees beauty and grace where others see ugliness and deformity. Give me the man who believes in the ultimate triumph of truth over error, of harmony over discord, of love over hate, of purity over vice, of light over darkness, of life over death. Such men are the true nation-builders.

Jay Cooke, many times a millionaire at the age of fifty-one, at fifty-two practically penniless, went to work again and built another fortune. The last of his three thousand creditors was paid, and the promise of the great financier was fulfilled. To a visitor who once asked him how he regained his fortune, Mr. Cooke replied, "That is simple enough: by never changing the temperament I derived from my father and mother. From my earliest experience in life I have always been of a hopeful temperament, never living in a cloud; I have always had a reasonable philosophy to think that men and times are better than harsh criticism would suppose. I believed that this American world of ours is full of wealth, and that it was only necessary to go to work and find it. That is the secret of my success in life. Always look on the sunny side."

"Everything has gone," said a New York business man in despair, when he reached home. But when he came to himself he found that his wife and his children and the promises of God were left to him. Suffering, it was said by Aristotle, becomes beautiful when any one bears great calamities with cheerfulness, not through insensibility, but through greatness of mind.

When Garrison was locked up in the Boston city jail he said he had two delightful companions,—a good conscience and a cheerful mind.

"To live as always seeing
The invisible Source of things,
Is the blessedest state of being,
For the quietude it brings."

"Away with those fellows who go howling through life," wrote Beecher, "and all the while passing for birds of paradise! He that cannot laugh and be gay should look to himself. He should fast and pray until his face breaks forth into light."

Martin Luther has told us that he was once sorely discouraged and vexed at himself, the world, and the church, and at the small success he then seemed to be having; and he fell into a despondency which affected all his household. His good wife could not charm it away by cheerful speech or acts. At length she hit upon this happy device, which proved effectual. She appeared before him in deep mourning.

"Who is dead?" asked Luther.

"Oh, do you not know, Martin? God in heaven is dead."

"How can you talk such nonsense, Käthe? How can God die? Why, He is immortal, and will live through all eternity."

"Is that really true?" persisted she, as if she could hardly credit his assertion that God still lived.

"How can you doubt it? So surely as there is a God in heaven," asserted the aroused theologian, "so sure is it that He can never die."

"And yet," said she demurely, in a tone which made him look up at her, "though you do not doubt there is a God, you become hopeless and discouraged as if there were none. It seemed to me you acted as if God were dead."

The spell was broken; Luther heartily laughed at his wife's lesson, and her ingenious way of presenting it. "I observed," he remarked, "what a wise woman my wife was, who mastered my sadness."

Jean Paul Richter's dream of "No God" is one of the most somber things in all literature,—"tempestuous chaos, no healing hand, no Infinite Father. I awoke. My soul wept for joy that it could again worship the Infinite Father.... And when I arose, from all nature I heard flowing sweet, peaceful tones, as from evening bells."

Taking Your Fun Every Day as You Do Your Work

Ten things are necessary for happiness in this life, the first being a good digestion, and the other nine,—money; so at least it is said by our modern philosophers. Yet the author of "A Gentle Life" speaks more truly in saying that the Divine creation includes thousands of superfluous joys which are totally unnecessary to the bare support of life.

He alone is the happy man who has learned to extract happiness, not from ideal conditions, but from the actual ones about him. The man who has mastered the secret will not wait for ideal surroundings; he will not wait until next year, next decade, until he gets rich, until he can travel abroad, until he can afford to surround himself with works of the great masters; but he will make the most out of life to-day, where he is.

"Why thus longing, thus forever sighing,
For the far-off, unattained and dim,
While the beautiful, all round thee lying,
Offers up its low, perpetual hymn?
"Happy the man, and happy he alone,
He who can call to-day his own;
He who, secure within himself, can say:
'To-morrow, do thy worst, for I have lived to-day!'"

Paradise is here or nowhere: you must take your joy with you or you will never find it.

It is after business hours, not in them, that men break down. Men must, like Philip Armour, turn the key on business when they leave it, and at once unlock the doors of some wholesome recreation. Dr. Lyman Beecher used to divert himself with a violin. He had a regular system of what he called "unwinding," thus relieving the great strain put upon him.

"A man," says Dr. Johnson, "should spend part of his time with the laughers."

Humor was Lincoln's life-preserver, as it has been of thousands of others. "If it were not for this," he used to say, "I should die." His jests and quaint stories lighted the gloom of dark hours of national peril.

"Next to virtue," said Agnes Strickland, "the fun in this world is what we can least spare."

"When the harness is off," said Judge Haliburton, "a critter likes to kick up his heels."

"I have fun from morning till night," said the editor Charles A. Dana to a friend who was growing prematurely old. "Do you read novels, and play billiards, and walk a great deal?"

Gladstone early formed a habit of looking on the bright side of things, and never lost a moment's sleep by worrying about public business.

There are many out-of-door sports, and the very presence of nature is to many a great joy. How true it is that, if we are cheerful and contented, all nature smiles with us,—the air seems more balmy, the sky more clear, the earth has a brighter green, the trees have a richer foliage, the flowers are more fragrant, the birds sing more sweetly, and the sun, moon, and stars all appear more beautiful. "It is a grand thing to live,—to open the eyes in the morning and look out upon the world, to drink in the pure air and enjoy the sweet sunshine, to feel the pulse bound, and the being thrill with the consciousness of strength and power in every nerve; it is a good thing simply to be alive, and it is a good world we live in, in spite of the abuse we are fond of giving it."

"I love to hear the bee sing amid the blossoms sunny;
To me his drowsy melody is sweeter than his honey:
For, while the shades are shifting
Along the path to noon,
My happy brain goes drifting
To dreamland on his tune.
"I love to hear the wind blow amid the blushing petals,
And when a fragile flower falls, to watch it as it settles;
And view each leaflet falling
Upon the emerald turf,
With idle mind recalling
The bubbles on the surf.
"I love to lie upon the grass, and let my glances wander
Earthward and skyward there; while peacefully I ponder
How much of purest pleasure
Earth holds for his delight
Who takes life's cup to measure
Naught but its blessings bright."

Upon every side of us are to be found what one has happily called—

Unworked Joy Mines

And he who goes "prospecting" to see what he can daily discover is a wise man, training his eye to see beauty in everything and everywhere.

"One ought, every day," says Goethe, "at least to hear a little song, read a good poem, see a fine picture, and, if it were possible, to speak a few reasonable words." And if this be good for one's self, why not try the song, the poem, the picture, and the good words, on some one else?

Shall music and poetry die out of you while you are struggling for that which can never enrich the character, nor add to the soul's worth? Shall a disciplined imagination fill the mind with beautiful pictures? He who has intellectual resources to fall back upon will not lack for daily recreation most wholesome.

It was a remark of Archbishop Whately that we ought not only to cultivate the cornfields of the mind, but the pleasure-grounds also. A well-balanced life is a cheerful life; a happy union of fine qualities and unruffled temper, a clear judgment, and well-proportioned faculties. In a corner of his desk, Lincoln kept a copy of the latest humorous work; and it was frequently his habit, when fatigued, annoyed, or depressed, to take this up, and read a chapter with great relief. Clean, sensible wit, or sheer nonsense,—anything to provoke mirth and make a man jollier,—this, too, is a gift from Heaven.

In the world of books, what is grand and inspiring may easily become a part of every man's life. A fondness for good literature, for good fiction, for travel, for history, and for biography,—what is better than this?

The Queen of the World

This title best fits Victoria, the true queen of the world, but it fits her best because she is the best type of a noble wife, the queen of her husband's heart, and of a queen mother whose children rise up and call her blessed.

"I noticed," said Franklin, "a mechanic, among a number of others, at work on a house a little way from my office, who always appeared to be in a merry humor; he had a kind word and smile for every one he met. Let the day be ever so cold, gloomy, or sunless, a happy smile danced on his cheerful countenance. Meeting him one morning, I asked him to tell me the secret of his constant flow of spirits.

"'It is no secret, doctor,' he replied. 'I have one of the best of wives; and, when I go to work, she always has a kind word of encouragement for me; and, when I go home, she meets me with a smile and a kiss; and then tea is sure to be ready, and she has done so many little things through the day to please me that I cannot find it in my heart to speak an unkind word to anybody.'"

Some of the happiest homes I have ever been in, ideal homes, where intelligence, peace, and harmony dwell, have been homes of poor people. No rich carpets covered the floors; there were no costly paintings on the walls, no piano, no library, no works of art. But there were contented minds, devoted and unselfish lives, each contributing as much as possible to the happiness of all, and endeavoring to compensate by intelligence and kindness for the poverty of their surroundings. "One cheerful, bright, and contented spirit in a household will uplift the tone of all the rest. The keynote of the home is in the hand of the resolutely cheerful member of the family, and he or she will set the pitch for the rest."

"Young men," it is said, "are apt to be overbearing, imperious, brusque in their manner; they need that suavity of manner, and urbanity of demeanor, gracefulness of expression and delicacy of manner, which can only be gained by association with the female character, which possesses the delicate instinct, ready judgment, acute perceptions, wonderful intuition. The blending of the male and female characteristics produces the grandest character in each."

The woman who has what Helen Hunt so aptly called "a genius for affection,"—she, indeed, is queen of the home. "I have often had occasion," said Washington Irving, "to remark the fortitude with which woman sustains the most overwhelming reverses of fortune. Those disasters which break down the spirit of a man, and prostrate him in the dust, seem to call forth all the energies of the softer sex, and give such intrepidity and elevation to their character that at times it approaches sublimity."

If a wife cannot make her home bright and happy, so that it shall be the cleanest, sweetest, cheerfulest place her husband can find refuge in,—a retreat from the toils and troubles of the outer world,—then God help the poor man, for he is virtually homeless. "Home-keeping hearts," said Longfellow, "are happiest." What is a good wife, a good mother? Is she not a gift out of heaven, sacred and delicate, with affections so great that no measuring line short of that of the infinite God can tell their bound; fashioned to refine and soothe and lift and irradiate home and society and the world; of such value that no one can appreciate it, unless his mother lived long enough to let him understand it, or unless, in some great crisis of life, when all else failed him, he had a wife to reënforce him with a faith in God that nothing could disturb?

Nothing can be more delightful than an anecdote of Joseph II. Choate, of New York, our Minister at the Court of St. James. Upon being asked, at a dinner-party, who he would prefer to be if he could not be himself, he hesitated a moment, apparently running over in his mind the great ones on earth, when his eyes rested on Mrs. Choate at the other end of the table, who was watching him with great interest in her face, and suddenly replied, "If I could not be myself, I should like to be Mrs. Choate's second husband."

"Pleasant words are as a honeycomb, sweet to the soul and health to the bones." It is the little disputes, little fault-findings, little insinuations, little reflections, sharp criticisms, fretfulness and impatience, little unkindnesses, slurs, little discourtesies, bad temper, that create most of the discord and unhappiness in the family. How much it would add to the glory of the homes of the world if that might be said of every one which Rogers said of Lord Holland's sunshiny face: "He always comes to breakfast like a man upon whom some sudden good fortune has fallen"!

The value of pleasant words every day, as you go along, is well depicted by Aunt Jerusha in what she said to our genial friend of "Zion's Herald":—

"If folks could have their funerals when they are alive and well and struggling along, what a help it would be"! she sighed, upon returning from a funeral, wondering how poor Mrs. Brown would have felt if she could have heard what the minister said. "Poor soul, she never dreamed they set so much by her!

"Mis' Brown got discouraged. Ye see, Deacon Brown, he'd got a way of blaming everything on to her. I don't suppose the deacon meant it,—'twas just his way,—but it's awful wearing. When things wore out or broke, he acted just as if Mis' Brown did it herself on purpose; and they all caught it, like the measles or the whooping-cough.

"And the minister a-telling how the deacon brought his young wife here when 't wa'n't nothing but a wilderness, and how patiently she bore hardship, and what a good wife she'd been! Now the minister wouldn't have known anything about that if the deacon hadn't told him. Dear! Dear! If he'd only told Mis' Brown herself what he thought, I do believe he might have saved the funeral.

"And when the minister said how the children would miss their mother, seemed as though they couldn't stand it, poor things!

"Well, I guess it is true enough,—Mis' Brown was always doing for some of them. When they was singing about sweet rest in heaven, I couldn't help thinking that that was something Mis' Brown would have to get used to, for she never had none of it here.

"She'd have been awful pleased with the flowers. They was pretty, and no mistake. Ye see, the deacon wa'n't never willing for her to have a flower-bed. He said 't was enough prettier sight to see good cabbages a-growing; but Mis'

Brown always kind of hankered after sweet-smelling things, like roses and such.

"What did you say, Levi? 'Most time for supper? Well, land's sake, so it is! I must have got to meditating. I've been a-thinking, Levi, you needn't tell the minister anything about me. If the pancakes and pumpkin pies are good, you just say so as we go along. It ain't best to keep everything laid up for funerals."

It is the grand secret of a happy home to express the affection you really have.

"He is the happiest," it was said by Goethe, "be he king or peasant, who finds peace in his home." There are indeed many serious, too serious-minded fathers and mothers who do not wish to advertise their children to all the neighbors as "the laughing family." If this be so, yet, at the very least, these solemn parents may read the Bible. Where it is said, "provoke not your children to wrath," it means literally, "do not irritate your children;" "do not rub them up the wrong way."

Children ought never to get the impression that they live in a hopeless, cheerless, cold world; but the household cheerfulness should transform their lives like sunlight, making their hearts glad with little things, rejoicing upon small occasion.

"How beautiful would our home-life be if every little child at the bed-time hour could look into the faces of the older ones and say: 'We've had such sweet times to-day.'"

"To love, and to be loved," says Sydney Smith, "is the greatest happiness of existence."

Finding What You Do Not Seek

Dining one day with Baron James Rothschild, Eugene Delacroix, the famous French artist, confessed that, during some time past, he had vainly sought for a head to serve as a model for that of a beggar in a picture which he was painting; and that, as he gazed at his host's features, the idea suddenly occurred to him that the very head he desired was before him. Rothschild, being a great lover of art, readily consented to sit as the beggar. The next day, at the studio, Delacroix placed a tunic around the baron's shoulders, put a stout staff in his hand, and made him pose as if he were resting on the steps of an ancient Roman temple. In this attitude he was found by one of the artist's favorite pupils, in a brief absence of the master from the room. The youth naturally concluded that the beggar had just been brought in, and with a sympathetic look quietly slipped a piece of money into his hand. Rothschild thanked him simply, pocketed the money, and the student passed out. Rothschild then inquired of the master, and found that the young man had talent, but very slender means. Soon after, the youth received a letter stating that charity bears interest, and that the accumulated interest on the amount he had given to one he supposed to be a beggar was represented by the sum of ten thousand francs, which was awaiting his claim at the Rothschild office.

This illustrates well the art of cheerful amusement even if one has great business cares,—the entertainment of the artist, the personation of a beggar, and an act of beneficence toward a worthy student.

It illustrates, too, what was said by Wilhelm von Humboldt, that "it is worthy of special remark that when we are not too anxious about happiness and unhappiness, but devote ourselves to the strict and unsparing performance of duty, then happiness comes of itself." We carry each day nobly, doing the duty or enjoying the privilege of the moment, without thinking whether or not it will make us happy. This is quite in accord with the saying of George Herbert, "The consciousness of duty performed gives us music at midnight."

Are not buoyant spirits like water sparkling when it runs? "*I have found my greatest happiness in labor,*" said Gladstone. "I early formed a habit of industry, and it has been its own reward. The young are apt to think that rest means a cessation from all effort, but I have found the most perfect rest in changing effort. If brain-weary over books and study, go out into the blessed sunlight and the pure air, and give heartfelt exercise to the body. The brain will soon become calm and rested. The efforts of Nature are ceaseless. Even in our sleep the heart throbs on. I try to live close to Nature, and to imitate her in my labors. The compensation is sound sleep, a wholesome digestion, and powers that are kept at their best; and this, I take it, is the chief reward of industry."

"Owing to ingrained habits," said Horace Mann, "work has always been to me what water is to a fish. I have wondered a thousand times to hear people say, 'I don't like this business,' or 'I wish I could exchange it for that;' for with me, when I have had anything to do, I do not remember ever to have demurred, but have always set about it like a fatalist, and it was as sure to be done as the sun was to set."

"One's personal enjoyment is a very small thing, but one's personal usefulness is a very important thing." Those only are happy who have their minds fixed on some object other than their own happiness. "The most delicate, the most sensible of all pleasures," says La Bruyère, "consists in promoting the pleasures of others." And Hawthorne has said that the inward pleasure of imparting pleasure is the choicest of all.

"Oh, it is great," said Carlyle, "and there is no other greatness,—to make some nook of God's creation more fruitful, better, more worthy of God,—to make some human heart a little wiser, manlier, happier, more blessed, less accursed!" The gladness of service, of having some honorable share in the world's work, what is better than this?

"The Lord must love the common people," said Lincoln, "for he made so many of them, and so few of the other kind." To extend to all the cup of joy is indeed angelic business, and there is nothing that makes one more beautiful than to be engaged in it.

"The high desire that others may be blest savors of heaven."

The memory of those who spend their days in hanging sweet pictures of faith and trust in the galleries of sunless lives shall never perish from the earth.

Doing Good by Stealth, and Having it Found out by Accident

"This," said Charles Lamb, "is the greatest pleasure I know." "Money never yet made a man happy," said Franklin; "and there is nothing in its nature to produce happiness." To do good with it, makes life a delight to the giver. How happy, then, was the life of Jean Ingelow, since what she received from the sale of a hundred thousand copies of her poems, and fifty thousand of her prose works, she spent largely in charity; one unique charity being a "copyright" dinner three times a week to twelve poor persons just discharged from the neighboring hospitals! Nor was any one made happier by it than the poet.

John Buskin inherited a million dollars. "With this money he set about doing good," says a writer in the "Arena." "Poor young men and women who were struggling to get an education were helped, homes for working men and women were established, and model apartment houses were erected. He also promoted a work for reclaiming waste land outside of London. This land was used for the aid of unfortunate men who wished to rise again from the state in which they had fallen through cruel social conditions and their own weaknesses. It is said that this work suggested to General Booth his colonization farms. Ruskin has also ever been liberal in aiding poor artists, and has done much to encourage artistic taste among the young. On one occasion he purchased ten fine water-color paintings by Holman Hunt for $3,750, to be hung in the public schools of London. By 1877 he had disposed of three-fourths of his inheritance, besides all the income from his books. But the calls of the poor, and his plans looking toward educating and ennobling the lives of working men, giving more sunshine and joy, were such that he determined to dispose of all the remainder of his wealth except a sum sufficient to yield him $1,500 a year on which to live."

Our own Peter Cooper, in his last days, was one of the happiest men in America; his beneficence shone in his countenance.

Let the man who has the blues take a map and census table of the world, and estimate how many millions there are who would gladly exchange lots with him, and let him begin upon some practicable plan to do all the good he can to as many as he can, and he will forget to be despondent; and he need not stop short at praying for them without first giving every dollar he can, without troubling the Lord about that. Let him scatter his flowers as he goes along, since he will never go over the same road again.

No man in England had a better time than did Du Maurier on that cold day when he took the hat of an old soldier on Hampstead road, and sent him away to the soup kitchen in Euston to get warm. The artist chalked on a blackboard such portraits as he commonly made for "Punch," and soon gathered a great quantity of small coins for the grateful soldier; who, however, at once rubbed out Du Maurier's pictures and put on "the faithful dog," and a battle scene, as more artistic.

"Chinese Gordon," after serving faithfully and valiantly in the great Chinese rebellion, and receiving the highest honors of the Chinese Empire, returned to England, caring little for the praise thus heaped on him. He took some position at Gravesend, just below London, where he filled his house with boys from the streets, whom he taught and made men of, and then secured them places on ships,—following them all over the world with letters of advice and encouragement.

His Head in a Hole

"I was appointed to lecture in a town in Great Britain six miles from the railway," said John B. Gough, "and a man drove me in a fly from the station to the town. I noticed that he sat leaning forward in an awkward manner, with his face close to the glass of the window. Soon he folded a handkerchief and tied it round his neck. I asked him if he was cold. "No, sir." Then he placed the handkerchief round his face. I asked him if he had the toothache. "No, sir," was the reply. Still he sat leaning forward. At last I said, "Will you please tell me why you sit leaning forward that way with a handkerchief round your neck if you are not cold and have no toothache?" He said very quietly, "The window of the carriage is broke, and the wind is cold, and I am trying to keep it from you." I said, in surprise, "You are not putting your face to that broken pane to keep the wind from me, are you?" "Yes, sir, I am." "Why do you do that?" "God bless you, sir! I owe everything I have in the world to you." "But I never saw you before." "No, sir; but I have seen you. I was a ballad-singer once. I used to go round with a half-starved baby in my arms for charity, and a draggled wife at my heels half the time, with her eyes blackened; and I went to hear you in Edinburgh, and *you told me I was a man*; and when I went out of that house I said, 'By the help of God, I'll be a man;' and now I've a happy wife and a comfortable home. God bless you, sir! I would stick my head in any hole under the heavens if it would do you any good."

"Let's find the sunny side of men,

Or be believers in it;
A light there is in every soul
That takes the pains to win it.
Oh! there's a slumbering good in all,
And we perchance may wake it;
Our hands contain the magic wand:
This life is what we make it."

He indeed is getting the most out of life who does most to elevate mankind. How happy were those Little Sisters of the Poor at Tours, who took scissors to divide their last remnant of bedclothing with an old woman who came to them at night, craving hospitality! And how happy was that American school-teacher who gave up the best room in the house, which she had engaged long before the season opened, at a mountain sanitarium, during the late war, taking instead of it the poorest room in the house, that she might give good quarters to a soldier just out of his camp hospital!

"Teach self-denial," said Walter Scott, "and make its practice pleasurable, and you create for the world a destiny more sublime than ever issued from the brain of the wildest dreamer."

Yet how many there are, ready to make some great sacrifice, who neglect those little acts of kindness which make so many lives brighter and happier.

"I say, Jim, it's the first time I ever had anybody ask my parding, and it kind o' took me off my feet." A young lady had knocked him down in hastily turning a corner. She stopped and said to the ragged crossing-boy: "I beg your pardon, my little fellow; I am very sorry I ran against you." He took off the piece of a cap he had on his skull, made a low bow, and said with a broad smile: "You have my parding, Miss, and welcome; and the next time you run agin me, you can knock me clean down and I won't say a word."

One of the greatest mistakes of life is to save our smiles and pleasant words and sympathy for those of "our set," or for those not now with us, and for other times than the present.

"If a word or two will render a man happy," said a Frenchman, "he must be a wretch indeed who will not give it. It is like lighting another man's candle with your own, which loses none of its brilliancy by what the other gains."

Sydney Smith recommends us to make at least one person happy every day: "Take ten years, and you will make thirty-six hundred and fifty persons happy; or brighten a small town by your contribution to the fund of general joy." One who is cheerful is preeminently useful.

Dr. Baffles once said: "I have made it a rule never to be with a person ten minutes without trying to make him happier." It was a remark of Dr. Dwight, that "one who makes a little child happier for half an hour is a fellow-worker with God."

A little boy said to his mother: "I couldn't make little sister happy, nohow I could fix it. But I made myself happy trying to make her happy." "I make Jim happy, and he laughs," said another boy, speaking of his invalid brother; "and that makes me happy, and I laugh."

There was once a king who loved his little boy very much, and took a great deal of pains to please him. So he gave him a pony to ride, beautiful rooms to live in, pictures, books, toys without number, teachers, companions, and everything that money could buy or ingenuity device; but for all this, the young prince was unhappy. He wore a frown wherever he went, and was always wishing for something he did not have. At length a magician came to the court. He saw the scowl on the boy's face, and said to the king: "I can make your son happy, and turn his frowns into smiles, but you must pay me a great price for telling him this secret." "All right," said the king; "whatever you ask I will give." The magician took the boy into a private room. He wrote something with a white substance on a piece of paper. He gave the boy a candle, and told him to light it and hold it under the paper, and then see what he could read. Then the magician went away. The boy did as he had been told, and the white letters turned into a beautiful blue. They formed these words: "Do a kindness to some one every day." The prince followed the advice, and became the happiest boy in the realm.

"Happiness," says one writer, "is a mosaic, composed of many smaller stones." It is the little acts of kindness, the little courtesies, the disposition to be accommodating, to be helpful, to be sympathetic, to be unselfish, to be careful not to wound the feelings, not to expose the sore spots, to be charitable of the weaknesses of others, to be considerate,—these are the little things which, added up at night, are found to be the secret of a happy day. How much greater are all these than one great act of noteworthy goodness once a year! Our lives are made up of trifles; emergencies rarely occur. "Little things, unimportant events, experiences so small as to scarcely leave a trace behind, make up the sum-total of life." And the one great thing in life is to do a little good to every one we meet. Ready sympathy, a quick eye, and a little tact, are all that are needed.

This point is happily illustrated by this report of an incident upon a train from Providence to Boston. A lady was caring for her father, whose mental faculties were weakened by age. He imagined that some imperative duty called on him to leave the swift-moving train, and his daughter could not quiet him. Just then she noticed a large man watching them over the top of his paper. As soon as he caught her eye, he rose and crossed quickly to her.

"I beg your pardon, you are in trouble. May I help you?"

She explained the situation to him.

"What is your father's name?" he asked.

She told him; and then with an encouraging smile, she spoke to her venerable father who was sitting immediately in front of her. The next moment the large man turned over the seat, and leaning toward the troubled old man, he addressed him by name, shook hands with him cordially, and engaged him in a conversation so interesting and so cleverly arranged to keep his mind occupied that the old gentleman forgot his need to leave the train, and did not think of it again until they were in Boston. There the stranger put the lady and her charge into a carriage, received her assurance that she felt perfectly safe, and was about to close the carriage door, when she remembered that she had felt so safe in the keeping of this noble-looking man that she had not even asked his name. Hastily putting her hand against the door, she said: "Pardon me, but you have rendered me such service, may I not know whom I am thanking?" The big man smiled as he turned away, and answered:—

"Phillips Brooks"

"What a gift it is," said Beecher, who was the great preacher of cheerfulness, "to make all men better and happier without knowing it! We do not suppose that flowers know how sweet they are. These roses and carnations have made me happy for a day. Yet they stand huddled together in my pitcher, without seeming to know my thoughts of them, or the gracious work they are doing. And how much more is it, to have a disposition that carries with it involuntarily sweetness, calmness, courage, hope, and happiness. Yet this is the portion of good nature in a large-minded, strong-natured man. When it has made him happy, it has scarcely begun its office. God sends a natural heart-singer—a man whose nature is large and luminous, and who, by his very carriage and spontaneous actions, calms, cheers, and helps his fellows. God bless him, for he blesses everybody!" This is just what Mr. Beecher would have said about Phillips Brooks.

And what better can be said than to compare the heart's good cheer to a floral offering? *Are not flowers appropriate gifts to persons of all ages, in any conceivable circumstances in which they are placed? So the heart's good cheer and deeds of kindness are always acceptable to children and youth, to busy men and women, to the aged, and to a world of invalids.*

"Thus live and die, O man immortal," says Dr. Chalmers. "Live for something. Do good, and leave behind you a monument of virtue, which the storms of time can never destroy. Write your name in kindness, love, and mercy, on the hearts of those who come in contact with you, and you will never be forgotten. Good deeds will shine as brightly on earth as the stars of heaven."

What is needed to round out human happiness is a well-balanced life. Not ease, not pleasure, not happiness, but a man, Nature is after. "There is," says Robert Waters, "no success without honor; no happiness without a clear conscience; no use in living at all if only for one's self. It is not at all necessary for you to make a fortune, but it is necessary, absolutely necessary, that you should become a fair-dealing, honorable, useful man, radiating goodness and cheerfulness wherever you go, and making your life a blessing."

"When a man does not find repose in himself," says a French proverb, "it is vain for him to seek it elsewhere." Happy is he who has no sense of discord with the harmony of the universe, who is open to the voices of nature and of the spiritual realm, and who sees the light that never was on sea or land. Such a life can but give expression to its inward harmony. Every pure and healthy thought, every noble aspiration for the good and the true, every longing of the heart for a higher and better life, every lofty purpose and unselfish endeavor, makes the human spirit stronger, more harmonious, and more beautiful. It is this alone that gives a self-centered confidence in one's heaven-aided powers, and a high-minded cheerfulness, like that of a celestial spirit. It is this which an old writer has called the paradise of a good conscience.

"I count this thing to be grandly true,
That a noble deed is a step toward God;
Lifting the soul from the common clod
To a purer air and a broader view.

"We rise by the things that are under our foot;
By what we have mastered of good or gain;
By the pride deposed and the passion slain,
And the vanquished ills that we hourly meet."

"My body must walk the earth," said an ancient poet, "but I can put wings on my soul, and plumes to my hardest thought." The splendors and symphonies and the ecstacies of a higher world are with us now in the rudimentary organs of eye and ear and heart. Much we have to do, much we have to love, much we have to hope for; and our "joy is the grace we say to God." "When I think upon God," said Haydn to Carpani, "my heart is so full of joy that the notes leap from my pen."

Says Gibbons:—

"Our lives are songs:
God writes the words,
And we set them to music at leisure;
And the song is sad, or the song is glad,
As we choose to fashion the measure.

"We must write the song
Whatever the words,
Whatever its rhyme or meter;
And if it is sad, we must make it glad,
And if sweet, we must make it sweeter."

"Looking Pleasant"—A Thing to Be Worked from the Inside

Acting on a sudden impulse, an elderly woman, the widow of a soldier who had been killed in the Civil War, went into a photographer's to have her picture taken. She was seated before the camera wearing the same stern, hard, forbidding look that had made her an object of fear to the children living in the neighborhood, when the photographer, thrusting his head out from the black cloth, said suddenly, "Brighten the eyes a little."

She tried, but the dull and heavy look still lingered.

"Look a little pleasanter," said the photographer, in an unimpassioned but confident and commanding voice.

"See here," the woman retorted sharply, "if you think that an old woman who is dull can look bright, that one who feels cross can become pleasant every time she is told to, you don't know anything about human nature. It takes something from the outside to brighten the eye and illuminate the face."

"Oh, no, it doesn't! *It's something to be worked from the inside.* Try it again," said the photographer good-naturedly.

Something in his manner inspired faith, and she tried again, this time with better success.

"That's good! That's fine! You look twenty years younger," exclaimed the artist, as he caught the transient glow that illuminated the faded face.

She went home with a queer feeling in her heart. It was the first compliment she had received since her husband had passed away, and it left a pleasant memory behind. When she reached her little cottage, she looked long in the glass and said, "There may be something in it. But I'll wait and see the picture."

When the picture came, it was like a resurrection. The face seemed alive with the lost fires of youth. She gazed long and earnestly, then said in a clear, firm voice, "If I could do it once, I can do it again."

Approaching the little mirror above her bureau, she said, "Brighten up, Catherine," and the old light flashed up once more.

"Look a little pleasanter!" she commanded; and a calm and radiant smile diffused itself over the face.

Her neighbors, as the writer of this story has said, soon remarked the change that had come over her face: "Why, Mrs. A., you are getting young. How do you manage it?"

"It is almost all done from the inside. You just brighten up inside and feel pleasant."

"Fate served me meanly, but I looked at her and laughed, That none might know how bitter was the cup I quaffed. Along came Joy and paused beside me where I sat, Saying, 'I came to see what you were laughing at.'"

Every emotion tends to sculpture the body into beauty or into ugliness. Worrying, fretting, unbridled passions, petulance, discontent, every dishonest act, every falsehood, every feeling of envy, jealousy, fear,—each has its effect on the system, and acts deleteriously like a poison or a deformer of the body. Professor James of Harvard, an expert in the mental sciences, says, "Every small stroke of virtue or vice leaves its ever so little scar. Nothing we ever do is, in strict literalness, wiped out." *The way to be beautiful without is to be beautiful within.*

Worth Five Hundred Dollars

It is related that Dwight L. Moody once offered to his Northfield pupils a prize of five hundred dollars for the best thought. This took the prize: "Men grumble because God put thorns with roses; wouldn't it be better to thank God that he put roses with thorns?"

We win half the battle when we make up our minds to take the world as we find it, including the thorns. "It is," says Fontenelle, "a great obstacle to happiness to expect too much." This is what happens in real life. Watch Edison. He makes the most expensive experiments throughout a long period of time, and he expects to make them, and he never worries because he does not succeed the first time.

"I cannot but think," says Sir John Lubbock, "that the world would be better and brighter if our teachers would dwell on the duty of happiness as well as on the happiness of duty."

Oliver Wendell Holmes, in advanced years, acknowledged his debt of gratitude to the nurse of his childhood, who studiously taught him to ignore unpleasant incidents. If he stubbed his toe, or skinned his knee, or bumped his nose, his nurse would never permit his mind to dwell upon the temporary pain, but claimed his attention for some pretty object, or charming story, or happy reminiscence. To her, he said, he was largely indebted for the sunshine of a long life. It is a lesson which is easily mastered in childhood, but seldom to be learned in middle life, and never in old age.

"When I was a boy," says another author, "I was consoled for cutting my finger by having my attention called to the fact that I had not broken my arm; and when I got a cinder in my eye, I was expected to feel more comfortable because my cousin had lost his eye by an accident."

"We should brave trouble," says Beecher, "as the New England boy braves winter. The school is a mile away over the hill, yet he lingers not by the fire; but, with his books slung over his shoulder, he sets out to face the storm. When he reaches the topmost ridge, where the snow lies in drifts, and the north wind comes keen and biting, does he shrink and cower down by the fences, or run into the nearest house to warm himself? No; he buttons up his coat, and rejoices to defy the blast, and tosses the snow-wreaths with his foot; and so, erect and fearless, with strong heart and ruddy cheek, he goes on to his place at school."

Children should be taught the habit of finding pleasure everywhere; and to see the bright side of everything. "Serenity of mind comes easy to some, and hard to others. It can be taught and learned. We ought to have teachers who are able to educate us in this department of our natures quite as much as in music or art. Think of a school or classes for training men and women to carry themselves serenely amid all the trials that beset them!"

"Joy is the mainspring in the whole
Of endless Nature's calm rotation.
Joy moves the dazzling wheels that roll
In the great timepiece of Creation." —Schiller

The "Don't Worry" Society

was organized not long ago in New York; it is, however, just as well suited to other latitudes and longitudes. It is intended for people who "cannot help worrying."

If really you can't help it, you are in an abnormal condition, you have lost self-control,—it is a mild type of mental derangement. You must attack your bad habit of worrying as you would a disease. It is definitely something to be overcome, an infirmity that you are to get rid of.

"Be good and you will be happy," is a very old piece of advice. Mrs. Mary A. Livermore now proposes to reverse it,—"Be happy and you will be good." If unhappiness is a bad habit, you are to turn about by sheer force of will and practice cheerfulness. "Happiness is a thing to be practiced like a violin."

Not work, but worry, fretfulness, friction,—these are our foes in America. You should not go here and there, making prominent either your bad manners or a gloomy face. Who has a right to rob other people of their happiness? "Do not," says Emerson, "hang a dismal picture on your wall; and do not deal with sables and glooms in your conversation."

If you are not at the moment cheerful,—look, speak, act, as if you were. "You know I had no money, I had nothing to give but myself," said a woman who had great sorrows to bear, but who bore them cheerfully. "I formed a resolution never to sadden any one else with my troubles. I have laughed and told jokes when I could have wept. I have always smiled in the face of every misfortune. I have tried never to let any one go from my presence without a happy word or a bright thought to carry away. And happiness makes happiness. I myself am happier than I should have been had I sat down and bemoaned my fate."

"'Tis easy enough to be pleasant,
When life flows along like a song;
But the man worth while is the one who will smile
When everything goes dead wrong;
For the test of the heart is trouble,
And it always comes with the years;
And the smile that is worth the praise of the earth
Is the smile that comes through tears."

A Pleasure Book

"She is an aged woman, but her face is serene and peaceful, though trouble has not passed her by. She seems utterly above the little worries and vexations which torment the average woman and leave lines of care. The Fretful Woman asked her one day the secret of her happiness; and the beautiful old face shone with joy.

"'My dear,' she said, 'I keep a Pleasure Book.'

"'A what?'

"'A Pleasure Book. Long ago I learned that there is no day so dark and gloomy that it does not contain some ray of light, and I have made it one business of my life to write down the little things which mean so much to a woman. I have a book marked for every day of every year since I left school. It is but a little thing: the new gown, the chat with a friend, the thoughtfulness of my husband, a flower, a book, a walk in the field, a letter, a concert, or a drive; but it all goes into my Pleasure Book, and, when I am inclined to fret, I read a few pages to see what a happy, blessed woman I am. You may see my treasures if you will.'

"Slowly the peevish, discontented woman turned over the book her friend brought her, reading a little here and there. One day's entries ran thus: 'Had a pleasant letter from mother. Saw a beautiful lily in a window. Found the pin

I thought I had lost. Saw such a bright, happy girl on the street. Husband brought some roses in the evening.'

"Bits of verse and lines from her daily reading have gone into the Pleasure Book of this world-wise woman, until its pages are a storehouse of truth and beauty.

"'Have you found a pleasure for every day?' the Fretful Woman asked.

"'For every day,' the low voice answered; 'I had to make my theory come true, you know.'"

The Fretful Woman ought to have stopped there, but did not; and she found that page where it was written—"He died with his hand in mine, and my name upon his lips." Below were the lines from Lowell:—

"Lone watcher on the mountain height:
It is right precious to behold
The first long surf of climbing light
Flood all the thirsty eat with gold;
"Yet God deems not thine aeried sight
More worthy than our twilight dim,
For meek obedience, too, is light,
And following that is finding Him."

In one of the battles of the Crimea, a cannon-ball struck inside the fort, crashing through a beautiful garden; but from the ugly chasm there burst forth a spring of water which is still flowing. And how beautiful it is, if our strange earthly sorrows become a blessing to others, through our determination to live and to do for those who need our help. Life is not given for mourning, but for unselfish service.

"Cheerfulness," says Ruskin, "is as natural to the heart of a man in strong health as color to his cheek; and wherever there is habitual gloom there must be either bad air, unwholesome food, improperly severe labor, or erring habits of life." It is an erring habit of life if we are not first of all cheerful. We are thrown into a morbid habit through circumstances utterly beyond our control, yet this fact does not change our duty toward God and toward man,—our duty to be cheerful. We are human; but it is our high privilege to lead a divine life, to accept the joy which our Lord bequeathed to his disciples.

Our trouble is that we do not half will. After a man's habits are well set, about all he can do is to sit by and observe which way he is going. Regret it as he may, how helpless is a weak man, bound by the mighty cable of habit; twisted from tiny threads which he thought were absolutely within his control. Yet a habit of happy thought would transform his life into harmony and beauty. Is not the will almost omnipotent to determine habits before they become all-powerful? What contributes more to health or happiness than a vigorous will? A habit of directing a firm and steady will upon those things which tend to produce harmony of thought will bring happiness and contentment; the will, rightly drilled,—and divinely guided,—can drive out all discordant thoughts, and usher in the reign of perpetual harmony. It is impossible to overestimate the importance of forming a habit of cheerfulness early in life. The serene optimist is one whose mind has dwelt so long upon the sunny side of life that he has acquired a habit of cheerfulness. "Talk happiness. The world is sad enough Without your woes. No path is wholly rough; Look for the places that are smooth and clear, And speak of those who rest the weary ear Of earth, so hurt by one continuous strain Of human discontent and grief and pain.

"Talk faith. The world is better off without Your uttered ignorance and morbid doubt. If you have faith in God, or man, or self, Say so; if not, push back upon the shelf Of silence all your thoughts till faith shall come; No one will grieve because your lips are dumb.

"Talk health. The dreary, never-changing tale Of mortal maladies is worn and stale. You cannot charm, or interest, or please, By harping on that minor chord, disease. Say you are well, or all is well with you. And God shall hear your words and make them true."

The Sunshine-Man

"There's the dearest little old gentleman," says James Buckham, "who goes into town every morning on the 8.30 train. I don't know his name, and yet I know him better than anybody else in town. He just radiates cheerfulness as far as you can see him. There is always a smile on his face, and I never heard him open his mouth except to say something kind, courteous, or good natured. Everybody bows to him, even strangers, and he bows to everybody, yet never with the slightest hint of presumption or familiarity. If the weather is fine, his jolly compliments make it seem finer; and if it is raining, the merry way in which he speaks of it is as good as a rainbow. Everybody who goes in on the 8.30 train knows the sunshine-man; it's his train. You just hurry up a little, and I'll show you the sunshine-man this morning. It's foggy and cold, but if one look at him doesn't cheer you up so that you'll want to whistle, then I'm no judge of human nature."

"Good morning, sir!" said Mr. Jolliboy in going to the same train.

"Why, sir, I don't know you," replied Mr. Neversmile.

"I didn't say you did, sir. Good morning, sir!"

"The inborn geniality of some people," says Whipple, "amounts to genius." "How in our troubled lives," asks J. Freeman Clarke, "could we do without these fair, sunny natures, into which on their creation-day God allowed nothing sour, acrid, or bitter to enter, but made them a perpetual solace and comfort by their cheerfulness?" There are those whose very presence carries sunshine with them wherever they go; a sunshine which means pity for the poor, sympathy for the suffering, help for the unfortunate, and benignity toward all. Everybody loves the sunny soul. His very face is a passport anywhere. All doors fly open to him. He disarms prejudice and envy, for he bears good will to everybody. He is as welcome in every household as the sunshine.

"He was quiet, cheerful, genial," says Carlyle in his "Reminiscences" concerning Edward Irving's sunny helpfulness. "His soul unruffled, clear as a mirror, honestly loving and loved, Irving's voice was to me one of blessedness and new hope."

And to William Wilberforce the poet Southey paid this tribute: "I never saw any other man who seemed to enjoy such perpetual serenity and sunshine of spirit."

"I resolved," said Tom Hood, "that, like the sun, so long as my day lasted, I would look on the bright side of everything."

When Goldsmith was in Flanders he discovered the happiest man he had ever seen. At his toil, from morning till night, he was full of song and laughter. Yet this sunny-hearted being was a slave, maimed, deformed, and wearing a chain. How well he illustrated that saying which bids us, if there is no bright side, to polish up the dark one! "Mirth is like the flash of lightning that breaks through the gloom of the clouds and glitters for a moment; cheerfulness keeps up a daylight in the soul, filling it with a steady and perpetual serenity." It is cheerfulness that has the staying quality, like the sunshine changing a world of gloom into a paradise of beauty.

The first prize at a flower-show was taken by a pale, sickly little girl, who lived in a close, dark court in the east of London. The judges asked how she could grow it in such a dingy and sunless place. She replied that a little ray of sunlight came into the court; as soon as it appeared in the morning, she put her flower beneath it, and, as it moved, moved the flower, so that she kept it in the sunlight all day.

"Water, air, and sunshine, the three greatest hygienic agents, are free, and within the reach of all." "Twelve years ago," says Walt Whitman, "I came to Camden to die. But every day I went into the country, and bathed in the sunshine, lived with the birds and squirrels, and played in the water with the fishes. I received my health from Nature."

"It is the unqualified result of all my experience with the sick," said Florence Nightingale, "that second only to their need of fresh air, is their need of light; that, after a close room, what most hurts them is a dark room; and that it is not only light, but direct sunshine they want."

"Sunlight," says Dr. L. W. Curtis, in "Health Culture," "has much to do in keeping air in a healthy condition. No plant can grow in the dark, neither can man remain healthy in a dark, ill-ventilated room. When the first asylum for the blind was erected in Massachusetts, the committee decided to save expense by not having any windows. They reasoned that, as the patients could not see, there was no need of any light. It was built without windows, but ventilation was well provided for, and the poor sightless patients were domiciled in the house. But things did not go well: one after another began to sicken, and great languor fell upon them; they felt distressed and restless, craving something, they hardly knew what. After two had died and all were ill, the committee decided to have windows. The sunlight poured in, and the white faces recovered their color; their flagging energies and depressed spirits revived, and health was restored."

The sun, making all living things to grow, exerts its happiest influence in cheering the mind of man and making his heart glad, and if a man has sunshine in his soul he will go on his way rejoicing; content to look forward if under a cloud, not bating one jot of heart or hope if for a moment cast down; honoring his occupation, whatever it be; rendering even rags respectable by the way he wears them; and not only happy himself, but giving happiness to others.

How a man's face shines when illuminated by a great moral motive! and his manner, too, is touched with the grace of light.

"Nothing will supply the want of sunshine to peaches," said Emerson, "and to make knowledge valuable you must have the cheerfulness of wisdom."

"Wondrous is the strength of cheerfulness," said Carlyle; "altogether past calculation its powers of endurance. Efforts to be permanently useful must be uniformly joyous,—a spirit all sunshine, graceful from very gladness, beautiful because bright."

"The cheerful man carries with him perpetually, in his presence and personality, an influence that acts upon others as summer warmth on the fields and forests. It wakes up and calls out the best that is in them. It makes them stronger, braver, and happier. Such a man makes a little spot of this world a lighter, brighter, warmer place for other people to live in. To meet him in the morning is to get inspiration which makes all the day's struggles and tasks easier. His hearty handshake puts a thrill of new vigor into your veins. After talking with him for a few minutes, you feel an exhilaration of spirits, a quickening of energy, a renewal of zest and interest in living, and are ready for any duty or service."

"Great hearts there are among men," says Hillis, of Plymouth pulpit; "they carry a volume of manhood; their presence is sunshine; their coming changes our climate; they oil the bearings of life; their shadow always falls behind them; they make right living easy. Blessed are the happiness-makers: they represent the best forces in civilization!"

If refined manners reprove us a little for ill-timed laughter, a smiling face kindled by a smiling heart is always in order. Who can ever forget Emerson's smile? It was a perpetual benediction upon all who knew him. A smile is said to be to the human countenance what sunshine is to the landscape. Or a smile is called the rainbow of the face.

"This is a dark world to many people," says a suggestive modern writer, "a world of chills, a world of fogs, a world of wet blankets. Nine-tenths of the men we meet need encouragement. Your work is so urgent that you have no time to stop and speak to the people, but every day you meet scores, perhaps hundreds and thousands of persons, upon whom you might have direct and immediate influence. 'How? How?' you cry out. We answer: By the grace of physiognomy. There is nothing more catching than a face with a lantern behind it, shining clear through. We have no admiration for a face with a dry smile, meaning no more than the grin of a false face. But a smile written by the hand of God, as an index finger or table of contents, to whole volumes of good feeling within, is a benediction. You say: 'My face is hard and lacking in mobility, and my benignant feelings are not observable in the facial proportions.' We do not believe you. Freshness and geniality of the soul are so subtle and pervading that they will, at some eye or mouth corner, leak out. Set behind your face a feeling of gratitude to God and kindliness toward man, and you will every day preach a sermon long as the streets you walk, a sermon with as many heads as the number of people you meet, and differing from other sermons in the fact that the longer it is the better. The reason that there are so many sour faces, so many frowning faces, so many dull faces, is because men consent to be acrid and petulant, and stupid. The way to improve your face is to improve your disposition. Attractiveness of physiognomy does not depend on regularity of features. We know persons whose brows are shaggy, eyes oblique, noses ominously longitudinal, and mouths straggling along in unusual and unexpected directions; and yet they are men and women of so much soul that we love to look upon them, and their faces are sweet evangels."

It was N. P. Willis, I think, who added to the beatitudes—"Blessed are the joy-makers." "And this is why all the world loves little children, who are always ready to have 'a sunshine party,'—little children bubbling over with fun, as a bobolink with song.

"How well we remember it all!—the long gone years of our own childhood, and the households of joyous children we have known in later years. Joy-makers are the children still,—some of them in unending scenes of light. I saw but yesterday this epitaph at Mount Auburn,—'She was so pleasant': sunny-hearted in life, and now alive forever more in light supernal.

"How can we then but rejoice with joy unspeakable, as the children of immortality; living habitually above the gloom and damps of earth, and leading lives of ministration; bestowing everywhere sweetness and light,—radiating upon the earth something of the beauty of the unseen world."

What is a sunny temper but "a talisman more powerful than wealth, more precious than rubies"? What is it but "an aroma whose fragrance fills the air with the odors of Paradise"?

"I am so full of happiness," said a little child, "that I could not be any happier unless I could grow." And she bade "Good morning" to her sweet singing bird, and "Good morning" to the sun; then she asked her mother's permission, and softly, reverently, gladly bade "Good morning to God,"—and why should she not?

Was it not Goethe who represented a journey that followed the sunshine round the world, forever bathed in light? And Longfellow sang:

"'Tis always morning somewhere; and above
The awakening continents, from shore to shore,
Somewhere the birds are singing evermore."

"The darkness past, we mount the radiant skies,
And changeless day is ours; we hear the songs
Of higher spheres, the light divine our eyes
Behold and sunlight robes of countless throngs
Who dwell in light; we seek, with joyous quest,
God's service sweet to wipe all tears away,
And list we every hour, with eager zest,
For high command to toils that God has blest:
So fill we full our endless sunshine day."